4113710800

D1756591

A Diffuse Murmur of History

Literary Memory Narratives of Civil War and Dictatorship in Spanish Novels after 1990

P.I.E. Peter Lang

Bruxelles · Bern · Berlin · Frankfurt am Main · New York · Oxford · Wien

Fiona SCHOUTEN

A Diffuse Murmur of History

Literary Memory Narratives of Civil War and Dictatorship in Spanish Novels after 1990

Cover image: Medallion of Francisco Franco, Plaza Mayor, Salamanca, Spain. Photograph by Wouter Prummel.

© P.I.E. PETER LANG S.A.,
Éditions scientifiques internationales
Brussels, 2010
1 avenue Maurice, B-1050 Brussels, Belgium
info@peterlang.com;   www.peterlang.com

Printed in Germany

ISBN 978-90-5201-590-3
D/2010/5678/07

Library of Congress Cataloging-in-Publication Data
Schouten, Fiona. A diffuse murmur of history : literary memory narratives of
civil war and dictatorship in Spanish novels after 1990 / Fiona Schouten.
        p. cm. Includes bibliographical references.
   ISBN 978-90-5201-590-3   1.   Spanish fiction—20th century—History and
criticism. 2.   Memory in literature. 3.   Spain—History—Civil War, 1936-
1939—Literature and the war. 4.   Spain—History—1939-1975—In literature.
        5.   Literature and history—Spain.   I. Title.
   PQ6144.S37 2000   863'.64094584608—dc22   2009050951

CIP also available from the British Library, GB.

Bibliographic information published by "Die Deutsche Nationalbibliothek"
"Die Deutsche Nationalbibliothek" lists this publication in the "Deutsche National-
bibliografie"; detailed bibliographic data is available on Internet at <http://dnb.d-nb.de>.

For Jorge

Mais *repérer*, dans un texte, des points d'ancrage de systèmes de valeurs ne renseigne pas, d'emblée, sur leur *localisation et origine énonciative*, sur leur *attribution* (qui les profère, les parle), ni sur leur *interprétation* (qui les assume, lequel est assumé préférentiellement). Tout ce qu'on saisit là, peut-être, c'est une 'rumeur' diffuse de l'idéologie (de l'Histoire).

Philippe Hamon

Contents

CHAPTER 1

Introduction

It is often said that the way we remember the past says more about us than it does about the past. We always choose which aspects we fondly remember and which events we would rather forget in answer to our current needs, so that the story of the past we construct is the story that best fits our present. In this light, the current obsession with memory in Spain, the "moda de la memoria" with its "scores of best-selling novels, memoirs, and studies, as well as widely viewed feature films, television programs, exhibits, and documentaries" (Faber 206) suggests a sudden need for change. Apparently, Spain is experiencing a sort of identity shift that calls for a redefinition and reappropriation of the past – a painful and violent past, moreover, which encompasses the Civil War of 1936-1939 and the dictatorship of Francisco Franco that followed it, ending only with the dictator's death in 1975.

In general, it is assumed that when the dictatorship ended and Spain carefully set democratisation processes in motion, it purposefully set out to *forget* about its undemocratic history. In this commonly shared view, the memory of the painful past was consciously suppressed in the young Spanish democracy. As Cardús i Ros polemically puts it, Spain suffered from an "intentional forgetting and […] the manufacturing of a great lie" (19). The past even became a downright taboo "del que sólo se discutía abiertamente en privado" (Cifre Wibrow 176). A conflict between public and private memory came into being (Resina, "Short of Memory" 99): the younger generations' knowledge of francoism was limited to what they were told by family members (Labanyi, "History and Hauntology" 67) because politics, but also the media and cultural production, actively reinforced the process of forgetting, or, as it was euphemistically called, *desmemorización*.

Of course, much is to be said for this view of transitional and early democratic Spain as a forgetful country that tried to ignore the past. It is undeniably true that in politics, a remarkable tendency towards consensus and progress manifested itself: the formerly illegal or newly instated left-wing parties co-operated with the right as peacefully as possible to turn the country into a democracy. Patricia Cifre Wibrow points out that "[e]se consenso no fue […] casual, ni surgió espontáneamente, sino que resultó de los debates y las discusiones que se llevaron a cabo durante los últimos años del régimen" (175). Consensus politics and the willing-ness to forget culminated in the ensuing *pacto de silencio* or *pacto del olvido* (176), silence pact or pact of forgetting, which was established even before Franco's death and was the result of a conscious political decision to bury the hatchet and keep quiet about the painful past.

At the same time, though, the past was not and could not be sup-pressed and 'forgotten' entirely. Very often, Spain's transitional gov-ernment simply had no choice but to deal with certain painful memories or remnants of the dictatorial era and the Civil War. On these occasions, it made a conscious effort to prevent them from causing any real discus-sion or conflict. The fortieth anniversary of the bombing of the Basque town of Guernica was commemorated in 1977, two years after Franco's death, and could not be avoided, even if it was only for the highly symbolic meaning the event had acquired through Picasso's iconic painting. The government managed to contain any feelings of discom-fort this might arouse by turning the commemoration into a symbol of rehabilitation for the *vencidos*, the War's 'defeated', in general, and for the repressed Basque people in particular. In this way, it dealt cleanly and quickly with the Basque feelings of resentment, and by thus recog-nising their sufferings without poking into them more than strictly necessary, facilitated the integration of the Basque people into the democratisation process (Aguilar Fernández 277). In a similar vein, the *Desfile de la Victoria* (Victory Parade) that celebrated the nationalist victory in the Civil War with a military parade was rebaptised *Día de las Fuerzas Armadas* (Day of the Armed Forces) soon after Franco's death – a more neutral name that at the same time would not provoke the army's protests (278). And in 1985, a monument was erected dedicated to all those who had died in the war, both the defeated republicans and the victorious nationalists (283). The government did its best to recon-cile both the left and the right wing with democracy and with each other, while at the same time going out of its way not to offend anyone or stir up deeper conflicts.

In an analogous way, the media adopted a soothing manner in deal-ing with the memory of francoism. Paloma Aguilar Fernández illustrates the "papel fundamentalmente moderador" (288) of the press with an analysis of the two biggest newspapers, *El País* and *ABC*, from which she concludes that neither printed any really shocking or conflictive stories of the Civil War, and that the subject was only touched with the utmost delicacy "para no abrir las mal cauterizadas heridas" (310). Only on a cultural level, perhaps, had the theme of francoism developed into a real taboo (Steenmeijer 141). Literature of the 1980s was distinctly a-political in nature, characterised by an orientalist and neo-spiritualist exoticism and a marked narcissism. Often, the works of the new writers were called "novelas ensimismadas" (introverted novels) because of their subjective and superficial content (Langa Pizarro 56). Still, however, Walther Bernecker points out that memory did not come to a complete standstill here, either:

> War eine kritische Auseinandersetzung mit der jüngsten spanischen Vergangenheit bis vor kurzem nicht Thema für eine breitere Öffentlichkeit, so existierten doch stets Rand- und Teilöffentlichkeiten, in denen die Erinnerung an Krieg und Diktatur durchaus präsent war. An vordester Stelle ist hier neben dem Spielfilm vor allem die Literatur zu nennen. (19)

It seems, then, that to depict Spain after 1975 as a country that embraced the future and never looked back is to exaggerate matters. It is highly probable that the use of such appealing yet categorical terms as 'silence pact' and 'pact of forgetting' has contributed greatly to the idea that the past was simply and squarely forgotten. That other notion, *desmemorización* or dememorisation, also contributes to this image of Spain as an amnesiac country. Such a reductive image of a complex reality does no justice to memory discourses that were necessarily always going on, even in the most silent and forgetful times. What is more, such metaphors are implicitly normative. For that reason, it might be preferable to replace the image of a personified Spain suffering from memory loss with that of a nation where the past was remembered reluctantly, and where memory discourses which threatened to destabilise society were neutralised as much as possible.

This need for neutralising the past can be explained by a number of related reasons, the most important of which was an acute fear of a new civil war. Paloma Aguilar Fernández shows that the situation in the late 1970s was reminiscent of that in the early 1930s, when an internally divided republican government's attempt to establish a democracy, the Second Republic, escalated into the Civil War. Like then, an international economic crisis struck Spain particularly hard (Aguilar Fernández 211). And like then, the new democracy had to be built on a basis that was far from firm. According to Aguilar Fernández, it was "la memoria del infortunio histórico y el miedo a los peligros de la radicalización" (211) that led to a politics of consensus. "Der Bürgerkrieg wurde als abschreckendes Beispiel immer dann beschworen, wenn die Angst vor inneren Unruhen akut wurde", Walther Bernecker agrees. "Insofern kann man von einer klaren Funktionalisierung der Bürgerkriegserinnerung im Dienste einer ganz bestimmten Demokratisierungsstrategie sprechen" (12). Needless to say, any wishes to polemicise the memory of the past once democracy was in place were silenced by the attempted coup of Lieutenant Colonel Tejero, in 1981: the frightening image of Tejero breaking into the Congress of Deputies and firing shots was captured on camera and broadcast for all Spaniards to see.

The need to gloss over the most painful aspects of the shared past was further pressed upon Spanish society by the power the former francoists still had. When Franco died, no real political rupture took place (Cardús i Ros 25): the process of democratisation had already started within the dictatorial system and was continued after the death of the dictator by the very politicians who had initiated it. The former supporters of the regime were able to continue unchanged within the new democracy, without having to account for what had happened before. As a famous example, Franco's minister for Information and Tourism, Manuel Fraga Iribarne, became president of Galicia between 1987 and 2005 after a prosperous political career under the dictatorship. During the entire Franco regime, left-wing activists, Basque and Catalan nationalists, and other opponents of the state had been oppressed and hunted down. The weakness of the only recently legalised left allowed the powerful right to maintain much of its political control (Bernecker 15). The oppressors and the oppressed worked together in relative harmony, preferring consensus and compromise to the settling of old scores.

There were other reasons for the development of a discourse of neu-tralisation in favour of consensus between left and right: a market emerged that asked for a modern, Western state (Resina, "Short of Memory" 91), and the Spanish people had a strong wish for peace no matter what political shape it had (Aguilar Fernández 353). The combi-nation of these factors led to a smooth democratisation of Spain. Ac-cording to Joan Ramon Resina, "[c]ertainly, the Spanish Transition was not a win-win game [...] [but] the Transition satisfied a majority" ("Short of Memory" 88). The end, a stable democracy that would help Spain move forward into a new era, justified the means: "el olvido o amnesia oficialista de lo ocurrido durante la Guerra Civil y la larguísima posguerra posterior, fue la condición *sine qua non* pactada para la democratización del país" (Izquierdo 104).

The Spanish *Transición* thus offers a prime example of how memory is moulded in answer to present needs. Official memory discourses were, in the first one and a half decades after the death of Franco, di-rected at consensus, at creating a version of the past that would avoid polarisation of the Civil War's winners and losers. Bernecker describes two particularly influential versions of the dictatorial past. One holds that the dictatorship was necessary to end the chaos that reigned in the country during the Republic that preceded the Civil War. This view admits that the dictatorship lasted too long, and that repression of the left was too severe; but, as Bernecker states indignantly, these were considered but "Schönheitsfehler" (15). The other version points out that, during the Civil War, both sides committed equally horrid crimes that are best forgotten. "Diese Version postuliert eine Äquidistanz

14

beider Lager zu den Verantwortlichkeiten für die Grausamkeiten" (15), Bernecker explains. Altogether, the past was seen as dangerous matter that was quickly becoming obsolete in the light of the brilliant democratic future. Transition culture was dominated by what Resina calls "ugly duckling-rhetoric" ("Introduction" 11): Spain's development into a democracy was displayed as a fairytale-like metamorphosis into a dazzling, modern nation. "Enlightenment reason and modern bourgeois values" (12) inspired a further focus on the promising future that did not allow a reconsideration of the much less glamorous past. The purposeful glossing-over of the past was necessary for Spain to adopt a new identity: that of a modern, Western democracy.

Once democracy was in place, this ugly duckling-rhetoric did not hold. After years of uninterrupted government since the first democratic elections of 1983, the socialist PSOE (Partido Socialista Obrero Español) became involved in a series of corruption scandals. Worse still, it became known that the PSOE had run so-called GAL (Grupos Antiterroristas de Liberación), which combated terrorist group ETA through equally illegal terrorist attacks. These new facts, combined with economic difficulties, made Spaniards feel that democracy was not as enlightened or brilliant as it had seemed before. The initial excitement and jubilation made way for a generally felt *desencanto*, disenchantment (Masoliver 39). Spain fell out of love with democracy and faced its reality as one democratic nation among others, struggling with a whole new array of problems. As democracy lost its halo, it also lost its novelty, and the fear of new disturbances or even a civil war diminished. Correspondingly, the need for neutralisation became less urgent: a changeover from desmemorización to remembering the past without attempting to take the sting out of it became tangible around 1990, as Jo Labanyi shows ("History and Hauntology" 65).

The consolidation of democracy enabled a renewed interest in those aspects of the past that had earlier been deemed too conflictive to heed. Recently, this interest has evolved into the memory boom described at the beginning of this chapter. But just as the neutralisation of the past did not automatically lead to its being forgotten entirely, this boom by no means implies a straightforward progress towards a coming to terms with war, dictatorship, and transition. Indeed, although there is much more room now for critical remembering and attention for the war's *vencidos*, the discourse of consensus is still viable from the 1990s onward. According to Ulrich Winter, the press still tends to "no [...] olvidar, pero sí [...] neutralizar y fantasear el pasado" (U. Winter 31).

The *Transición*'s discourse of neutralisation is omnipresent, but it is still especially recognisable in the acts and speeches of the PP (Partido Popular); it is the PSOE that has proved most eager to stir up things past.

This is shown particularly clearly by the controversy surrounding the excavation, from the year 2000 onwards, of republican mass graves from the Civil War. A private initiative of the Asociación para la Recuperación de la Memoria Histórica (ARMH), it touched a society-wide nerve and led to a network of volunteers, scholars and other collaborators involved in the tracing of mass graves, their excavation, and the identification of those buried there. In this case, attempts at neutralising or soothing the question were not an option; once the excavations started, the very real and tangible presence of the soldiers' bodies forced the Spaniards to face up to the forgotten past. As Ulrich Winter puts it: "La reaparición de los muertos es, pues, un regreso del hecho traumático mismo" (25-26). Unsurprisingly, the PP government of the time was unwilling to support the movement (Blakeley 55).

There was no stopping to the matter, however. According to Georgina Blakeley, initiatives like the ARMH emerged due to national as well as international factors:

> A number of factors, both exogenous and endogenous, can explain the timing of attempts in Spain to recover the disappeared of the Civil War [...]. In terms of the former, the key factor is the change in the international environment [...]: a well-developed body of international human rights law [...]; a well-established network of non-governmental organizations NGOs) [...] which benefited from the development of new communication tools such as the internet [...]. At a domestic level, attempts to recover historical memory coincided with numerous anniversaries celebrating the fact that Spain has lived through the longest democratic period of its history. (45-46)

With Spain's new identity as a Western democracy came the importance of human rights, and the buried past became a global as well as a local matter. Following Jo Labanyi, Spain has been criticised "for refusing to confront the traumas of the past" ("History and Hauntology" 65). This criticism was particularly loud when Spanish judge Baltasar Garzón had former Chilean dictator Pinochet arrested, as it was felt that Spain first ought to hold its own dictator accountable (Blakeley 46). Under the pressure of these developments on a national and international level, the PP caved in and promised its support to the excavation of Civil War graves; but, expressing itself in what may be called a textbook example of transitional rhetoric, the 2003 PP government imposed the condition "that these excavations will not be used to reopen old wounds and revive old grudges" (55).

The current memory boom is, thus, not a phenomenon that Spain feels fully comfortable with. It is made up of a whole spectrum of memory narratives, most of which are either grouped around the transitional notion that remembering is dangerous, or around the discourse that comes with Spain's new democratic identity, which wants to remember the past and give a voice to the *vencidos*. Apart from these two memory narratives, a host of versions of the past and convictions as to how it is best approached can be found, and often, those who want to face the past are willing to neutralise it as they go along. One intermediary approach is visible, for example, in the discussion about Franco's burial place, the monumental Valle de los Caídos, built by republican prisoners of war and other forced labourers ("El Gobierno confirma"). This monument, a dangerously significant spot, has been left alone for decades. Now, its fate is open to debate. At the same time, though, this debate appears to head in a rather neutralising direction: the monument is to be provided with an educational "Centro de Interpretación del Franquismo" (El Gobierno convertirá"). Another such intermediary view is contained even in the *Ley de la Memoria Histórica* (Law of Historical Memory), an otherwise very typical product of the democratic discourse, approved by the Spanish government on the 31 October 2007. This law promises, among other things, recognition of *all* Civil War victims and victims of the dictatorship.

Yet in spite of such conciliatory endeavours, Spain and its memory discourses now appear to be characterised above all by polarisation. The silence pact of the *Transición* is partly to blame for this, as the careful avoidance of difficult subjects did nothing to really bring together the two halves of Spain that had fought each other in the War. The fact that Spain has what is essentially a two-party political system, and that the two major parties are always facing each other in government and opposition, does nothing to lessen this division. It is clear that the country is still divided into what are traditionally called "las dos Españas" (U. Winter 23). What is more, the memory boom causes Spain's disharmony to increase as differences are stressed and responses provoked. The PSOE has for some time advocated the reworking of the painful past, removing francoist symbols like the statue of Franco from the Plaza de San Juan de la Cruz in Madrid, and polemically changing street names that echo francoism. These types of action, however, always cause extensive media debates and diametrically oppose the PSOE and the PP. Moreover, they have given rise to a very vocal revisionist movement on the right wing that abandons the PP's careful, transitional stance of dealing with the past as little as possible. This movement is led by Pío Moa, remarkably a former member of antifrancoist resistance, whose best-selling *Los mitos de la Guerra Civil* (2003) and *Franco: un balance histórico* (2005) present a view of Franco's coup as a necessary answer to the Second Republic, which Moa portrays as increasingly communist and undemocratic.

Even the tragedy of 11 March 2004, has become a subject of dispute and discordance between the two parties, and plainly illustrates the reigning polarisation of the two Spains. After 191 people had been

killed in a terrorist attack on passenger trains in Madrid, the PSOE surprisingly won the elections only days later. The number of voters was
far greater than usual in these elections, and the result could be read as a
reproach to the PP for not only maintaining that the attack had been
performed by left-wing Basque terrorist group ETA, long after it had
become clear that Muslim organisation Al Qaeda was behind the bombings, but also for provoking Al Qaeda in the first place by openly supporting the USA's Iraq war despite mass protests. While the tragedy thus
inspired anger in PSOE voters, right-wing media began, in turn, to circulate all manner of conspiracy theories suggesting that ETA, not Al Qaeda,
was behind it. In Spanish media, examples of these two opposed interpretations of events abound – one need only compare an article like that
of García-Abadillo, who refuses to see the hand of Al Qaeda in the
"11-M" bombing, to that of Yoldi and Rodríguez, who criticise this
attitude. The 2007 commemoration of the train bombing was preceded
by a PP protest march against PSOE politics.

What is visible in contemporary Spanish society, then, is on the one
hand a great need to remember the past and to find justice for its victims, which causes debates, polarisation, and the occasional rise of
radical right-wing revisionism. On the other hand, though, there is still a
tendency to want to continue treating the past with the utmost care if it
cannot be left alone altogether. That this transitional discourse is still so
strong may hardly be called surprising. It was a strategy that had proved
immensely successful during the democratisation of Spain – and why
change a winning team? Indeed, Sebastiaan Faber asks himself: "Why
should any nation 'come to terms' with its past at all?". (210) In answer
to this question, he provides a number of reasons: remembering is a
moral duty, it is a legal duty, the truth must be known for scholarly
reasons, as well as for didactic ones; we can learn from it, so that it need
not repeat itself. Finally, Faber mentions the often felt suspicion that
what is repressed must come back to haunt. Faber calls this a psychological argument with "a clear Freudian genealogy" and rightly points
out that this assumption departs from a "health-related metaphor" (210),
where the Spanish nation is the traumatised patient whose repressed
memories disturb his everyday life (a metaphor in line with the discourse of amnesia I discussed earlier). All of the reasons mentioned
here, except perhaps that of the scholarly search for truth, appear to be
linked to a specifically Western democratic discourse that values human
rights and echoes the debates on personal and national trauma, on guilt
and responsibility, that took place in the wake of the Second World War
and the Holocaust. Yet the idea that human rights must come before all
else, even if they cause discord between the 'two Spains', is not necessarily one shared by all Spaniards in the light of their specific history.

Moreover, there is the slowly growing feeling, even among those who openly support a reconsideration of the past and recognise the moral duty to do right by those who lost the war and suffered repression, that the enormous attention generated for Spain's painful past is leading to an overkill, an "empacho de memoria" (Rosa, "Empacho de memoria"). On the occasion of the 2006 *Año de la Memoria Histórica* (Year of Historical Memory), Isaac Rosa writes that even though the memory movement per se is not a bad thing, chances are that "algunos acaben el año con la barriga llena de pasteles y, pasada la fiesta, rechacen otro bocado agitando una mano y palmeándose la abultada tripa mientras disimulan un regüeldo ahíto y dicen: no más memoria, por favor". Due to the sheer force of the movement and the accompanying commercial interest, as well as the institutionalisation and thus neutralisation of the past, Rosa notes that the publications and events, the television series and anniversaries are often "como golosinas, engordan pero no alimentan". Rosa's re-editing of his 1999 novel *Malamemoria* illustrates his point of view. Eight years after the first version had been published, he found the original title had become redundant, and named the new, reworked version *¡Otra maldita novela sobre la Guerra Civil!*

It is noteworthy that scholarly contributions to this discussion, even those that only deal with the phenomenon of the memory trend itself, do not remain impartial in the debate: they all insist that the past must be dealt with. As we have seen, Walther Bernecker does not exactly hide his indignation as he talks of revisionist memory narratives of the *Transición*, which branded the crimes of the dictatorship 'minor flaws'. Sebastiaan Faber, in turn, appears to agree fully with all five of his arguments (the moral, scholarly, legal, didactic and psychological reasons to remember). As he states that, to the question of *why* a past should be come to terms with, "the answer may seem too obvious for words", he shows a clear bias for the discourse of 'healthy' remembering. Moreover, he himself reverts to the sickness-to-health metaphor by stating:

> There are two ways to interpret Spain's recent obsession with its violent twentieth-century past: as a symptom of collective pathology or as a sign of sociopolitical health. In the first reading, Spain is finally beginning to pay the price for its almost thirty-year long *pacto del silencio* or *pacto del olvido* [...]. In the second reading, Spain's democracy – increasingly stable and vibrant [...] – is poised to face its final challenge: working through its past, reconciling remaining differences, and establishing a truly national collective memory. Can one imagine a more convincing sign of the nation's rock-solid health than its vigorous civil society [...]? (205)

Literary scholar Ana Luengo is also explicit in her opinion on the necessity of remembering the Spanish past: "Parecía que con crear una democracia consensuada ya estaba todo superado [...]. La cuestión es que no es así, quedaban muchas cosas por resolver" (274).

This study is, of course, subject to the same risk of bias. Not a Spanish product but, rather, a study from the outside, performed within a Western European nation with a strong pro-democratic and humanitarian identity, it could easily imply a similar preference for 'working through' painful pasts, and letting human rights prevail. The author is never fully in control of his or her work, as the following chapter will make clear, and the reader may well discover traces of such bias. At the same time, though, I will at least avoid such firm statements as that of Bernecker and stress once again that, while careful neutralisation may be uncomfortable, especially when developments all over society suggest a nationally felt need to face the past, a massive memory explosion may not be any more comfortable, either. As Jo Labanyi and Isaac Rosa have pointed out, the fact that the past is talked about does not necessarily lead to anything other than a lot of talk. Indeed, if one looks at contemporary Spanish society with Faber's Freudian metaphor of the sick and traumatised country in mind, one cannot help but be reminded of the Holocaust victim who, by talking ceaselessly about his trauma, turns his interlocutors against him (Langer 28). While it seems that the very urgency of memory discourse in Spain shows that the past can no longer be glossed over, there may be no adequate way to speak about its worst sides, either.

Above all, it is the consequences of such a clear opinion about what the Spanish are to do with their past, namely, to remember it and deal with it, that the present study wants to investigate and challenge. Many scholars of contemporary Spanish cultural phenomena in general, and of literature in particular, seem to suggest that it is the task of the artist, of the writer, both to clear the way for such a healing process and to make a head start with the actual process of coming to terms with the past. After all, as Bernecker mentions, literature is above other media the place where "Rand- und Teiloffentlichkeiten" (19) are present. Luckily, Bernecker finds, Spanish literature has done exactly that: it has touched upon a taboo subject before it was raised anywhere else. To her satisfaction, Anna Caballé also points out that in Spanish literature of the 1990s, "ciñiéndonos al ámbito hispánico, la escritura memorialística [...] ha dado un vuelco impresionante, generando un movimiento [...] expansivo" (11-12). Ulrich Winter sees things differently: Spanish memory media are characterised, he says, by processes of reconciliation that are visible precisely in cinema and literature (33). He classifies a number of contemporary Spanish novels as "arte del olvido", nostalgic books with a predilection for the surreal and fantastic and full of "imágenes borrosas" (32). The novels present a "premeditada revisión del pasado que libera el futuro" (34) and thus, while broaching a difficult subject, do so in the careful way that is typical of transitional discourse. Winter finds that authors such as Antonio Muñoz Molina, Rafael Chirbes and Javier Marías write this type of literature. Ana Luengo agrees, and openly criticises novels in which "la Guerra Civil aparece como un episodio muy antiguo" (273). She claims, moreover, that both the writers and their readers have a responsibility to deal with the past 'morally', not using it for commercial benefit:

> En realidad, toda producción literaria sobre la Guerra Civil y la Dictadura se encuentra en una encrucijada entre el replanteamiento político-histórico del pasado, y el aprovechamiento simplemente efectista del mismo. Cada *homo agens* será, pues, responsable del camino que prefiera escoger, y parece que existe una tendencia a elegir el segundo. No sólo por los escritores, sino también por los lectores: las novelas que proponen una construcción contemplativa tienen mayor éxito editorial en España que las novelas que proponen la desconstrucción como incómoda relectura del pasado. La responsabilidad estriba en elegir de qué forma se quieren sentar las bases morales para el presente, y para el futuro. (274)

This ethical obligation of authors and other artists to break taboos is not an idea restricted to the Spanish scholarly context. Criticism of those who show too little *engagement* in times of ideological struggles, or who fail to pay attention to what has been repressed and 'forgotten', is of all times and places. In the context of Spanish literary studies, the call for a working-through of the past, in which the writer has an important responsibility, a task to perform, is so frequent that it needs to be challenged. Why should we expect of an author, after all, that he or she sides with the advocates of stirring up the past? And even if authors intend to write such 'responsible' literature, how can we be sure that they actually do this successfully?

For an important problem which is inherent in such expectations, is that the relationship between remembering as it takes place in society and the way memory takes shape within a novel is so problematic that it is really difficult to speak of a relationship at all, as the following chapter will attempt to explain. Whereas I will show in the same chapter that it is possible for memory narratives to find their way wholly into a work of literature, their literary recombination may lead to all kinds of complications and readings which the author may never have intended. The act of writing a literary work, or, indeed, of writing a text in general, is so hard to control that it may end up saying either what the author intended it to say, or the opposite; or, as frequently happens, both at the same time, and a whole lot of other things, too.

Yet the question is whether the 'unreadability' of texts, and particularly of literary texts, is really such a bad thing in the face of a subject as difficult as the recent Spanish past. Perhaps, the complexity of this subject is better addressed by allowing for complexities within the literary work, and perhaps a clear and normative stance of a 'responsible' author would fail to do justice to the uncomfortable aspects of the past that the literary work engages with. Perhaps, in other words, an 'ethical' treatment of the past is not one that aims for a direct and unproblematic reading experience, but rather, one that allows for uncertainty and otherness.

The body of texts I will investigate here consists of a number of recent Spanish novels that deal with the memory of the country's undemocratic past, and with the memory narratives of contemporary Spanish society. I will try and establish the part the novels played in passing on, developing, creating and reworking the memory of the Civil War and the dictatorship of Franco, and in the process, I will come across many questions about the role of literature in addressing painful histories. Instead of looking at the contribution literary works make or attempt to make to 'healing' a nation or to trading in 'forgetting' for 'remembering', I will instead look upon the texts themselves, enquiring how they incorporate memory narratives from Spanish society and how this incorporation affects the works' positions in relation to extra-literary memory processes. In doing so, I will study these novels not as symptoms of processes of forgetting or remembering, but as literary works which exist in and relate to a complex environment of memory struggles.

PART I

THEORY

CHAPTER 2

Literature, Trauma, and Ethics

Reconciling Post-Structuralism
and Collective Memory Studies

Collective Memory Studies
and the Crisis of Representation

Should art in general, and literature in particular, serve a taboo-breaking purpose? Can it be expected to engage with, respond to, and direct, memory discourses in society? As they address these types of questions, which become pertinent precisely in the face of such a difficult past as that of Spain, scholars like Ana Luengo, Walther Bernecker, and Sebastiaan Faber betray an interest in the function of literature in society, and a concern with ethics and literary responsibility, which are certainly not unique to the Spanish situation. In fact, these scholars start from a research branch that is relatively new, but quite influential already. This branch, collective memory studies, looks upon memory as a collective phenomenon, and upon literature as a medium that plays an important role in transmitting views of the past. In the words of memory scholar Astrid Erll:

> Literarische Texte […] erfüllen vielfältige erinnerungskulturelle Funktionen, wie die Herausbildung von Vorstellungen über vergangene Lebenswelten, die Vermittlung von Geschichtsbildern, die Aushandlung von Erinnerungskonkurrenzen und die Reflexion über Prozesse und Probleme des kollektiven Gedächtnisses. Literatur *wirkt* in der Erinnerungskultur. (142)

Collective memory studies emerged together with a memory boom in the whole of the Western world (Huyssen) – a boom attributed to many causes, but said above all to be the consequence of the Holocaust's impact and the prospect that, soon, nobody will remain to testify to it first hand. According to Joan Ramon Resina, "the current interest in memory goes back to the 1990s-1980s, a decade that saw […] the disappearance of the generation that had experienced the dramatic mid-century events, most notably the survivors of extermination camps" ("Introduction" 1). However, as Jos Perry suggests, the importance of memory culture nowadays could also be explained by its commercial possibilities (13), and this may be especially true now, considering the wealth, health and prolonged lifespan of the older generations (11). The reasons may vary from country to country, but Erll mentions three factors that seem to apply generally: historical transformation processes, changes in media technologies and media functioning, and the scholarly interest in memory (4). Erll, herself an exponent *par excellence* of collective memory studies, thus shows that this research branch is both fed by the memory boom and is keeping it, and itself, alive and vibrant. And alive it is, particularly in the humanities: Aleida Assmann calls memory a leading concept of cultural studies ("Gedächtnis"), Wulf Kansteiner talks of a sudden "memory wave in the humanities" (179).

Since its beginnings, collective memory studies has developed a whole set of theories and terms in order to study, classify and understand the phenomenon of memory. One important point of departure was egyptologist Jan Assmann's re-introduction, in 1992, of the term 'collective memory', which was coined by Maurice Halbwachs as early as 1925. This concept made it possible to look upon memory not as a personal, individual and psychological phenomenon, but as a shared entity that united groups and cultures. Assmann found that, while the concept was highly useful, its definition as "the active past that forms our identities" (Halbwachs 111) could do with some clarification. After dismissing it as "overly vague" (45), he set out to expand on the term and on other useful insights Halbwachs provided. Assmann adopted Halbwachs's view that memory is never truly individual, but that it exists within what he calls a *cadre social*, the system of communication and interaction of a specific social group. Individual memory is determined by the thought patterns, norms, presuppositions and experiences of the group the rememberer is a part of. "Individuell im strengen Sinne sind nur die Empfindungen, nicht die Erinnerungen", Jan Assmann states (37).

Still following Halbwachs, Assmann then assumed that every social group knows a sort of consensus on how the past is to be narrated, which depends on the necessities of the group at that particular moment in time. This collective memory, constantly developing as society and its needs change, both obeys and determines the group's identity process. Assmann added a classification of different types of memory to Halbwachs's theory: memory can either be cultural (52), if the remembered is in the distant past – the Napoleonic wars, Ancient Egypt – and becomes part of the foundational stories and myths upon which a group identity or nation is founded; or communicative, if the past is still remembered, talked about and passed on by those who lived it (50). Collective memory is thus a dynamic phenomenon, which includes certain aspects of the past and excludes others, depending on the need for identity building, and which shifts as communicative memory either becomes cultural memory, or is forgotten, as time passes.

After Assmann's influential publication there followed a long-standing confusion as to how collective memory could be defined. It seemed clear that it described the phenomenon of group memory, but due to its shifting nature and its dependence on individual memory processes it could never be fully pinned down. The confusion was worsened by the simultaneous emergence of such synonyms, derivatives and subcategories as social, cultural, or historical memory (Olick and Robbins 111). However, this did not prevent a sudden "overuse of the term" (112); indeed, as Aleida Assmann puts it, "a whole new discourse has been built around the term [...] that fills extended library shelves" ("Four Formats of Memory" 1). Gradually, the focus shifted from debating the validity of the notion and its actual ontological status to searching for methods to apply it to cultural studies.

As a research branch, collective memory studies has developed a great many new and useful concepts and insights, and it has changed our views on memory processes in society. As an added benefit in the field of literary studies, moreover, it has provided a functionalistic perspective that views literature as a medium of memory. Collective memory, as is now widely accepted, is a group phenomenon; for that reason, in order to be shared and understood by this group, it must always be mediated. In Kansteiners words, "All memories [...] only assume collective relevance when they are structured, represented, and used in a social setting" (190). Erll states:

> Kollektives Gedächtnis ist ohne Medien nicht denkbar. [...] Es gehört zu den Grundannahmen der kulturwissenschaftlichen Gedächtnisforschung seit Halbwachs und Warburg, dass kollektives Gedächtnis weder eine vom Individuum abstrahierte Instanz noch ein Resultat biologischer Mechanismen wie Vererbung ist [...]. Genau deshalb müssen Medien als Vermittlungsinstanzen und Transformatoren zwischen individueller und kollektiver Dimension des Erinnerns gedacht werden. So können persönliche Erinnerungen erst durch mediale Repräsentation und Distribution zu kollektiver Relevanz gelangen. [...] Umgekehrt erlangt das Individuum nur über Kommunikation und Medienrezeption Zugang zu soziokulturellen Wissensordnungen und Schemata. (123)

Memory media are pivotal in the sense that they are the bridge between individual and collective memory, and they are as varied as they are many. Memory can be transmitted through oral narration, through a photograph or work of art, through television or the internet, but also, in a broader sense, through rituals and monuments. In this context, Pierre Nora's famous concept of *lieu de mémoire* is significant. Nora's groundbreaking study *Les lieux de mémoire (1984-1992)* describes a

27

great number of memory sites, which are "les lieux où se cristallise et se réfugie la mémoire" (xvii) and which are characterised by their symbolic function as memory media, transmitting a sort of shared conception of the past. Nora includes not only commemorations, museums and celebrations, but also the Larousse dictionary or the Marseillaise hymn in his work. Memory media pass on memory and shape it at the same time; Astrid Erll underlines the far-reaching importance of media in memory studies by modifying Halbwachs's term of *les cadres sociaux* into *les cadres médiaux de la mémoire* (140).

Literature is one of these memory media, and this new awareness is in itself enough to inspire a new direction in literary studies that follows the memory tendency of cultural studies as a whole. The reception of a literary work, its election as a canonical work, and the changed perception of it over time, are fruitful subjects of study, the more so since the literary canon and the changes it undergoes are indicative of identity processes on national, religious or other levels. So, Ann Rigney's article "Portable Monuments", on the long-term reception of Walter Scott's historical novel *The Heart of Midlothian*, shows the novel's beginnings as a part of popular culture, and its consequent inscription in, and transformation of, history writing. In general, the study of the development of memory media over time and their contribution and adaptation to various memory discourses does not just lay bare ongoing memory processes, but also serves the investigation of the continually changing role, place, appreciation and function a work of literature can have in society. As for the work itself, new aspects of it that are highlighted in new eras may help us to appreciate its complexity and explain its canonisation, or the lack thereof.

Both for cultural studies in general and for literary studies in particular, then, the scholarly turn to memory has been of great benefit. However, it has been criticised severely at the same time. As I mentioned earlier, collective memory studies developed out of a concern for the victims of difficult pasts, and particularly out of the move that the Holocaust is now undergoing from communicative into cultural memory. It is noteworthy that particularly Holocaust historians, who studied the Shoah well before the memory boom took off, are highly critical of memory's popularity both in scholarly circles and in society at large. On the one hand, these scholars often recognise that the turn to memory has been a natural consequence of the developments in their own field, that of historiography, after the Holocaust. On the other hand, though, they often conceive of it as a movement that allowed a hollowing-out and weakening of their own terms and theories. It is therefore not unusual for historians, particularly Holocaust historians, to react against the study of memory or the centrality of the concept in the humanities. Historian Charles Maier phrases this competition of history and memory most forcefully: "[M]emory, we can claim, has become the discourse that replaces history", he states (142). In his view, the discourse on memory is an impoverished version of that of history, and the two are in serious competition as one tries to replace the other.

It is the commercial success of memory that seems to worry historians like Maier, and particularly the danger of oversimplification that comes with it. Maier openly expresses his concern about what he calls "memory industry" (143), and Holocaust historian Saul Friedlander remarks that we are faced with a "stream of representations which [...] swings between the mythical and the banal" (50). Dominick LaCapra, in turn, underlines the warnings of historians against "the danger of an obsession with, or fixation on, memory" (12). He mentions that "the immersion in memory and its sites may at times have the quality of junk-Proustian *Schwärmerei*" (*History and Memory* 9), and his description of a particular side effect of the interest in memory, which elaborates on the Proust reference, immediately calls to mind Isaac Rosa's "empacho de memoria". Discussing Charles Maier's article, LaCapra states with approval: "[Maier] is preoccupied not simply with a quantitative excess that signals a morbid preoccupation [...]. Indeed the memory that upsets him is itself something one indulges in [...]. It is the chocolate-covered madeleine of the psyche on which one overdoses" (14).

The question is, of course, whether these scholars are justified in their protests against memory's commercialisation. Admittedly, popular culture can reduce the central idea of memory itself, and commerce may indeed produce a form of memory that is sentimental and overly sweet. But that does not mean that the centrality of memory per se is a bad thing. Indeed, as I have mentioned earlier, the turn to memory has brought new insights and approaches to the analysis of culture, so that it is at least a fruitful scholarly direction. Still, historians are not exactly in the wrong when they warn against the dangers of memory. If we only look at the terms and concepts that are used to describe memory processes, particularly the body of psychological terms such as 'trauma', 'repression' or 'forgetting', we see that they are taken out of their psychological context and employed in a way that is often simplistic and schematic, so that they do not end up doing justice to the complexity of the historical realities they cover. As we have seen in the Spanish case, such use is not restricted to everyday life. As scholars talk of 'trauma' and 'repression', they often impose a sort of positivistic view on memory processes, a sickness-to-health metaphor that is clearly normative. And if we compare this frequently unthinking use of such notions to the treatment they originally received, in post-Holocaust historiography, we can only note that the memory boom has led to the danger of these concepts becoming hollow even in scholarly texts.

This is the more striking when we consider that, when psychoanalytic terms were first used to describe collective processes in the works of historians of the Holocaust, their importance lay precisely in their complexity. At the time, historiography faced a crisis of representation that was not inspired, but certainly greatly intensified, by the Holocaust, that mid-twentieth century "watershed", as it has been called (Felman and Laub, xiv). After the Holocaust, one of the concerns that emerged in Western thought was the problem of representing what was soon considered 'unrepresentable'. French philosopher Jean-François Lyotard famously described the impact of Auschwitz, in its acquired role as *pars pro toto* of the entire Shoah, in analogy to an earthquake which destroyed the instruments that could measure its destructive force:

> Supposez qu'un séisme ne détruise pas seulement des vies, des édifices, des objets, mais aussi les instruments qui servent à mesurer directement et indirectement les séismes. L'impossibilité de le quantifier n'interdit, pas, mais inspire aux survivants l'idée d'une force tellurique très grande. (91)

Referring to this analogy, Sidra DeKoven Ezrahi remarks that "the camp [...] constitutes the very center of evil but is located in a realm just beyond the borders of civilised speech and behavior". As a consequence, "at the postmodern end of our millennium, a new aesthetics and ethics of representation are being forged with Auschwitz as the ultimate point of reference" ("Representing Auschwitz" 121). In the wake of the Holocaust, the reductive and inadequate nature of language came to the foreground: the Holocaust, it became clear, was a limit-event whose sheer terror consisted in the fact that it *escaped* words.

The felt unspeakability of Auschwitz as a historical reality had some major consequences in a number of areas. First and foremost, it inspired a further rethinking of historiography, which all of a sudden saw itself faced with the impossible task of historicising the Holocaust. While the late nineteenth century was already marked by a "crisis of historicism, that is, the notion that history is linear or progressive" (Voloshin 70), this crisis reached new heights when, particularly from the 1960s onwards and with a peak in the late 1980s and early 1990s, historiography began dealing with the Shoah. Promptly, history's emphasis on fact-finding and the reconstruction of 'truth' was once again sincerely questioned, not in the least place by historians themselves. Saul Friedlander, a prominent Holocaust historian, thematises the "*inadequacy* of traditional historiographical representation" and the dilemma it entails for the historian who wants to "keep records of events" (x). The 1985 *Historikerstreit* of German historians such as Jürgen Habermas and Ernst Nolte, whose subject was that of the comparability or exceptionality of the Holocaust, arose, in essence, out of the very same question of 'unspeakability', challenged by Nolte and defended by Habermas: was it 'allowed' to apply normal schemes of comparison and comprehension to this unique historical phenomenon? Altogether, historiography was unmasked as much less objective than it made itself appear: as a narrative, it contained a certain level of the fictionality that comes with narrative organisation. Eminent historian Hayden White, particularly, problematised the narrativity of historiography in his influential 1987 study *The Content of the Form*, and pondered whether narrative, with its emplotment and schematisation of the 'real' past, was really the most suitable form for addressing it.

Faced with this crisis of representation, historiography felt its own inadequacy and began developing new instruments to deal with a reality which could no longer be approached objectively and in a positivistic way. Historians turned increasingly to memory as a subjective form of history, and their interest in subjectivity and search for modes of narration other than that of traditional historiography converged with the importance that survivor testimony and survivor trauma gained in the aftermath of the Holocaust. The symptoms and sufferings of a wholly new category of trauma patients, the concentration camp survivors, gave way to a new field known as 'trauma studies' or 'trauma theory', and the medical discourse that was developed in this branch of psychology, sociology, and psychiatry resonates in the 'writing' of the Holocaust. So, terms like 'working through', 'trauma', 'mourning', or 'repression' became applicable to entire nations and large-scale collective processes. The influential 1967 work *Die Unfähigkeit zu Trauern* by psychoanalysts Alexander and Margarete Mitscherlich and literary scholar Shoshana Felman's 1992 *Testimony*, a collaboration with psychiatrist Dori Laub, are but the clearest examples of the extent to which psychoanalytic terminology became applicable to collective processes. As time passed and more became known about the workings of individual trauma, scholars applied Freudian and other clinical terms more and more frequently to processes in society, and used them in their descriptions of the Holocaust as a traumatic event from which entire peoples, most notably the Jews, suffered. Saul Friedlander's *Memory, History, and the Extermination of the Jews of Europe* (1993) is one such instance.

Dominick LaCapra famously analysed this use of a new narrative and defended it against its critics. LaCapra finds the new trauma narrative useful in the study of the Holocaust, and suggests the use of psychoanalysis as a perspective which enables the historian to reformulate traditional historiography (*Representing the Holocaust* 8). He argues in favour of the application of originally clinical psychoanalytic concepts, designed by Freud to describe individual cases, onto collective processes. In fact, he writes:

> My basic premise [...] is that the fundamental concepts of psychoanalysis (such as transference, resistance, denial, repression, acting-out, and working-through) undercut the binary opposition between the individual and society, and their application to individual or collective phenomena is a matter of informed argument and research. Freud developed these concepts in a clinical context and thought they applied to collective processes only through analogy; a recurrent concern is how it is possible to extend them to collectivities. I believe that this concern, both in Freud and in others, is based on mistaken individualistic ideological assumptions [...]. These concepts refer to processes that always involve modes of interaction, mutual reinforcement, conflict, censorship, orientation toward others, and so forth, and their relative individual or collective status should not be prejudged. (*History and Memory* 43)

For LaCapra, the Holocaust and its aftermath are so complex and so difficult to understand that the use of psychoanalytic terms is not only permitted, but actually *called for*, to enable us to grasp this complexity without reducing it to a binary opposition.

Yet LaCapra is aware that such individual psychoanalytic concepts need to be handled with care in a collective context. If they are borrowed unthinkingly and used to describe new, collective processes, concepts like 'trauma', 'repression', or 'working-through' may obscure as much as they reveal. This is a danger Dominick LaCapra acknowledges and warns against: he states that "in the (curiously named) field of 'trauma theory', there is a great temptation to trope away from specificity and to generalize hyperbolically" (*History and Memory* 23). Robert Eaglestone also quite rightly points to "the risk [...] that the term trauma [...] if it is invoked with all the rest of the analytic and therapeutic tools, will overcode the accounts of the Holocaust with a discourse of healing analysis or therapy" (33).

This risk is certainly strong when it comes to collective memory studies, a branch of research that developed around the time when the discourse of psychoanalysis thus gained in importance within historiography. Interestingly, as Wulf Kansteiner points out, the combination of psychoanalytic notions and the very concept of collective memory itself is problematic. After all, one of the key insights this field has produced is precisely that collective memory processes do not function in a similar way to, or have the same status as, the processes of individual memory, so that concepts like these must be used with the necessary caution. Indeed, Kansteiner finds their use so risky that he prefers to avoid it altogether. In his eyes, they cause the impression that the concept of collective memory is made up of individual memories which then 'add up' to a sort of society-wide pathological profile. For this sum of memories, he prefers the term of *collected memory*:

A collected memory is an aggregate of individual memories which behaves and develops just like its individual composites, and which can therefore be studied with the whole inventory of neurological, psychological, and psychoanalytical methods and insights concerning the memories of individuals. [...] But on a collective scale, especially on the scale of larger collectives, such assumptions are misleading. (Kansteiner 186)

As Kansteiner explains, *collective* memory is a non-individual phenomenon. The use of psychoanalytic terms to describe it would obscure the actual dependence of memory not on mechanisms like repression, but on actual political and social factors of the present (187).

Kansteiner's emphatic remarks on the misleading nature of psychoanalytical methods in the study of collective processes already imply that not all scholars of collective memory share his scruples. And indeed, it has become habitual for memory scholars to speak of 'collective trauma' or of the 'repression' of painful pasts, often in the very hollowed-out way that LaCapra wanted to avoid at all cost. The question is whether collective memory studies can actually do without the tools and terms it takes from the study of individual memory. After all, as I have shown above, this is the toolkit that collective memory studies has inherited from the crisis of representation that led to the memory boom, and it is clear that such a pervasive legacy cannot be shaken off all that easily.

While these terms are difficult to avoid, it is clear that they need to be used carefully when applied to collective processes. To use a discourse of psychological illness in reference to a nation or context is to describe it in normative terms. This has its consequences, not only for that which is talked of, but also for those who do the talking: historians and other scholars who speak of trauma and painful pasts assume an ethical role of their own. Joan Ramon Resina's description of the ideal "alternative historian" summarises the ethical part historians are to play. The alternative historian, says Resina, "rejects the metaphysics of traditional history – the history of the state", and performs an ethical task that is almost heroic: "Recovering tracts of historical amnesia for the collective memory is comparable to filling the ocean with polders" ("Short of Memory" 119). If this in itself noble goal is embedded in a health-related discourse, the historian who wants to fulfil such an ethical and responsible role easily becomes a sort of doctor or psychiatrist who can 'heal' the traumatised nation by rescuing the forgotten. In the process, the historian becomes an authority on 'truth-finding'.

Even if it appears to lead to exaltation of the own importance, the ethical stance of the historian or the memory scholar is entirely understandable and even laudable, in the sense that it tries to lay bare 'tracts of historical amnesia' that were repressed by official versions of memory. Particularly in a context where a painful past is 'silenced' by official memory narratives and where the victims' voices are allowed no place, the historian is right to assume an ethical responsibility. Yet if psychoanalytic metaphors are used unthinkingly, the actual outcome is not an alternative historiography. Rather, discourses of forgetting are simply replaced with a new narrative of trauma and health. Joan Ramon Resina warns that it is not enough to uncover certain narratives about the past as myths: "it is not sufficient to discover in it a simulacrum [...]. A simulacrum cannot be merely denounced, for that implies that one is in possession of a sounder paradigm of truth" ("Introduction" 5). Scholars who grant themselves the power of 'truth-finders' and judges actually operate according to a mechanism of exclusion that Michel Foucault would call the "volonté de vérité" (*L'ordre du discours* 16): they themselves are among those authorised to find out and expose the 'truth' about the past, and as a consequence, alternatives are overlooked or forbidden.

When scholars combat official memory discourses in their role of alternative historians, the tendency to want to replace one memory narrative with another, a 'truer' one, is already dubious. It is perhaps even more problematic in the context of the memory boom. These days, the urge to remember has become *part* of official memory narratives. Instead of filling an ocean with polders, scholars of the past may have trouble finding spots that are still flooded by the sea of the forgotten. As a consequence, those who insist on confronting the nation with its painful past can be said to *reinforce* official memory narratives rather than to look for the elements that are excluded by such an official version. So, scholars of history and memory may unwittingly be adhering to official health-related images of the past, combating versions of neutralisation and silencing, and end up in competition and binary opposition.

When scholars lose themselves in a sickness-to-health discourse, this also leads to a particular blindness towards the object of study that I have noted at the beginning of this chapter. Scholars of memory media, not in the last place literary scholars, can easily be tempted to look primarily upon the way their medium has functioned or is still functioning in society. Their authority as 'truth-finders' or doctors lends them the air of judges, and they may be tempted to subject the object they are appreciating to the rules and norms of the official discourse that they are promoting. Often, a literary scholar will thus look upon novels written in the period just before the memory boom took off and point out to what extent these novels have behaved 'as they should', placing the painful, 'traumatic past', back on the agenda. In the process, contemporary scholars expect their objects of study to assume a vanguard position in what was, in hindsight, a process towards remembering. Bernecker's

remark about the "Rand- und Teilöffentlichkeiten" of art, and of literature and film in particular, is illustrative of this expectation. So is the
following statement of literary scholar Ernestine Schlant: "[L]iterature
projects the play of the imagination, exposing levels of conscience and
consciousness that are part of a culture's unstated assumptions and
frequently acknowledged elsewhere" (3). Literature, in other words, can
legitimately push the boundaries of what is permitted. Art is privileged
in the sense that it says things differently, so that it is allowed the freedom to say more or other things than those dictated by official discourses. If it has not performed the ethical task that arises out of this
privilege, the literary scholar may condemn it according to the rules that
are valid nowadays in the domain of memory.

The memory medium, the work of fiction, will thus be seen in terms
of its function within the greater whole and judged according to certain
rules. As a consequence, the novel is reduced to one link in a chain of
cause and effect, and even when its specificity as a literary utterance is
not forgotten, it is read in a way that does not do full justice to the
peculiarity of the work itself. Michel Foucault warned against such a
view of discursive statements in terms of the question "selon quelles
règles tel énoncé a-t-il été construit" (*L'archéologie du savoir* 39). He
would rather we attempt to "restituer à l'énoncé sa singularité
d'événement" (40). Only if we look at a novel as it occurs, we can see it
in its own, discontinuous and peculiar light.

Perhaps, then, the literary scholar had better avoid a psychoanalytic
discourse and its implications, not because this will lead to any degree
of objectivity, but because this particular discourse has become bound
up inextricably with official, conciliatory memory narratives and a set of
norms and values which imply the healing of the nation. Rather, the
literary scholar's equivalent of Resina's 'alternative historian' may
come to see the individual works of art not in function of the sickness-
to-health metaphor, but as individual utterances at a particular place and
time. So, the optimism that is implied by psychoanalysis in the simplified form frequently found in memory studies, will not have to determine the study of contemporary Spanish fiction – and the literary works
themselves are appreciated in their complexity.

Collective Memory Studies and the Legacy
of Post-Structuralism

Literary scholars who belong to the field of collective memory studies
can thus be affected by the popularity and omnipresence of memory
nowadays, and historians like LaCapra, Maier or Friedlander do well to
warn them against a risk of hollowed-out metaphors and their impact on
the positions scholars choose in relation to their objects. But there is yet

another aspect of collective memory studies' inheritance from historiography and trauma studies that causes its scholars to struggle, and it particularly affects those who take literature as their subject. Due to a simplistic and schematic interpretation of post-Holocaust, twentieth-century theory, particularly of post-structuralist thought, memory scholars tend to jump to conclusions about the relationship between text and context, a relationship that is particularly central when it comes to dealing with texts about difficult historical realities. Interestingly, their conclusions are based on an unnecessarily harsh view of twentieth-century theory that also surfaces in the original, post-Holocaust historians' debates.

The crisis of historiography that reached a boiling point in the wake of the Holocaust was a crisis of representation in general, and what went for historiographical texts also went for all other kinds of texts. Friedlander states, speaking for his fellow historians: "Ultimately we are confronted with the problem of language as such" (57). It appeared that not just historiography, but any form of representation could not lay claim to truth, no matter how faithfully it wanted to portray historical reality. Words, it seemed, would only form an obscuring layer over a chaotic reality. As Ernst van Alphen phrases it: "The problem is not that historical reality does not exist; rather, it is that our talking about it does not make it present but, on the contrary, causes it to recede behind the rhetorical and narrative effects of our discourse" (32). Language itself, a sign system, was not capable of grasping this reality; worse still, it obscured it and pushed it to the background. Representation of a horrifying event like the Holocaust, which must always take place in a system of signs, became fundamentally problematic.

Such insights into and thoughts on the nature of language resonated with other, partly simultaneous, partly anterior developments in Western philosophical discourses. Criticism of the transparency and objectivity of language and other systems of signs already marked the structuralist movement that began stirring itself way before the dramatic events in Nazi Germany unfolded. As early as 1916, Ferdinand de Saussure had published *Cours de linguistique générale*, a pivotal, structuralist study in linguistics which conceived of language as a system of signs that does not refer to reality directly, but that is self-referential. The essentially French structuralist and post-structuralist approaches of the 1950s and 1960s investigated the consequences of this problem of referentiality in a multitude of domains. For instance, Roland Barthes famously pronounced the Death of the Author in 1967: a text, made out of language, did not mirror and obey an authorial intention, and the author's power was partially transposed onto the reader, now the principal constructor of meaning. In post-structuralism, Jacques Derrida stressed the extent to which the self-referential text could turn against its author by showing how uncontrollable and dangerous language is to the writer (*De la grammatologie*), and Michel Foucault pointed out how utterances are not subject to external laws, but generate their own norms and values (*L'archéologie du savoir*, *L'ordre du discours*).

Educated in this post-structuralist tradition, scholars of memory, and among them, those who take Spanish literature about the Civil War as their subject, are very much aware of the limited referentiality of language, and of the particular problems this leaves them with when studying memory, often mediated through language. Remarkably, it has become rather a habit in the scholarly debate on memory to incorporate an awareness of the nature of language and, what is more, to interpret it as a downright law, a strict boundary thrown up between a text, made of language, and its context. Memory scholars tend to assume post-structuralism has severed all links between a text and a context, and in doing so, perform a schematic and harsh reading of poststructuralist theory.

This reading turns out to be of great hindrance in memory studies, particularly in literary memory studies, for it does not allow scholars to discuss or analyse a work and then connect their findings unproblematically to a contextual reality. Of course, to read a contemporary Spanish novel without any regard for its context, while in it, the francoist dictatorship is remembered and thematised in ways remarkably similar to memory processes going on outside it, is not a satisfactory option. What is more, scholars and critics inspired by collective memory studies do not *want* to read such novels without paying attention to their contexts, since the rapports between literature and society are in fact what interests them most. And while looking at the function of a literary work as a memory medium in a certain memory culture has proved, as mentioned before, a worthy subject of study, the actual *text* and the memory processes described within, must not be overlooked.

Yet if we look more closely, we find that the interpretation of structuralism and post-structuralism shared by these memory scholars is simply all too strict. To conclude from the impressive body of theoretical and philosophical works on language which the twentieth century produced that theory has somehow robbed language of all its 'relevance', is to simplify matters greatly. Rather, it must be suspected that the contrary is true: the pervasive legacy of the twentieth century is profoundly marked by the Holocaust, and its 'irrational', 'relativist' and deconstructivist force can be seen as a response to the very event. "These understandings of the postmodern fail to take into account both its central and consistent commitment to ethics and its rigorous, rational side", Eaglestone argues, "that is, postmodernism does not reject rationality, but is aware of the limits and processes of rationality" (3). Seen in this way, literature in general, and contemporary Spanish novels in particular, may be non-referential in that they are made of language, but they still have a particular connection to, and ethical responsibility towards, historical events.

It is plain, however, that many scholars of collective memory do conceive of twentieth-century theory as relativist, as a wedge between a text and a context. In fact, some of them enjoy the thought that collective memory studies *challenges* structuralism and post-structuralism, and that this is precisely what makes collective memory studies such an attractive direction of research – along with the dearly missed 'social relevance' to which the humanities can now once more lay a claim. Wulf Kansteiner phrases the satisfaction scholars experience as follows:

> On the one hand, the study of memory turns academics into concerned citizens who share the burdens of contemporary memory crises. As "memory experts" we can explore the social impact of rapidly evolving communication technologies, the uncertainties of collective belonging after the end of the Cold War, and the challenges of coming to terms with war and genocide. On the other hand, the study of memory is a bona fide intellectual exercise, one that allows academics to respond to the most interesting philosophical legacies of the last century. In particular, through the concept of memory, we can demonstrate to the few remaining postmodern critics how representations really work and how the power of representations can be explained. The rare combination of social relevance and intellectual challenge explains the popularity of the field. (179-180)

Erll phrases things less polemically when she states: "Unter dem Gedächtnis-Paradigma wird nun die Bezugnahme auf Vergangenheit mit den Einsichten postmoderner Theoriebildung vereint" (4). Hers is an attitude frequently found among memory scholars: that of a slight discomfort when faced with the legacy of (post-)structuralist theories – and with the prohibition of connecting text and context that these theories are felt to imply.

This perceived intellectual confrontation of collective memory studies and twentieth century theory entails a struggle for the many scholars who want to study memory processes in literature. In the Spanish context, this is illustrated by works like Bettina Bannasch and Christiane Holm's collection *Erinnern und Erzählen*, which describes the narrative staging of the Civil War in a large number of recent Spanish novels, or Ana Luengo's *La encrucijada de la memoria*, on memory in recent Spanish fiction. These scholars discover memory narratives in their objects of investigation that are very similar to those in contemporary Spanish society. Even so, they feel they have to be aware at all times that their analysis of memory construction in fiction does not necessarily and directly lead to any real knowledge about memory processes outside of the work of fiction. The problem is, of course, that such memory processes may enter into a literary work; but, as Astrid Erll makes clear, their very literary configuration brings with it a separation between the original memory context and the fiction it is turned into. The fictional world has its own rules, which can be imaginary and unrealistic (147). Erll warns that literature has only a "stark eingeschränkte[n] Anspruch auf Referenzialität" (148).

In itself not a problem, this perceived non-referentiality of fiction strongly diminishes the so-called 'social relevance' of literary collective memory studies that, following Kansteiner, attracts memory scholars to their subject in the first place. Worse still, it interferes with the general suspicion not only among readers, but also among scholars, that there must be a connection between the memory context outside, and memory processes inside the text. It is clear that most memory scholars, certainly those in the field of contemporary Spanish fiction, are not satisfied with an analysis that only reaches as far as the pages of the novel. Bettina Bannasch, for instance, tries to heighten the social relevance of her volume by adding a paragraph on the novel's "erinnerungskulturelle Positionierung" to every analysis. Ana Luengo in turn attempts to determine through text analysis how six contemporary Spanish novels "cooperaban al avance en la recuperación de la memoria que tanto se anunciaba en los medios de comunicación a finales del siglo XX" (273). Antonio Gómez López-Quiñones only studies "algunas claves temáticas y estéticas de esta generación de textos y filmes que, quizá, sea una de las últimas en tener a la Guerra Civil como un referente moral, histórico y cultural ineludible para la identidad española" (12), handily staying within the limits of his subject while pointing out its importance in the construction of a kind of collective Spanish identity. Others, such as María-Teresa Ibáñez Ehrlich and Patricia Cifre Wibrow, simply content themselves with the fact that connections can be suggested, and analogies pointed out, letting the reader's common sense fill in the gap.

Such attempts at connecting text and context are understandable, but the wish to combine collective memory studies' social relevance and the supposed theoretical rigour of structuralism and post-structuralism leads to all kinds of uncomfortable compromises and even the occasional methodical *faux pas*, as Ana Luengo's *La encrucijada de la memoria* clearly illustrates. Luengo assumes that to make a direct connection between context and text is problematic, and she seems to have sought her way out of a problem which might turn her study into nothing more socially relevant than a textual analysis. Inspired by Halbwachs, Assmann, and a host of other prominent memory scholars, she sets out to find collective memory in contemporary Spanish literature: the subtitle of her study, *La memoria colectiva de la Guerra Civil Española en la novela contemporánea*, leaves little room for doubt as to her purpose. Oddly, Luengo applies a method from what she terms socio-political sciences, developed by Winter and Sivan, to the characters and narrators in her novel, dividing them into categories (*homo psychologicus, homo sociologicus, homo agens*) according to their more or less social role in remembering. Luengo defends her choice of theoretical model by stating: "Si se parte de la idea de que la memoria es un proceso neurológico y existencial, lo más relevante será su dimensión autobiográfica" (22). She describes her attempt at reaching collective through individual memory as follows: "[p]ropongo comenzar con algo tan sencillo como la forma en que cada individuo accede a su propia infancia, para después poder ver de qué forma se organizan los recuerdos del pasado a un nivel social, colectivo" (15). But neither in literature, nor in the real world do individual memories ever add up to a collective memory. Luengo actually studies collected memory, and the method she chooses is thus only suitable for individual memories, governed by the laws of psychology. What is more, she problematically studies literary characters, constructed of language, using methods developed for use on individuals outside literature.

The Spanish case makes clear that wishful thinking may lead to mistaken assumptions. Scholars really *want* to connect text and context, they really *wish* to see in the memory processes described in literature the same ones that are present in society, to the extent, in Luengo's case, of treating literary characters as actual people; and they *assume* that structuralism and post-structuralism's highlighting of the self-referential nature of language prohibits one-on-one connections from being made. Rather than an interesting challenge, then, the confrontation of collective memory studies and the legacy of twentieth-century theory proves more like a headache to literary scholars. And it is an unnecessary headache: structuralism and post-structuralism in no way forbid the connection between texts and their contexts.

It is plain that the self-referentiality of language puts literary scholars with an interest in memory in a tight spot: they may feel that twentieth-century theorists allow them little room for linking literary memory to memory processes in the real world. But if we conceive of postmodernism as critical of language's capacities of reference, we should not, at the same time, exaggerate this criticism and interpret it as a strict separation of fiction and the outside world. After all, its non-referential nature does not imply that fiction comes to exist within a vacuum. It is still something which is created, something which arises from something else: the language in which a novel is written, its logic and inner laws all exist prior to it. If a writer can lose control over his writings, as Derrida suggested, this is precisely because he does not control their language. Behind this system of language, there is no ultimate referent, but more discourse, as Foucault stresses: "On ne cherche donc pas à passer du texte à la pensée, du bavardage au silence, de l'extérieur à l'intérieur, de la dispersion spatiale au pur recueillement de l'instant, de la multiplicité superficielle à l'unité profonde. On demeure dans la dimension du discours" (*L'archéologie du savoir* 101). Still, if that which precedes the discourse is also discursive, then the text can unproblematically relate to that prediscursive non-referent.

It is not just in the Spanish context that a restrictive view on structuralism and post-structuralism is held. Memory scholar Astrid Erll also passes over the genealogy of (post-)structuralism too lightly, interpreting it as a prohibition against connecting text and context. With a mind to bridge the gap between memory processes in novels and those in the real world, often so remarkably similar, but unable to converge completely, she turns to Paul Ricœur's acclaimed *Temps et récit* (1983-1985). In doing so, Erll performs a fundamental paradigm shift: she moves from a post-structuralist approach of the text into the realm of hermeneutics. This is not surprising, considering the fact that Ricœur himself forcefully criticises the structuralist barrier thrown up between text and context, 'inside' and 'outside', literally using the term prohibition (*interdit*):

> Je voudrais montrer [...] ce rapport de l'extérieur à l'intérieur que la poétique moderne réduit trop vite à une simple disjonction, au nom d'un prétendu interdit jeté par la sémiotique sur tout ce qui est tenu pour extra-linguistique. Comme si le langage n'était pas dès toujours jeté hors de lui-même par sa véhémence ontologique! (80)

Ricœur proposes a hermeneutic model which Astrid Erll characterises as "[e]in literaturwissenschaftliches Modell, das den komplexen Zusammenhang von kollektivem Gedächtnis, Literatur und ihre Wirkung in der Erinnerungskultur veranschaulichen kann" (149-150).

Ricœur's model spans the whole hermeneutic circle and includes not only the text but also its production in and its reception into the extraliterary world. It departs from the Aristotelian concept of mimesis, which he defines as "l'imitation ou la représentation de l'action" (59) and pairs with the idea of *muthos*, emplotment or "l'agencement des faits" (60). Ricœur makes his definition of mimesis palatable to the postmodern reader by stating that by imitation, he means an "imitation créatrice" that is more than a mere copy of a reality; and that by representation, he means not "quelque redoublement de présence" but "la coupure qui ouvre l'espace de fiction" (76). Essentially, Ricœur's model takes into account not just the literary configuration of the narrative, but also "l'amont et l'aval" (76), the prefiguration as well as the reconfiguration of a text, while not departing from the textual realm. He stresses that literary plot construction is grounded in a basic knowledge of temporal and action structures and of symbolic resources with which a text can be understood, so that prenarrative norms out of the context are felt in the text. Also, the plot construction guides the reader, so that it contains its own potential 'postnarrative' reading to a certain extent.

It is the inclusion of the two sides of mimesis in this model that enables Astrid Erll to conceive of a relationship between literature and memory culture, as she uses the threefold definition of mimesis to describe memory literature in its context: "Die Unterscheidung dreier Stufen der Mimesis ermöglicht, drei zentrale [...] Aspekte analytisch voneinander zu trennen: 1. die erinnerungskulturelle Präfiguration, 2. die Konfiguration neuartiger Gedächtnisnarrative und 3. deren leserseitige, kollektive Refiguration" (150). Memory literature, in other words, can be studied as a textual configuration that relates to and depends on its context, both because it incorporates and produces the norms and values of the memory culture that precedes it and because it anticipates a particular reconfiguration in the reception context. Erll goes on to point out that when already existing narratives of memory of the real world enter into a work of fiction, no transition from the paradigmatic nonlinearity of 'reality' to the syntagmatic order of narrative is necessary, precisely due to these narratives' *already narrative* form:

> Ricœur's Unterscheidung zwischen kultureller Wirklichkeit als paradigmatischer und dem literarischen Text als syntagmatischer Ordnung ist mit Blick auf Erinnerungskulturen sicherlich zu modifizieren. Denn wie bereits aufgeführt, haben wir es in weiten teilen der Erinnerungskultur bereits mit narrativen Strukturen zu tun. Angesichts einer Vielzahl koexistenter und konkurrierender Gedächtnisse in jeder Erinnerungskultur kann mit Ricœur davon ausgegangen werden, dass literarische Werke auf ein Netz von Bedeutungen zugreifen – nur eben mit dem Unterschied, dass Teile dieses Netzes bereits konfiguriert sind. (151)

The memory narratives that find their way into fiction are already configured narratively; their temporal and causal order is determined in the extra-literary world. Yet, since they are separated from their original context and replaced or recombined in the fictional world, Erll maintains that there *is* still a configuration process going on: one in which "bestimmte Versionen von Kollektivgedächtnis auf poietische Weise konstruiert werden" (152). In other words, a re-arranging of memory versions (in themselves already configured) takes place, which the reader can follow thanks to his knowledge of pre-existing structures and symbols.

It is easy to see why Erll turns to Ricœur's mimetic model in an attempt to combine text and context, and to explain the relation between memory narratives preceding the literary work and the reappearance of those narratives within the work. But if her choice for Ricœur implies, and it certainly seems that way, that she considers structuralism and post-structuralism to undercut all links between text and context, this choice may be made on an equivocal basis. As a matter of fact, Michel Foucault's influential contribution to post-structuralist theory, far from seeing language as separate from the 'real world', describes how discourse, the individual utterances that are made (or are allowed to be made) within social groups and structures, creates norms, for instance through mechanisms of in- and exclusion and prohibition. As a consequence, the norms and values Ricœur calls prenarrative are created by discourse and thus made of language, so that nothing stands in the way of these norms' entering into a work of literature that inscribes itself into that discourse and thus contains and produces the very norms and values which reign outside the text.

Particularly seen in the light of Michel Foucault's works, then, the difficulties Ana Luengo, Wulf Kansteiner or Astrid Erll seem to experience with the strict text-context separation are unnecessary. While it is true that twentieth century theory has problematised the referential nature of language, it has in no way claimed that a text is not preconditioned by, and that it does not itself constitute, norms, values, and discourse in general. The text does not copy its context, but it does not exist independently of it, either. Playful and relativist as postmodern theories may seem, their concern with contexts cannot be overlooked.

Reading Ethically

Memory scholars, and particularly literary scholars of memory, may thus feel free to abandon an all too radical interpretation of post-structuralism as well as the methodological issues that such an interpretation entails. Contrary to what is often assumed, twentieth-century theory does not see the text as independent of its context and without any obligations to it whatsoever. Instead, there is a profoundly ethical side to post-structuralism that has come to the foreground particularly in the 'ethical turn' many diagnosed postmodernism with in the 1980s and 1990s. In a nutshell, postmodern ethics centres around difference, otherness, and specificity: "One could say that, for [Derrida and Foucault], *alterity* emerges as the sign of intersubjective relations and the *ethical subject of discourse* as its necessary corollary", Peter Baker states (3). This very difference and complexity is difficult to combine with the wish for 'responsibility' that we often find in the works of scholars dealing with memory media.

Implicitly, many works on literary memory may perhaps be said to be Aristotelian at heart, when it comes to ethics. They depart from an assumption that literature has a function in society and that an author can control the work to such an extent that he or she can determine the way it will be read and exercise influence through it. The ethical consequences of such an assumption are elaborated by Paul Ricœur, whose work memory scholar Astrid Erll, at least, cites appreciatively. In Ricœur, the organisation of the text (the *muthos*) is, as we have seen, performed according to pre-existing structural, temporal and symbolic understandings, and these understandings make the composition digestible to its readers, who use their knowledge to decipher the text and interpret its meaning. The composing entity which Ricœur describes is a narratological instance that brings to mind Wayne Booth's concept of the implied author, because it seems to be highly humanised.

In Booth, the implied author is the organiser of a text, who incorporates the (prefigured) values and norms of the novel. The implied author is almost a human being, or at least a God: "Even the novel in which no narrator is dramatized creates an implicit picture of an author who stands behind the scenes, whether as stage manager, as puppeteer, or as an indifferent God, silently paring his fingernails" (Booth 151). Like actual humans, this author implied by the text undergoes emotions, and ranks and judges whatever the work of fiction describes. Indeed, Booth contends: "The emotions and judgments of the implied author are [...] the very stuff out of which great fiction is made" (86). Though Ricœur does not state explicitly that his view of the emplotter of a novel is similar to Booth's implied author, this lies enclosed, first of all, in his description of it as an ethical being. It is suggested, secondly, by Ricœur's inclusion in his theory of a fictional implied reader: the implied author's equally emotional and personified counterpart.

The implied author's ethical nature stems from his ability to build emotions into his work that affect the reader; here, Ricœur comes to rely outright on Aristotle's treatment of tragedies in his *Poetics*. Following Aristotle, Ricœur finds that what the reader experiences is constructed in the work of fiction: "la réponse émotionnelle du spectateur est construite dans le drame, dans la qualité des incidents destructeurs et douloureux pour les personnages eux-mêmes" (71). The reader feels for the characters and shares their pain to some extent. In this context, Ricœur speaks of "concordance discordante" (72): the plot's concordance, its neat construction as a legible whole, is temporarily mixed with discordance as one or more emotions (fear, pity, or surprise) complicate it and "constituent la menace majeure pour la cohérence de l'intrigue" (71). Nevertheless, the Aristotelian tragedy always remains concordant: "L'art de composer consiste à faire paraître concordante cette discordance. [...] C'est dans la vie que le discordant ruine la concordance, non dans l'art tragique" (72).

It must be noted here that Ricœur does not provide the clearest of definitions for his concepts of concordance and discordance. As it appears, a concordant text is a fully comprehensible and whole construction, whose meaning is clear and whose interpretation straightforward. Discordance appears to be defined negatively: it is everything that is disturbing in a text, that leads to uncertainty or instability – it is everything that is *not* concordant. Seen in this way, concordance becomes a sort of ideal wholeness, which a text can never fully maintain; but, at the same time, it seems to be possible for concordance to keep discordance in check. This is the case with certain emotional forces, Ricœur says, following Aristotle.

These forces, the main emotions which may be called up in a work of fiction, are what Aristotle calls fear and pity, the tragic emotions that constitute our "sens de l'humain" (Ricœur 75). In accordance with Aristotle, Ricœur is convinced that the human, the emotional, is uncontrollable and therefore discordant to a degree, threatening to undermine the coherence of the logically and rationally unfolding plot; but that, on the other hand, it functions as a concordant factor at the same time. The plot unfolds depending on this emotionality; the emotion is part of the plot constructed by the implied author and reconstructed by the reader. "C'est en incluant le discordant dans le concordant", Ricœur states, "que l'intrige inclut l'émouvant dans l'intelligible" (74). Emotions, uncontrollable as they may be, are at the same time essential to emplotment strategies. This is precisely because of their humaneness:

> Dans la mesure, en effet, où ces émotions sont incompatibles avec le répugnant et le monstrueux, comme avec l'inhumain (le manque de cette 'philantropie' qui nous fait reconnaître des 'semblables' dans les personnages), elles jouent le rôle principal dans la typologie des intrigues. (74)

The tragic emotions inspire a reader to 'philanthropy', and the intrigue of the literary work is determined by their capacity to make the reader sympathise with its characters.

Ricœur's conception of philanthropy[1] thus designates the empathy a reader may experience for a character, which is awakened by the tragic emotions an implied author builds into the plot. Eaglestone also discusses such empathy in his work on the Holocaust, opting for the illuminating term of "identification" (26), and connects it to Martha Nussbaum's idea of "rational emotions" (53). Nussbaum, whom Robert Eaglestone calls "a neo-Aristotelian philosopher" (27), takes the effect of these same tragic emotions a step further when she argues that since they make the reader feel empathy for certain characters, they may

---

[1]   It is debatable whether all would agree with Ricœur's word choice here. D.W. Lucas remarks that Aristotle uses the term *eleos* for pity, not *philantropia*. He states: "The distinction between *eleos* and the milder *philantropia* [...] suggests that pity is a powerful emotion" (Aristotle, *Poetics* 273).

ultimately have an impact on the personality of the reader himself: literature teaches the real reader "a more external sort of sympathy" (66) which enlarges his moral and ethical conscience and makes him a better, more responsible citizen. Ricœur limits himself to the text when he discusses how a literary work tries to build in compassion and attempts to seduce the reader into constructing the plot in a certain way, and into accepting the text's values and judgements. At the same time, it is clear that when the implied author incorporates a certain humaneness, a certain philanthropy into his plot, he does acquire a decidedly ethical nature.

Ricœur points out that a constructed plot, made to appear concordant by its implied author, can contain forces that try to interrupt or undermine this concordance. Indeed, Ricœur follows Aristotle's view on this in recognising the emotions of fear and pity, as well as that of surprise, as *discordant* forces within the concordant plot. Ricœur stays very close to Aristotle in his appreciation of a tidy, concordant plot[2], but he is of the conviction that this temporary discordance is a risk that needs to be taken, for it is to ensure the attention and interest of the reader: it makes the reader accept the plot and perform its construction. According to Ricœur, these discordant forces form a necessary evil, and they pose no real danger to the unity or concordance of the plot as a whole: they only provide *temporary* discordance which is resolved as the *muthos* is further unrolled. They are, in Nussbaum's words, 'rational emotions'.

Ricœur's preference for concordance and his subsequent fear of discordance obviously stems from his (Aristotelian) idea of the ethical and educational function of reading, from the notion that a text may inspire the noble yet temperate feeling of empathy in a reader. But this view of literature as controllable and especially the idea of this control as ethical is entirely at odds with the post-structuralist conception of literature and ethics. Central to post-structuralist ethics, in fact, is the idea of *Otherness*, of a fundamental distance and difference between subjects. Feelings of empathy actually *rob* the 'Other' of this essence of Otherness: they suggest that the person who empathises can stand in another's shoes, feel as the Other does, and thus share in the Other's experience. This is precisely an unethical deed: we have only to think of the fundamental difference between the Holocaust survivor who testifies to his experiences and the sympathetic bystander who can never comprehend what it has really been like. As Eaglestone remarks,

---

[2] Aristotle has a rather strict conception of what plots ought to look like: "the plot, since it is the imitation of an action, must be the imitation of a unified action comprising a whole; and the events which are the parts of the plot must be so organized that if any one of them is displaced or taken away, the whole will be shaken and put out of joint" (Aristotle, *Aristotle's Poetics* 54).

Despite being at the centre of the Western experience of literature and reading, and described in a plethora of different ways, the process of identification is barely understood. Yet much rests on it: ideas about our enjoyment of
literature in general and for many, such as Martha Nussbaum and Wayne
Booth, the possibility of the moral power of literature. Centrally, in this context, identification is that against which [Holocaust survivor Primo] Levi
and others want to build a dyke: it is identification which leads to the illicit
'grasping' and 'assimilation' (to use Levi's word) of Holocaust survivor testimony. Survivors do not believe that they can or should be identified with,
even through their testimony. (28)

This appropriation or negation of Otherness is what Jacques Derrida,
in an essay on Emmanuel Levinas, calls "violence transcendantale"
("Violence et métaphysique 2", 434). The emotions of sympathy and
respect encapsulate a necessary violence: that which is sympathised with
is always forcefully made a part of the sympathetic intention of the
person who performs this sympathy, and thus reduced.

Ortwin de Graef cites Derrida and draws conclusions for a sympathetic view on literature, such as that of Nussbaum. According to him,
the text is appropriated and reduced by the sympathetic reader, who
turns it into a highly lisible (Ricœur would say concordant) object. In De
Graef's eyes, and no doubt also in those of Derrida, to read like this is to
refuse a text its essence of *unreadability* (37). Jacques Derrida described
the text as a sort of monster of Frankenstein which upon being created,
turns against its creator. As De Graef points out, there are good reasons
to believe that literariness can be described precisely as a refusal of
being understood (21). To put it in Ricœur's terms: texts in general, and
literature very particularly, have discordance at their core.

This idea of fiction as being fundamentally more complex and more
open to multiple interpretations than other texts is not new. It is also
visible in the post-Holocaust approach to fiction, which singled out
literature as more suitable to narrate the Holocaust than historiography.
Literature, it was and is often said, provides a better framework for
expressing the very inexpressible nature of the concentration camp
experience. Hayden White has said that "the Holocaust is no more
unrepresentable than any other event in human history. It is only that its
representation, whether in history or fiction, requires the *modernist*
style" (qtd. in Dunker 15). This "modernist", non-linear, subjective and
self-reflexive style (which can thus also be called a *postmodernist* style)
may well have its place in history books, but its reliance on fictionalisa-
tion makes it pertain to the realm of literature above all. The idea that
such forms of fiction lend themselves to problematic representation of a
problem of representation, making felt the difficulty and the very inde-
scribability of the concentration camp, is widespread. Ernestine Schlant
finds that particularly novels (and, as she admits, films) lend themselves

well to counteracting the limited nature of historiography: "Fiction is malleable and protean in its appropriation of the most diverse kinds of discourses. Even at its sparsest [...] [i]t is inclusive and panoramic" (3). Ernst van Alphen actually extends this view to figurative, non-literal art, stating: "Figurative expressions are more *precise*; they are able to represent situations and experiences that cannot be conveyed by literal expressions" (29).

Literature is thus ethically charged, but to Derrida and others, the responsible role lies with the reader. To read ethically then becomes to read *discordantly*, to seek multiple, often antagonistic readings, and to unfold the work's complexity instead of reducing it to a concordant whole. Seen in this light, it becomes highly doubtful whether concordance, allowing the simple and straightforward reading of a text as containing only one meaning, is such a valuable quality as Ricœur makes it out to be. For Derrida, the task of the reader is to disclose fundamental discordance, to read a text not as readable, but as unreadable. As Dominick LaCapra points out, "reading may keep alive the critical potential of certain texts and counteract the ways in which canonization mitigates or represses the role of texts in stimulating legitimately thought-provoking questions in the reader" (16).

This approach to ethics is at odds with Ricœur's emphasis on an implied ideal reader who performs the reading that a text 'prescribes'. Though Ricœur does acknowledge the existence and importance of real readers and their real worlds, he refers mostly to Jauß and Iser (117) for reception aesthetics and highlights their description of the text as "un ensemble d'*instructions* que le lecteur et le publique *exécutent*" (117). Ricœur sees the implied reader as an emotional being capable of grasping a text's tragic emotions. The implied reader will always be seduced by them, and he will in this way become a human being who is ethically conditioned. He simply obeys the implied author, whose organisation of a fictional text is set up to convey a particular meaning – so that the 'ethical' responsibility turns out to lie with the implied author and indirectly with the real author who must control the text. The real reader is largely relieved of any ethical tasks: he or she must manage to reconstruct the concordant message of the literary work. If many real readers fail to do so, the real author and the work itself are ultimately to blame. In the reality of memory discourses, this view could easily seem an oversimplification, as it would fail to do justice to the conflictive reception context of novels, where memory debates often remain unresolved.

For reasons such as these, it seems preferable, in the analysis of Spanish literature, to turn to post-structuralism and its conception of ethics, rather than to dismiss its theories as 'relativist'. Post-structuralist ethics does not bank on concordance or empathy, it does not appropriate trauma victims' experiences by making them collective and enabling identification, and it does not rely on a simplistic psychoanalytic discourse that demands 'responsibility' and 'working-through'. Yet how can we perform a reading that can be considered 'ethical', that shows the literary work as a complex whole and allows for its literariness, within the perspective of its memory context and the narratives that compete there? How can we establish the norms and values that the work shares with its discursive context, in order to be able to understand where they are transgressed?

In order to answer this question, I will turn to a heterogeneous group of francophone researchers – Ruth Amossy refers to "the French analytical tradition" ("Introduction to the Study of Doxa" 370) – who depart from a decidedly post-structuralist, in this case mostly Foucaultian perspective and who steer clear of collective memory studies, its ethics and assumptions on the difficult connection of text and context.

Like Ricœur, the scholars of this French narratological paradigm take into account a pre-existing reality shaping the narrative, but it is the reality of outertextual discourse – the values outside the text are also present inside it, due to Foucaultian discursivity. Literary scholar Vincent Jouve describes the link between values in and outside a text as follows:

> Si le texte propose sa propre vision du bien et du mal, il le fait en jouant sur des représentations qui existent hors de lui et indépendamment de lui – faute de quoi, il serait tout simplement illisible. Les valeurs inscrites dans le texte ne se laissent donc appréhender qu'à travers les relations implicites qu'elles entretiennent avec les valeurs extérieures au texte. (15)

Jouve states that the text's norms, its portrayal of the good and the bad, draw upon a similar distinction in the world outside the text; this means that the text is rendered readable to the reader who shares these values (and who overlaps wholly or partially with an implied reader), but also that it is potentially unreadable for those real readers unfamiliar with that particular set of norms.

Ruth Amossy, among others, takes the study of such pre-existing norms further as she distinguishes a collective set of ideas, which she identifies as *doxa*: the Aristotelian term used to designate "common knowledge and shared opinions" (Amossy, "Introduction to the Study of Doxa" 362). In Amossy's words:

To be sure, the specific term is not always used: doxa appears under various guises, such as public opinion, verisimilitude, commonsense knowledge, commonplace, *idée reçue*, stereotype, cliché. Broadly speaking, however, all that is considered true, or at least probable, by a majority of people endowed with reason, or by a specific social group, can be called doxic. (369)

Amossy's conception of a shared knowledge is reminiscent of the concept of collective memory. Amossy makes it quite clear that the study of doxa, widespread as it is, has mostly been a matter explored in francophone literary and linguistic theories (375). For that reason, we have to bear in mind that it stands at quite a distance from collective memory studies (which originated, above all, in the English- and German-speaking scholarly communities). Yet it seems that the notion of doxa and that of collective memory draw on similar assumptions. Both the study of doxa and collective memory studies accept the existence of a collective repertoire shared by a social group, which interacts with the individual's experience of reality, and both understand this repertoire to be mediated. Doxa is "[u]n va-et-vient incessant [...] entre les images logées 'dans notre tête' et celles que divulguent abondamment les textes et les media" (*Les idées reçues* 9), Amossy says. It is possible to consider collective memory as a part of doxa: it is the consensus existing within a group of what the past was like and how it is to be evaluated. As such, it is part of this group's 'common knowledge'. Simultaneously, though, the theoretical background of doxa makes clear that this is a collectively shared phenomenon in a dehumanised form, to which individual psychoanalytic concepts such as 'trauma' are hard to apply. Doxa is a collective's shared outlook rather than a collectively suffered disease.

The same francophone literary theorists describe a process which is remarkably similar to Ricœur's mimetic model, but which yet again starts from a very different point of view, when they talk of the act of creation, the act of reading and the actual text. The text is prefigured by doxa; it is organised by an "autorité, à l'origine de l'énonciation et qui coiffe la totalité du récit" which "renvoie à ce que certains théoriciens appellant 'l'auteur impliqué'" (Jouve 90); and it is the knowledge of the doxa, shared by real author and real reader, that makes the text understandable to the latter, although he is also free in his reading. As Dufays says, "la lecture comporte toujours deux dimensions: l'une, collective et contrainte [...], l'autre, sujette davantage aux variations individuelles" (*Stéréotype et lecture* 37). Here, we easily recognise Ricœur's prefiguration, configuration, and refiguration on the different mimetic levels. What is different, though, is the view of the text's authority, the implied author. This instance is seen as precisely that, an instance: a textual construct where specific ideas and valuations of the context enter into the novel, and which is in charge of organising the text. This enunciative authority does not, of course, decide the reception on the part of the real reader, but it contains indications as to how it wants the text to be read, "permettant de répérer, derrière l'œuvre, une intention dont le lecteur est la cible" (Jouve 89). As opposed to Ricœur's model, then, while French narratology does not eliminate the implied author, it does lessen its significance through de-personification. The text can simply be regarded as a discursive statement prefigured by equally discursive, doxic, collective elements, and the actual ethical consequences of reading lie with the real reader.

An added advantage is that the francophone theorists have not just developed a model for textual analysis. They have also designed a number of methods to study the processes of the configuration of doxa within a text, which we may now make use of. The general idea is that the prefiguring doxa, or, as Dufays calls it, the "codes" (*Stéréotype et lecture* 11), provide the text with a set of norms and values according to which it is fitted with a hierarchy, a ranking from good to bad. Philippe Hamon calls this the ideology a text produces, the textual "effet-idéologie" (9):

> L'*effet-idéologie*, dans un texte (et non: l'*idéologie*) passe par la construction et mise en scène stylistique d'*appareils normatifs* textuels incorporés à l'énoncé. [...] On peut cependant poser, comme hypothèse affinée, que ces appareils évaluatifs peuvent apparaître et se laisser localiser en des *points textuels* particuliers [...]. Ces lieux peuvent être définis comme lieux d'une *évaluation*, [...] comme des foyers relationnels complexes [...]. (20)

According to Hamon, ideology as a textual effect comes into being in places in the text where evaluation is carried out. Hamon explains that every evaluative point in a text has its own specifics, or *appareils normatifs*: the form of the evaluation (positive or negative), the nature of what is evaluated (action or person), the instance or instances who perform the evaluation and the norms that are evoked may differ from evaluation to evaluation. Together, these four aspects produce what Hamon calls a *dominante normative* (28). From Hamon's description, we may conclude that ideology in a text is the result of constant comparison of norms, and that, since eventually a dominant norm results, the text's ideology is hierarchically structured.

Vincent Jouve works out a method to study Hamon's *effet-idéologie* or, as he prefers to call it, the "effet-valeur" (10). Jouve finds that there exists at least an implicit relation between values inside and outside the text (15), something which Hamon described poetically as the "'rumeur' diffuse de l'idéologie (de l'Histoire)" (Hamon 41). The textual value, he claims, cannot be studied without taking into account representations outside the text. Jouve proposes to first look at the individual characters in a novel. These can express their values through what they say and think, and, especially, through their actions: "Dans un roman, c'est surtout parce qu'il fait qu'un personnage affiche ses valeurs" (Jouve 66). By looking at what a character says, but also at how he behaves and what or who motivates him, one can discover his values. All the characters' values may then be studied in their hierarchical relationship to one another, and thus, one may discover "la valeur des valeurs: l'idéologie du texte" (89). The characters' position on the ideological scale of the novel then influences their authority as evaluators: when a character whose overall evaluation is that of a 'bad' person, pronounces a judgment, this judgment is likely not to be the *dominante normative*. Jouve points out that not every character has the same authority (105); and that often, but not always, the narrator is the most authoritative judge who imposes his values on the novel (92).

All in all, the French narratological method and the description of the textual value-effect by Hamon and Jouve stemming from it leave us with an adequate method to tackle the doxic elements within a novel. We now know that the novel's configuration, its plot or *muthos*, is hierarchically structured according to norms and values embodied by the implied author, but in correspondence with extra-literary doxa or collective views, which must somehow be acknowledged within the text to facilitate understanding and readability. If we simply look at evaluations in the novel, taking into account the status of the evaluator as well as his actions, we can deduce these values. On the whole, moreover, Jouve's description suggests a division of authority that makes it quite clear, generally, what the *dominante normative* really is, and which evaluator represents it – often, it is the narrator. As we look at this value hierarchy of doxic origin, we are able to see how memory narratives existing in society that have been absorbed into a novel wholly, without need for a narrative configuration due to their already narrative form, also become subject to the novel's hierarchisation. In a novel which addresses the past and thematises memory processes, the one considered doxic, or correct, may thus be qualified as 'good', and other, contesting views, as 'bad'. By looking at the textual hierarchy, the values and the normative dominant, we can discover which of the memory narratives present in the novel is privileged, and in this way, which version of the past is the doxic or collective one that the novel incorporates.

Apparently, in order to be able to pinpoint the doxic within a novel, one has only to study the hierarchy that organises it and deduce the pre-narrative norms and values that control it; these norms also extend to collective narratives that are ranked accordingly in the novel. But this, then, is the ranking of memories by the implied author, which the author intends; and not always does a novel present us with an unproblematic concordant structure that, without any inner conflicts, follows the authorial intention to the letter.

Towards a Discordant Reading of Contemporary Spanish Memory Novels

The Aristotelian take on ethics underlying the works of many scholars of collective memory focuses strongly on what Ricœur terms concordance: on the capability of a literary work to convey a clear message, present a particular take on social debates, and be readable to its readers. In this way, a work may indeed be called responsible or irresponsible at a glance. And if we look at Jouve's and Hamon's descriptions of value hierarchies in a novel, we are forced to conclude that many works of fiction, in spite of being literary and discordant at heart, present us with a very concordant appearance. It is plain that an ethical, 'discordant' reading is made difficult by such elements as value hierarchies, not to mention other comforting, recognisable structures and stereotypes that guide the reader. Where does one start in an attempt to read novels 'ethically', looking for the places where this concordance collapses?

In fact, the very Aristotelian model advocated by Ricœur provides us with a starting point. After all, while Ricœur exposes his ideas on the concordance of texts, his descriptions of such concordance make felt, at times, that there are some aspects of the Aristotelian model he is uncomfortable with. Though Ricœur maintains throughout his study that concordance may remain intact in texts, he does admit the possibility of its being threatened and becoming more problematic. In general, Ricœur becomes a tad defensive and argumentative whenever he discusses how plot linearity and regularity must sometimes make way for emotion. Ricœur himself has to admit that even the most concordant of works, following Aristotle, must contain the 'temporary discordance' of the 'tragic emotions'. Fear, surprise, and pity threaten the wholeness of the plot: through them, a sort of arbitrariness, an uncontrollability enters into the novel.

Whereas Aristotle still convinced his readers that this disturbance was only temporary, this way of looking upon fictional texts becomes rather difficult against the background of post-structuralism. It is doubtful whether it is really possible for a text to keep such emotions in check, or whether they introduce a level of discordance that heightens the openness and complexity of a text. The question becomes, in other words, whether it is possible for any text, let alone any literary text, to seem entirely concordant – and whether or not it might be preferable to look at the *discordant* consequences, at the *irrationality*, of rational emotions. It might be a good idea, then, to start our analysis by looking at what makes a novel appear concordant, whether this be a predictable plot structure or the calling up of fear, pity, or surprise – and then to investigate whether this appearance of concordance holds.

At the same time, we might do well to direct our attention towards a phenomenon Ricœur describes as an outright threat to concordance. In Ricœur, emotion is the force that threatens to undermine the concordance of a plot most. Ricœur finds that even the supposed 'rational' emotions can cause discordance. Unsurprisingly, he is all the more apprehensive when it comes to emotions that are much less contained and much more straightforwardly violent in nature, and which thus become the opposite of 'humane'. The tragic emotions Ricœur lists as temporarily discordant forces in a concordant whole "sont incompatibles avec le répugnant et le monstrueux, comme avec l'inhumain" (74). The inhuman, or rather, the non-human, becomes a deeply disruptive and therefore 'unethical' force of 'non-rational' emotions. And it is precisely in novels dealing with a painful, 'traumatic' past, that the inhuman can appear: that which is repressed can return to haunt. Interestingly, this possibility of haunting, or the spectral, in a text is a concept which, in Derrida, has a decidedly *ethical* function.

Paradoxically, the spectral is defined precisely by the fact that it cannot be defined. Derrida deals with this paradox in *Spectres de Marx*, as well as in a number of essays. In one of those essays, "Marx, c'est quelqu'un", Derrida points out: "La question des spectres est donc la question de la vie, de la limite entre le vivant et le mort, partout où elle se pose" (23). Julian Wolfreys interprets this quote as follows: "the spectre is something between life and death, though neither alive nor dead" (x). The spectre, and the spectral in general, is thus what ghost literature and films would call the 'undead'. Like a vampire, the spectre can manifest itself in the world of the living, and therefore, it is not dead; nor, however, is it a living part of that world. It is only an apparition in it. The spectral cannot be, just as it cannot *not* be: it has no ontological status. It has its own category, which Derrida calls "hantologie".

This hauntology, "le discours sur la fin", instead of ontology, "le discours de la fin" (Derrida, *Spectres de Marx* 31) is what causes the paradox of the spectral. There is no way of defining it, because it simply *is* not. In Derrida's words: the spectral is a concept without concept ("Marx, c'est quelqu'un" 23). At most, it can be described by analogy, as Fredric Jameson does. To him, spectrality is "what makes the present waver: the vibrations of a heat wave through which the massiveness of the object world – indeed of matter itself – now shimmers like a mirage" (38). Jameson's "vibrations" are the manifestations of the spectral that we can observe in our world, and that produce a certain distorting effect. Julian Wolfreys considers this analogy particularly well-chosen, because not only does it not comprise a definition as such (the spectral is, of course, indefinable), it also illustrates how we can perceive the spectral, even if we cannot see it: "A trace registers itself in the field of vision but this trace is not that which causes the registration. Caused by that which affects the visible it is the trace of something else, something which cannot be seen, as such" (77). Wolfreys appears to take his own description of haunting from this image of the spectral: "Haunting might best be described as the ability of forces that remain unseen to make themselves felt in everyday life" (110). The manifestation of this haunting is not the spectre, or ghost, but its trace: the ghost retracts itself as soon as it manifests itself. Simon Critchley calls this "the ghosting of the ghost" (10).

Haunting thus causes a sort of disruption: traces of ghosts oscillate in an invisible, but perceptible way. Derrida describes one such haunting process in *Spectres de Marx*. Borrowing Marx's famous line "Ein Gespenst geht um in Europa – das Gespenst des Kommunismus" (22), he argues that communism may have died, but that precisely communism's demise causes its return in the shape of a ghost. Derrida argues that, re-reading Marx, he finds that history and death of communism loom over the texts, investing them with a new significance: "[c]e qui s'y manifeste en premier lieu, c'est un spectre [...]. À la relecture du *Manifeste* et de quelques autres grands ouvrages de Marx, je me suis dit que je connaisais peu de textes, dans la tradition philosophique [...] dont la leçon parût plus urgente *aujourd'hui*" (35). Derrida points out that Marxism's death does not mean the end of it, but that, in a dialogue with its spectre, we can still find it to be of post-mortem relevance. Communism's ghostly return is one example of haunting; but it is a phenomenon that can occur in many places and on many levels.

The broad and all-enveloping nature of haunting becomes clear when we look at all the levels on which it can occur in modern life. Derrida's "quasi-concept" ("Marx, c'est quelqu'un" 23) of the spectral is, Wolfreys argues, characteristic of modernity. Indeed, Derrida himself has mentioned that modern technology is the locus *par excellence* of haunting (Wolfreys 1). The reason for this is that modern modes of communication – television, the telephone – constitute reproduction. And, as Derrida points out, reproduction is linked to repetition and representation, creating a phantom structure. What is reproduced is always altered, fragmented and reduced, and at the same time, it is perpetuated or prolonged. The copy, or simulacrum, is not a faithful reproduction, but exists independently of its original through a "liquidation de tous les référentiels" (Baudrillard 11), and becomes equivalent to the 'real' original in such a way that it can replace it. Simulacra, as copies without original, create awareness of the lack of such an original and are, in the words of Jo Labanyi, "fertile soil for ghosts" ("History and Hauntology" 78). Modern and postmodern culture in general are therefore open to haunting. So, too, is writing: since narrative is always a form of representation, and is potentially limitless yet constantly reproduced, Wolfreys concludes that "all forms of narrative are, in one way or another, haunted" (3). It seems that haunting is not only omnipresent in contemporary culture, but that it is also always present in a narrative. According to Wolfreys, "all stories are [...] ghost stories" (3).

Haunting is thus a very wide phenomenon that can occur on a big or small scale, in a novel or in a whole cultural discourse. As long as there is some trace of the absent in the present, a hint of the original in the copy, there is a potential for the spectral. In a text, of course, it is so natural, frequent and omnipresent an occurrence that it does not always disturb the plot. It can be present in the background or described, as a character experiences its forces. Yet it is certainly also possible for a process of haunting to pervade the very structure of the text itself, and to destabilise its core – and in such a case, haunting becomes a thoroughly discordant force that is experienced by fictional characters and readers alike.

It would appear, then, that to study haunting in a novel is a very complex task. Haunting processes can frequently be detected by looking at the strangest elements in stories or novels. Often, in a study on haunting, supernatural phenomena such as vampires, werewolves, and other living dead are looked at, and so are photographs of the dead, doublings, and other simulacra. This method is largely inspired by Sigmund Freud's influential essay, "The Uncanny", to which I will return in chapter 6; it is significant that while Derrida mentioned Freud's work only in a footnote, this footnote is quoted more frequently than many other parts of Derrida's study of Marxist haunting (*Spectres de Marx* 275). A problem of studying haunting like this, though, is that it depends very much on stereotypes: stereotypes exactly like the vampire or the werewolf, whose presence becomes so predictable that their uncanny force is strongly undermined.

To diagnose a novel with a haunting process is to demonstrate an undecidability, an unresolved doubleness, that is never easy to pinpoint because of its intangibility. In the case of memory novels that deal with a difficult past, though, haunting may be expected due to the presence of trauma. Trauma is, of course, very likely to return in a ghostlike manner: repressed and consciously forgotten, it is nevertheless still felt – and literary scholars often sense it in the literary works they analyse.

Haunting is a deeply complex process, fundamentally open and 'unreadable', and it is no wonder that Eaglestone states that haunting in Derrida is ethical in nature, "the grounding of a new form of hope and humanism, a humanism beyond humanism" (3). But here, too, a truly ethical reading in a Derridean sense requires an effort. Even scholars who discover haunting processes in novels can still be seduced to perform a reading that is concordant to a degree, burdening even such texts with a responsibility of 'dealing with' a past. One important reason for this is the psychoanalytic discourse that is evoked by the term 'trauma', and that leads, among other things, to a tendency to choose the side of the trauma's 'victims'. Jo Labanyi, for instance, investigates memory (particularly traumatic memory) and haunting in a large number of contemporary Spanish novels and films in her article "History or Hauntology", suggesting that "the current postmodern obsession with simulacra may be seen as a return of the past in spectral form" (64). The past thus returns, and leaning on Derrida's remark that ghosts must be exorcised "to grant them the right to a hospitable memory out of a concern for justice" (66), Labanyi argues strongly for a rehabilitation and re-remembrance of the past's nameless victims – the *desaparecidos* of Latin American regimes, for example. Labanyi connects Derrida's (quasi-)concept of the spectral to countries where a traumatic past is repressed, suggesting that its ghosts *should* really be allowed into memory. The works she studies, haunted as they may be, are thus endowed with the task of pointing out the nature of these ghosts and to begin allowing them a place in memory; the actual haunting processes taking place within them are all made dependent on this one intention.

Isabel Cuñado also links trauma to haunting. In a convincing study of the works of contemporary Spanish author Javier Marías, whom critics have often accused of writing "una obra extranjerizante, tanto en tono como en contenido" (9) which has avoided dealing with Spain's traumatic past, Cuñado demonstrates how even in the least 'Spanish' of his works, the author "ha tratado y sigue tratando cada vez más de la realidad española" (9). Cuñado shows how trauma haunts all works through elements that cause estrangement: the double, and photography, among other things (31). Though in itself, this view is well-maintained and supported by much evidence, it seems to want to redeem Marías, the 'un-Spanish' writer who never engaged much with the Spanish past. In Cuñado's study, we find out that Marías had been doing just that all along, which makes him a fore-runner in the performance of the ethical duty (ethical in the Aristotelian sense, that is) to deal with the repressed past. It is obviously easy to 'slip back' into concordant reading.

It has become clear in the above that to read a memory novel ethically, at least in the post-structuralist sense, is not to look upon plot construction per se, upon the 'instructions' given by the text and the norms expressed in it both implicitly and explicitly. Rather, it is to look at the text's hierarchy of values and to ask where such a text becomes discordant, where norms and values are abandoned or maintained while at the same time contradicted. In such a way, the real complexity of a novel may unfold – and in the process, not just the memory narrative it appears to want to convey is laid bare, but the whole complex discourse, complete with its limitations and shady boundaries, is traced as it is present in the one text. Such a way of reading looks not for one meaning, thus becoming a participant in discussions, but for many, and it allows the literary work to show how it reflects, but also how it recombines and uses, memory discourses in society.

This is the type of reading I intend to perform upon a selection of fourteen contemporary Spanish memory novels. Written after 1990, they all thematise the undemocratic past, and sometimes also the Civil War. What is more, they directly latch on to contextual memory narratives by describing a memory process themselves, whereby the past is looked upon from a post-dictatorial present, so that parallels between text and context are all the more obvious as the act of remembering itself becomes a subject of reflection. Naturally, it is difficult to strictly separate different stages of Spanish memory discourses, but it is clear that the general development from careful treatment of the past to memory boom converged with the novels' appearance. Luis Goytisolo's *Estatua con palomas* (1992), Julio Llamazares's *Escenas de cine mudo* (1994), Antonio Muñoz Molina's *El dueño del secreto* (1994), Manuel Vicent's *Tranvía a la Malvarrosa* (1994), Álvaro Pombo's *Aparición del eterno femenino* (1993) and Justo Navarro's *La casa del padre* (1994) all date from the early 1990s, when the subjects of the dictatorial past and the Civil War were first critically addressed; Rosa Regàs's *Luna lunera* (1999), Andrés Trapiello's *El buque fantasma* (1998) and Félix de Azúa's *Momentos decisivos* (2000) stem from a time when the memory discourse had gained considerably in strength, though it was not officially recognised; and Javier Cercas's *Soldados de Salamina* (2001), Carlos Ruiz Zafón's *La sombra del viento* (2001), Enrique Vila-Matas's *París no se acaba nunca* (2003), Rafael Chirbes's *Los viejos amigos* (2003) and Javier Marías's *Tu rostro mañana* (2002-2007) saw a context increasingly dominated by the new memory discourse and the conflicts it caused.

By selecting these works, I have tried to collect and study the main memory literature written since 1990. All authors are prominent writers, whose works are debated, studied and criticised. Indeed, all writers are included in one or more of four major works by the prominent literary critics José Antonio Masoliver Ródenas, José María Pozuelo Yvancos, Ignacio Echevarría, and Fernando Valls. Together, these critics' works create what may be called a canon of Spanish novelists around the turn of the millennium. By selecting from among the authors and novels they chose to incorporate in their overviews, using those works that thematise memory in the way explained above, I have attempted to come up with a corpus of novels that, while it does not pretend to be exhaustive in any way, does want to present as full an image as possible of Spanish memory novels after 1990.

In its totality, this body of works should allow us to formulate a hypothesis on the ways in which Spanish literature has, on the whole, been active in the reawakening of critical memory in Spanish society. The corpus, as has become clear from its description, consists of such works as actively deal with the memory of the past, and as such, these works are bound to incorporate or investigate their society's memory narratives: they may uncover the way the past is thought of, if it is thought of at all, and they may try to amplify this, modify it, or choose between the various versions of the past that circulate in the society which first sees them in print. Whether they manage to elaborate on this material at all, and to put forward clearly and unproblematically their own contribution to the debates, or whether the responsibility they do or do not assume is of a different nature altogether, will have to become clear in the course of this investigation.

In the following chapters, I will look more closely at the effect of a number of textual features, one by one, that can disturb the text's value hierarchy; and I will also show how concordance may be suggested in spite of such discordance. This study wants to focus on the essential unreadability of all texts under scrutiny, and read them in such a way that their complexity can be appreciated. It will occasionally make use of selected reception documents – reviews, newspaper articles, scholarly studies, and the like – to contrast or support such readings, so that the inner discordance of the literary text is shown. Its aim is to create a panorama of the forces at work when it comes to memory construction in literature, in relation to a vibrant memory culture like that in Spain.

In chapter 3, I will look at a phenomenon that is capable of providing a novel with a degree of predictability to the experienced reader of literature, and that is thus capable of guiding the reader and imposing concordance: the genre, and, in this particular case, the genre of the *Bildungsroman*. Whereas this stereotypical sequence creates expectations and provides a structure of understanding, it may also be parodied or otherwise highlighted. What is more, its typical structure may be used outside generic works and thus generate precisely a lack of concordance and a plurality of meanings that heightens the literariness of the work. Is this thematising and loosening of the genre, then, enough to disrupt any apparent concordance? Or, alternatively, does it impose concordance by introducing a strongly hierarchical structure? Is the use of genre, in other words, really a way of keeping up a concordant semblance in a novel?

In chapter 4, I will go on to study nostalgia, an emotion typically evoked by the process of remembering. I consider this emotion, part and parcel of the memory novel, as a feeling which relies above all on recognition, identification and human empathy in the reader. Indeed, it can be seen as a version of Aristotelian pity – particularly in cases where memory is rose-coloured and seductive, creating a sadness for lost times. In this chapter, it will become clear how seductive this emotion is, and how easily it lets discordance get out of hand in spite of attempts to combat it through irony or parody. This, of course, may impact the novel's value hierarchy, and the 'irrationality' of this rational emotion may allow a much higher level of discordance than a shallower reading would allow.

In chapter 5, I will deal with autobiography – another recurrent phenomenon in memory literature, especially in the form of autobiographical fiction, where it emerges in otherwise fictional surroundings. One of the tragic emotions Ricœur mentioned, following Aristotle, is that of surprise: the reader is faced with an unexpected plot twist, and this causes him or her to feel a discordant shock (temporary, according to Ricœur) while he or she is at the same time compelled to read on and see how the plot develops. I will argue that the introduction, or interruption, of a semblance of referentiality like that of autobiography may just have such a surprise or shock effect. The ensuing discordance may turn out to be less temporary than Ricœur assumed, and continue to be an undermining force throughout the work, structurally combating the implied author and its norms, values, and versions of the past. What is more, the 'aura' that comes with autobiography's apparent referentiality, the haunting suggestion of an original that is referred to, might heighten surprise and discordance. Here, too, a thorough reading may reveal a work's inner complexity.

In chapter 6, finally, I will look at the discordant force of the uncanny. In the novels discussed in this chapter, elements of the monstrous or the supernatural are included in the plot construction through the use of tropes of the gothic and the uncanny, thus opening up a specific form of the spectral that is connected to an entire cultural 'domain of fear'. Their presence might point to a strongly undermining tendency within the text that will make it difficult (but not impossible) for it to be read as a simple and concordant story; at the same time, though, these generic stereotypes may be overly familiar and thus have ceased to be uncanny, frightening, and strange. I will, therefore, attempt to establish whether the tropes of the fearsome are actually uncanny, and whether this uncanniness creates a heightened degree of discordance and a complexity of reading.

As mentioned before, this investigation departs from Ricœur, or, rather, from those places in Ricœur where he is made to feel uncomfortable as he comes across elements of texts that seem to threaten concordance severely. Since this occurs whenever the talk is about emotion, the analytical chapters are for the most part organised around emotions – except for that on the *Bildungsroman*, which studies a stereotypical genre structure that might be supposed to only heighten concordance. The following chapters, on nostalgia and autobiography, really also investigate the emotions of fear and pity, and of surprise, respectively – as they appear in their most common guise within these memory novels. In the final analytical chapter, I will turn to look at the most discordant of emotions, that of horror or the uncanny, even if the subjects of haunting and horror are bound to be addressed earlier on as well due to memory literature's openness to haunting. In this chapter, I will focus on the question of when and how exactly the uncanny as an emotion is called up within a narrative, so that I can deal with the mechanics of horror in a more extensive way here than in the context of previous analyses.

It is noteworthy that, in almost all of the chapters, to address an emotion turns out to mean confronting that emotion with a genre or mode. This creates an apparent lack of equilibrium between these chapters and may also raise the question of whether they deal with an emotion, a plot structure, or both. Only in the chapter on nostalgia, the genre or mode concept remains in the background: nostalgia's evocation does not depend on a move away from stereotypical plot structures, and it can actually be strengthened by them – for example, when it is called up in a typical *Bildungsroman* plot. However, since the surprise effect depends on the *interruption* of predictable plot structures, these need to be taken into account whenever this emotion is analysed – hence the focus on autobiography in this chapter. Finally, the emotion of horror or the uncanny is called up through stereotypical tropes, but it needs to *surpass* them. Since both the 'inhuman' and the surprising can thus only occur in relation to stereotypical structures that they disrupt or unbalance, their analysis cannot be executed without paying attention to these structures as well.

What will lie before us, ultimately, is the textual analysis of fourteen novels, all of which have been chosen to illustrate one particular aspect of discordance and concordance in a fictional plot. This does not mean, of course, that a nostalgic novel cannot contain a haunting process, that a highly uncanny novel does not pertain to a certain genre, or that the autobiographical shock effect is incompatible with nostalgia. In all cases, the novel's emplotment strategies can be distinguished, its discordant elements pointed out, its value hierarchy determined, its inner contradictions shown, and its complex connections to the memory context established. In the process, an overview is constructed of contemporary Spanish memory literature, its ethical potential, and the field of norms and values to which these novels relate both in a dependent and in a creative way. Finally, I will place all these works within the particular phase of the context they appeared in, and attempt to answer the question what role these major examples of Spanish memory literature can play, and have played in dealing with the past.

PART II

ANALYSES

CHAPTER 3

The *Bildungsroman* Genre as a Stereotype

Genres, Stereotypes and the *Bildungsroman*

In literature, one way of structuring and ordering a work, of making it 'readable' and concordant, is to make it pertain to a genre – to a sort of category of related works that helps the reader classify the text at hand. "Genre – with all its signs, both textual and extra or meta-textual – forms a horizon of expectations which illuminates (or conversely can cover over) texts", Eaglestone explains. "Genre is the context of a work that, as it were, both frames it and makes it comprehensible 'externally' and gives it a shape 'internally'" (38). As Hans Robert Jauß puts it,

> Ein literarisches Werk […] weckt Erinnerungen an schon Gelesenes, bringt den Leser in eine bestimmte emotionale Einstellung und stiftet schon mit seinen Anfang Erwartungen für 'Mitte und Ende', die im Fortgang der Lektüre nach bestimmten *Spielregeln der Gattung oder Textart* aufrechterhalten oder abgewandelt, umorientiert oder auch ironisch aufgelöst werden können. (175, my italics)

Judging by the genre concept's long history – already in Aristotle, we find the division of literature into the classic triad of lyric, epic, and drama – a need for such a classification has been common to readers and authors through the ages. The Aristotelian genre division was adhered to for centuries, and hardly questioned until the nineteenth century saw German Romanticism, whose "most pervasive legacy" was "the idea that it was possible to ignore altogether the doctrine of genres" (Duff 4). Nevertheless, the concept of genre has remained alive and well in the twentieth century, occupying an important place in the theories of the Russian Formalists, in those of Mikhail Bakhtin, and later, in reception studies, notably in the work of Jauß (Duff 14). Though the twentieth century also saw the genre concept further attacked by Maurice Blanchot and deconstructed by Jacques Derrida (Duff 5), David Duff cannot but note that genre concepts are still omnipresent in literary theory, and that there is even a decided confidence in the notion of genre (15). It seems that genre is an ineradicable construct used by readers and writers of all times.

Apparently, genre provides a literary work with an internal structure and renders it concordant to the eyes of the reader. This is why I begin my 'discordant' reading of Spanish memory novels by looking at genre: it constitutes a plot that seems concordant, and that is apparently only disturbed by any emotions the novel calls up. It may be wondered, however, whether this really is the case – if every work can be considered discordant in itself, this seeming concordance is only a guise. Genre, moreover, is certainly not as stable and clear a concept as it would seem, as the uncertainties that surround the term suggest. Nowadays, the term is used to describe both the novel as a whole and a wide range of specific forms of the novel. One such form is that of the *Bildungsroman*, to use the term coined by Karl Morgenstern in the early nineteenth century, but made known by Wilhelm Dilthey in his 1913 essay *Das Erlebnis und die Dichtung* (Jeffers 49). In the *Bildungsroman*, also known as the apprenticeship novel or the coming-of-age novel, a young person enters into adulthood through a series of formative experiences. As will become abundantly clear, this stress on the adolescence and experience of one of the main characters renders it a very attractive form for the memory novel, where an older narrator can look back on such a vital period in his or her youth.

Attempts at defining the *Bildungsroman* immediately show how confusing a term like genre itself is. David Duff describes the *Bildungsroman* as a "subgenre" (xvi) of the novel genre, and Randolph Shaffner calls it one of "a few commonly recognised types of the novel" (6), along with the Gothic novel, the detective story, etcetera. He, too, reserves the concept of genre for the novel as a whole. Others, however, call the *Bildungsroman* a genre in its own right, though they often apply other terms to it as well. Franco Moretti speaks of a "symbolic form" (5), but also of a genre (229), and Jerome Buckley quite simply calls the *Bildungsroman* a genre (17), while Thomas Jeffers appears to avoid the word genre altogether. Duff explains that precisely this terminological uncertainty is one of the most characteristic sides of contemporary genre theory: the close relation of genre to terms such as mode, form, type, or structure creates "one of the enduring problems of genre theory, namely, confusion of terminology". The lack of a "species", a body of identifiable genres, makes him warn the reader against entering into genre theory's jungle: "genre theory still awaits its Linnaeus" (17).

Ultimately, whether we call the *Bildungsroman* an independent genre or prefer to see it as a subgenre of the novel, it is clear that coming-of-age novels share certain characteristics which allow them to be admitted onto the list of (sub)generic works. But here, we immediately come across one of genre's most problematic sides: it stubbornly resists definition, since the connection between all individual characteristics and the genre as a whole is difficult to make. When does a fictional work on a young adolescent become a *Bildungsroman*? What elements does it need to evoke the genre, and which characteristics can it do without? Studies on the *Bildungsroman* struggle with this question, and they frequently provide us with ample lists of possible conventions and sample plots, often departing from what is generally considered the architextual *Bildungsroman*: Goethe's 1796 *Wilhelm Meisters Lehrjahre* (Buckley 12). Jerome Buckley describes the "broad outlines of a typical *Bildungsroman* plot" (17):

A child of some sensibility grows up in the country or in a provincial town, where he finds constraints, social and intellectual, placed upon the free imagination. [...] He therefore, sometimes at quite an early age, leaves the repressive atmosphere of home (and also the relative innocence), to make his way independently to the city [...]. There his real 'education' begins, not only his preparation for a career but also – and often more importantly – his direct experience of urban life. The latter involves at least two love affairs or sexual encounters, one debasing, one exalting, and demands that in this respect and others the hero reappraise his values. By the time he has decided, after painful soul-searching, the sort of accommodation to the modern world he can honestly make, he has left his adolescence behind and entered upon his maturity. (17-18)

Shaffner expands this list of traits by enumerating no less than twenty-three "concrete potentialities within the apprenticeship novel" (17), ranging from "a tendency toward the inner life" (17) to "the view of art solely as a partial means toward the unfolding of personality" (18). He also distinguishes five "presuppositions" (18) on life, the world, development and choice, and eight recurring themes of the apprenticeship novel (18), of which "[s]elf-culture or self-formation" is the "primary recurring theme" (22). Jeffers, in turn, finds Buckley's synopsis "adequate as far as it goes" but would "supplement it with a list of initiatory tests that every inwardly developing *Bildungsheld* must at least try to pass" (52): a sexual and a vocational test, and, finally, "that business of ruminating, but specifically about the *connections* between art, ethics, and metaphysics, the practical stress falling on the middle term" (53).

All of these scholars, however, feel that a simple enumeration of traits and conventions will not do to define the genre and its specific works. After describing the prototypical *Bildungsroman* plot, Buckley feels obliged to remark that "[n]o single novel, of course, precisely follows this pattern" (18), though he claims that it must not ignore "more than two or three of its principal elements – childhood, the conflict of generations, provinciality, the larger society, self-education, alienation, ordeal by love, the search for a vocation and a working philosophy" (18). Jeffers warns us that "[t]he coherence of the *Bildungsroman* tradition, then, can to some extent seem artificial – a line of authors who, wittingly or unwittingly, have organized their tales around some arbitrary conventions or semiotic flags" (54). He therefore abstains from defining the *Bildungsroman*: "It is best not to say too exactly" (49). At most, he finds, the *Bildungsroman* is recognisable by contrasting it to its nearest relations: it lies between the *Erziehungsroman*, the novel of education (with Rousseau's *Émile* as an example), and the *Entwicklungsroman*, where a hero moves from one stage of his life to another – an observation also made by Moretti (17). Shaffner similarly compares the *Bildungsroman* to a host of other 'types' of the novel, showing for example that the *Bildungsroman* differs from the picaresque novel through its focus on the hero's inner life (8-9). He feels forced to conclude, though, that "what it shares with any one of these unrelated or kindred types [...] is what frequently separates it and its sole companion from the others, with the result that its existence as a synthesis of all these shared traits is what makes it unique" (14-15). Clearly, comparison with other genres or types does not make the definition of the *Bildungsroman* a great deal easier.

In a 1930s essay, Mikhail Bakhtin already recognised this problem of definition as he compared the different conditions that have been used to determine whether or not a novel could be labelled a *Bildungsroman* or coming-of-age novel. He states: "It is clear even at first glance that this list [of *Bildungsromane*] contains phenomena that are too diverse [...]. All this forces us to sort out in a different way [...] the entire problem of the so-called *Bildungsroman*" ("The *Bildungsroman*" 20). His own solution to this problem is to describe genre not by summing up its standard ingredients, but by pointing out its specific temporal and spatial characteristics. Bakhtin here coins the term chronotope, a concept closely related to, but distinct from, the concept of genre. The chronotope is "the intrinsic connectedness of temporal and spatial relationships that are artistically expressed in literature" (84); and it is precisely the chronotope "that defines genre and generic distinctions" (85). Each chronotope has its own and distinguishing time-space, or plot-setting relationship: the chronotope of the Greek romance, for example, is that of "an alien world in adventure-time" (89) where protagonists do not age between adventures, in spite of their exotic travels and the huge geographical distances they cover.

Interestingly, though, Bakhtin's concept of the chronotope causes him to make a subdivision of the *Bildungsroman* into five different categories, each with its own particular chronotope. In *Bildungsromane* of the first category, time is cyclical and idyllic, and man's life is eternally repeating the same seasons of life and nature – Bakhtin finds this chronotope in eighteenth-century idyllists and in regionalist *Heimatskunst*. In the second type of *Bildungsroman*, cyclicality is still present, though the connection is not as close. A novel belonging to this second type usually "depicts the world and life as *experience,* as a *school*" (22). The chronotope of the third category is no longer determined by cyclical time: "Emergence takes place in biographical time, and it passes through unrepeatable, individual stages" (22). The fourth type of *Bildungsroman* adds a distinctly didactic dimension to this and departs from a pedagogic ideal (basically, this is what Jeffers calls the *Erziehungsroman*: Bakhtin mentions Rousseau's *Émile* as an example), and the fifth type links the individual, biographical emergence to a specific historical process of growth and change – Bakhtin calls this "the most significant [type]", since "[m]an's emergence is accomplished in real historical time, with all of its necessity, its fullness, its future, and its profoundly chronotopic nature" (23).

These five categories all fall under Bakhtin's description of the *Bildungsroman* as "the novel of human emergence" (21), and the broadness of the definition explains why it is much more inclusive than those of Moretti, Jeffers or Shaffner. In a work of this genre, the hero or protagonist is not a constant, but a variable (21). Along with this description come genre conventions connected to growth and development. The focus on a formative period, usually in the youth of the hero or protagonist, is a consequence of the importance of his development; and the troubled quest for identity full of obstacles he needs to overcome signifies his personal growth. In due course, first encounters with love, lust, betrayal and other elements of adulthood emerge as conventions, as well. All of these conventions are very similar to those described by such scholars as Jeffers, Shaffner, and Buckley – so that the use of the concept of the chronotope does not, in the case of the *Bildungsroman,* lead to a rather more concrete outcome as to how it can be defined. If anything, the division into five subtypes, each with their own time-place relationship, only adds to this genre's complexity.

Later in life, however, Bakhtin developed a view on the chronotope that sheds a great deal of light on the relationship between a genre and its conventions. Bart Keunen finds that, in Bakhtin, the term chronotope usually refers to genre, but that it may also "coincide with motifs" (2). Indeed, Bakhtin describes the *Bildungsroman* as a chronotope, but in an added conclusion dated 1973 (the preceding essay is from 1937-1938), states that

> [w]e have been speaking so far only of the major chronotopes, those that are most fundamental and wide-ranging. But each such chronotope can include within it an unlimited number of minor chronotopes; in fact, as we have already said, any motif may have a special chronotope of its own. (252)

Hence, as Bakhtin shows, the chronotope of the Gothic may be distinguished, but so may that of the gothic castle, a chronotope that is really a place "saturated through and through with [...] the time of the historical past" (246), whose old-fashioned furniture, family portraits and legends bring together the present and a many-layered past. Keunen states that, essentially, chronotopes are "cognitive strategies applied by specific readers and writers", drawing on their "prior knowledge" (1): in short, "the term 'chronotope' refers to the stereotypical semantic information that is used during the encoding or decoding of literary texts" (2). Keunen is not the only one to connect the concepts of genre and stereotype: Jean-Louis Dufays, whose *Stéréotype et lecture* engages with reception theories such as that of Jauß, sees genre as *"un ensemble plus ou moins organisé de sequences stéréotypées [...] et de topoi qui permet de structurer une série illimitée de discours"* (*Stéréotype et lecture* 92 : the italics are his). What is more, he calls it a *"macro-structure"* (93) of stereotyping.

If we conceive of genre as a (macro-)stereotype, we can now better explain the mechanisms and rapports of conventions and genre as a whole. Essentially, a stereotype is an image that emerges when we see a familiar scheme in a literary work or elsewhere. Ruth Amossy describes it as "la grille que l'esprit humain applique sur le monde pour mieux l'investir" (*Les idées reçues* 24). Each culture and every epoch has its own stereotypes, from that of the avid, scheming Jew to that of the over-emotional, weak woman whose domain is the house, to cite some of Amossy's examples (28). The stereotypical image is part of the "imaginaire social" (9) of a certain time and place; it belongs to "un stock préexistant de représentations collectives" (9) and draws upon the collective set of ideas Amossy identifies as *doxa*. Consequently, the emergence of the image may be triggered by elements that the reader or listener recognises, but the stereotype as a collective scheme or construct does not *depend* on these elements. Amossy puts it this way as she discusses the stereotype of the avaricious Jew:

> On voit donc que le détail et la substance verbale du texte peuvent varier indéfiniment à condition de se ramener à l'image initiale du vieux Juif avare. On peut imaginer cent descriptions différentes dont aucun terme ne serait répété littéralement, et qui néanmoins se rangeraient sous la même rubrique. Un même stéréotype se dessine dans la multitude des pièces, des romans, des pamphlets, des discours politiques consacrés aux Shylocks et aux Elie Magnus. Il y est à la fois omniprésent, et éternellement absent. (23)

This would certainly explain the dependence of the genre on its conventions and its simultaneous independence of them. Amossy does not go into the subject of genre, but her discussion of the 'industry of fear' does resemble the bakhtinian linking of the generic chronotope and the motif chronotope. Amossy describes a number of 'scary' motifs – remote castles, tombs, villains, and so on. Together, these individual motifs or conglomerates of motifs may call up a stereotype of the gothic, or the uncanny, or any related macro-stereotype of the fearsome. The motifs, however, can also become stereotypes themselves. The gothic castle can still remind us of the Gothic novel, but it has gone on to become what Amossy calls a more general 'stereotype of fear' (129). The haunted castle, indeed, is a clear case of a stereotypical *pars pro toto*: an essential trope of the Gothic genre and other such macro-stereotypes, its appearance *outside* of Gothic fiction or horror cinema makes it a stereotype in its own right. There, after all, the castle's presence is capable of calling up all other connotations – supernatural occurrences, villains and susceptible female protagonists – that traditionally come with the genre. This, then, is the key to explaining the relations between a genre and its motifs: the genre *is* a specific stereotype, and it is called up by (in themselves random) conventions which, in turn, may also be or become stereotypes by their very association with the genre. The genre is a macro-stereotype that can turn its own conventions into stereotypes which call it up inside but also outside the generic work.

As a stereotypical image, the genre is a mould that guides the reader in constructing the meaning of a work of literature: by referring to a knowledge of previous generic works, and by opening up the work to inter- or architextuality, it allows a degree of predictability. The use of genre, then, is one way of providing concordance within a novel. The immediate danger to such concordance that this stereotype brings with it, though, is that its very architextuality and intertextuality opens up a novel to such a wide frame of reference, to such a large body of texts, that the generic novel might be decidedly more complex and its reading much less straightforward as a result. Nonetheless, the fact remains that genre is always a stereotype, a simplified image rather than a complex web of references, and so, the general image of the genre that is called up does not necessarily lead to a reconsideration of all other works of the genre. Dufays points out that readers very often tend to accept the stereotypes called up by a text unproblematically, and use them merely as tools for constructing meaning. He convincingly argues that the stereotype is so essential to a reader's understanding of the text that frequently he is not bothered by its very stereotypical nature and accepts the reading of the text it suggests. For though a reader is free on principle to read a text in whichever way he wants, it is possible and even highly likely for a work to send him in a certain direction. Dufays states that the act of reading "devait être définie *à la fois* comme une création de sens dotée de tous les pouvoirs et comme la concrétisation de certaines virtualités de l'objet social" (10). Formally, in other words, the text may offer an infinite variety of options as to how it can be read, but the reader will usually choose to follow one of those options that the text suggests most strongly as a result of its historic and social positioning.

Still, the fact that genre can be seen as a stereotype does not necessarily make it a tool for providing concordance in a novel. In fact, it can do just the opposite, especially when it is *only partially* called up. As we have seen, the connection between the conventions of the *Bildungsroman* and the genre itself functions in two directions, so that a particular convention can come to stand for the entire genre, even if no other conventions are present to support it. It is therefore possible for a novel to call up the *Bildungsroman* genre through certain elements, but to depart from its standard plots and forms in other ways. Thus, if the genre is called up but not maintained throughout, discordance seems just as probable to occur as concordance, and it is possible to read such a novel both as a *Bildungsroman* and as distinct from a *Bildungsroman*. And since it is very unclear what a *Bildungsroman*-plot actually looks like, this double reading is quite likely to occur. Also, concordance does not hold whenever a stereotype is somehow thematised and uncovered in a text. As Dufays says (the italics are his), "la lecture [...] est nécessairement canalisée, modalisée, par *la manière dont ces stéréotypes se trouvent énoncés*: que les stéréotypes soient assumés par l'écriture ou qu'ils soient au contraire mis à distance par celle-ci compte énormément aux yeux du lecteur" ("Stéréotypes, lecture littéraire et postmodernisme" 86). Dufays shows that a stereotype can be parodied, ironised, or deconstructed (*Stéréotype et lecture* 233). It is, then, very well possible for a stereotype to become more than a textual figure through which a self-evident doxa speaks. Just as easily, it can become involved in a hierarchical struggle of different value systems. The stereotype comes to stand for an alternative value system that can be exposed, ridiculed, or deconstructed.

To complicate matters, though, the parodied, exposed text – the particular genre that is made fun of – is not always completely devalued. Linda Hutcheon, for one, shows that contemporary forms of parody need not always use its ironic inversion "at the expense of the parodied text" (*A Theory of Parody* 6). Instead, its use as well as its inversion of that text often lead to a "combination of respectful homage and ironically thumbed nose" (33) of that which is parodied. It is possible, moreover, for a parody of genre to really become the parody of something else. Parody, in Hutcheon's description, is always directed at text and limited to text, but it can function as a vehicle for social satire, too. This is what Hutcheon calls "parodic satire (a type of the *genre satire*) which aims at something outside the text, but which employs parody as a vehicle to achieve its satiric or corrective end" (62). The parodying and laying bare of the genre stereotype may very well be a way of criticising that which lies beyond the text. All in all, the genre parody may establish what at first looks like a concordance-imposing value hierarchy and a degree of predictability, but it really allows much more ambiguity than

72

its appearance may show. For the Spanish novels I study here, this means that the predictability and readability which the stereotypical conventions seem to call up, may be the very cause of disturbance and discordance. As a consequence, hierarchies of values or memory narratives may be unbalanced and undermined.

In the Spanish memory novels I want to analyse here, conventions of the *Bildungsroman* are present and they shape the way in which memory is portrayed. At the same time, though, the genre is either not maintained throughout the work, or it is parodied or otherwise highlighted. Does such heightened complexity and discordance lead to a more complex intertwining of normative discourses? And what are the consequences of the particular chronotope that is introduced into the novel – does it contrast with the memory discourses otherwise present in the work? The following analyses will try to clarify this.

Antonio Muñoz Molina, *El dueño del secreto*

It can hardly be called surprising that Georges Tyras discovers *Bildungsroman*-like qualities in Antonio Muñoz Molina's 1997 novel *El dueño del secreto* (143). The work presents us with a large number of conventions of the coming-of-age novel. Its narrator-protagonist and main evaluator looks back upon a formative period in his youth, when, as a village boy from Andalucía, he came to Madrid in 1974 to study Journalism. Upon arriving in the big city, he struggles to survive, but eventually lands a job as a typist with a man called Ataúlfo Ramiro. This Ataúlfo, a rich bon-vivant who introduces the young protagonist to a world of luxuries, is a confessed anarchist, and before he knows it, the protagonist finds himself involved in antifrancoist rebellion. Meanwhile, he starts taking part in student demonstrations, too, while learning about love, life, and revolution. He is deeply impressed with his first peek at a naked woman, with the first time he experiences fear, with the first time he enters into a self-service restaurant; and in between all these first times, he tries to follow his vocation to become a journalist. Place, here, also functions as a genre convention: the big city offers the protagonist the chance to taste 'real', complicated, full-on life, especially because it is opposed to the quiet, unchanging little village the protagonist comes from. The protagonist, all in all, reaches maturity in the period described in the novel.

As mentioned above, the genre conventions that call up the stereotypical stance of the *Bildungsroman* aid the reader in grasping the text, referring, as they do, to all the other literary works to which they stand in an architextual relationship. The fact that this is a *Bildungsroman* leads the reader to understand that there is a life lesson to be learnt here, and that the protagonist will learn it through experience. In this particu-

lar case, moreover, the year in which the narration is set is highly significant: 1974, the year of the Portuguese revolution, on the eve of
Franco's death. Bakhtin, who divides the *Bildungsroman* into five types,
states that it reached its culmination in the fifth and last one, where
man's emergence happens in historical real time; in other words,

> [man] emerges *along with the world* and he reflects the historical emergence
> of the world itself. He is no longer within an epoch, but on the border be-
> tween two epochs, at the transition point from one to the other. This transi-
> tion is accomplished in him and through him. He is forced to become a new,
> unprecedented type of human being. What is happening here is precisely the
> emergence of a new man. (23)

It would seem that *El dueño del secreto* belongs to this type of coming-
of-age novel: the protagonist matures in order to become a new person
in a new, democratic time.

But when we look at the *Bildung* of the protagonist-narrator, it becomes clear that this is quite another type of *Bildungsroman*. When he
sets out for Madrid, his expectations are sky-high: he expects to find the
adventure and the fast world that he, as an aspiring journalist, misses so
dearly in his home village with its aptly named tavern "*De aquí no paso*,
cuyos clientes, de un modo u otro, acababan siempre haciendo honor a
tal nombre" (77). By the end of the novel, however, he has returned to
his village, but not in the triumphant way Buckley allows the *Bildungsheld*, "to demonstrate by his presence the degree of his success or the
wisdom of his choice" (18). The hero of *El dueño del secreto* merely
resumes the village life he so despised. He marries his high school
sweetheart, settles down into a job with the company of his father-in-
law, and resigns to a life very different from the one he tried to find in
Madrid. The revolution and adventure he wanted to be a part of have
turned out to be an illusion that is long gone. The protagonist is hum-
bled: he has not managed to influence history, and he has learned that a
simple, insignificant existence is all he can aspire to.

From this point of view, it might be better to classify *El dueño del
secreto* as Bakhtin's second type of coming-of-age novel, which is
characterised by cyclical time – meaning that time and life are seen as
ever-repeating cycles, starting with birth, and ending with death, analogous to the passing of the seasons. This type of *Bildungsroman* "traces a
typically repeating path of man's emergence from youthful idealism and
fantasies to mature sobriety and practicality", Bakhtin remarks; in it,
"one becomes more sober, experiencing some degree of resignation"
("The *Bildungsroman*" 22).

The protagonist-narrator has learnt this sobering lesson and often repeats it throughout the novel. Frequently, he underlines the cyclicality of

the experience by highlighting that this lesson was learnt, not just by him, but by his entire generation:

> Parecía, en aquella primavera de 1974, antes de la revolución portuguesa de abril, que nada iba a cambiar nunca, y cuando alguien recordaba aquel verso de un poema de Brecht, *la más larga noche no es eterna*, uno pensaba que sí, que la noche franquista sí iba a serlo, porque nadie tendría la paciencia, la obstinación o el coraje de esperar su fin, y porque el fascismo, desde Chile, estaba volviendo a ensombrecer el mundo. Nuestra generación [...] fue la última en llegar al antifranquismo, y nos tocó la paradoja de heredar, con dieciocho años, la traición de derrota de las generaciones anteriores, de respirar un aire enrarecido por treinta y tantos años de desaliento y de invenciones gloriosas y absurdas de huelgas generales que no fueron vencidas porque nunca llegaron a existir. En el País Vasco se había impuesto el estado de excepción. Por algunos parques de Madrid, incluso por los pasillos de alguna facultad, llegó a verse el prodigio fugaz de una muchacha que corría desnuda: era una moda que venía de los campus universitarios de América, y que aquí no llegó a calar, y se llamaba el *streaking*, un cuerpo desnudo atravesando como un rayo los lugares más usuales y más tristes, y desapareciendo luego sin dejar ni un rastro de su resplandor. (130-131)

Here, the narrator describes his generation's futile attempts at revolting against the seemingly endless dictatorship. A fear of being stuck in an eternal night spurs its members into action, but their actions are never more than short rays of light that die down again, leaving the world as dark as it was before. It seems, then, that the lesson learnt in *El dueño del secreto* is a lesson learnt by a collective, and it is a forceful lesson for that reason. History is a cyclical movement, and individuals like the protagonist cannot really influence it, in spite of their revolutionary hopes and dreams. They have to accept their humility in the face of world events, and aim at nothing more than a life that is, as the narrator describes his own at the end of the novel, "una vida transparente, serena, en la que no falta algún privilegio ni ocurre casi nada" (167).

In due course, this novel's scholarly readers detect a responsible, moral tone in this work. It is read by many as a critique of transitional Spanish memory discourses, breathing a disillusionment caused by the way Spain became a democracy through compromise and forgetting. So, Fabienne Bradu finds that *El dueño del secreto* contains "la imagen misma del desencanto" (47), and Alicia Molero de la Iglesia also calls the protagonist "inadaptado y desencantado" (392). After all, the scholars stress, we are dealing here with an author "volcado hacia el rescate de la memoria" (Tyras 139), whom critics have singled out because of his "tradición [...] de luchar contra el olvido" (Oropesa 163). Tyras actually cites the author himself: "Lo peor de la dictadura [...] es que nos convirtieron en un país sin memoria" (139).

However, this reading is undermined by the protagonist-narrator himself. In spite of the fact that he stresses his own sobering-up repeatedly, he secretly adheres to a rather different version of what happened in 1974 than the supposed lesson of resignation would allow. The *Bildungsheld* believes that Ataúlfo's rebel group was on the verge of overthrowing the regime, and moreover claims his own, important part in the historical chain of events: he is convinced that he is personally "responsable del fracaso en España de una revolución como la de Portugal" (72). It was the protagonist himself who betrayed the secret of the conspiracy to his roommate Ramonazo, thus spreading the rumour that led to the dismantling of the conspirators' group. This view on past events, of course, highly contradicts the supposed maturity and sobriety of the protagonist-narrator, and it is at odds with the portrayal of time as cyclical and change as occurring only at the surface. It is suggested here that individuals *can* influence history, and that the protagonist-narrator has done just that, albeit with painful consequences which he still feels guilty of.

It is not that the scholarly readers of *El dueño del secreto* do not recognise this contradiction, but they explain it by pointing out that the narrator-protagonist remains humble and resigned even when he talks of his 'secret'. And in this, the critics and scholars who read Muñoz Molina's work as 'responsible' are certainly not mistaken. In the final chapter, the narrator looks back on the past and mentions that he still keeps one secret: that of his memory. "Nadie piensa ya en aquellos tiempos", he claims, "nadie se acuerda del invierno y de la primavera de 1974, ni de la ejecución de Puig Antich o del nombre del húngaro o polaco al que le dieron garrote vil en Barcelona. Yo sí me acuerdo de todo: ése es mi secreto" (167). But when he comes to speak of what he *actually* remembers, it seems that he occupies himself by reminiscing about facts of rather less general importance:

> No pueden saber que es en otra buena memoria disimulada tras la que ellos conocen, como en un doble fondo, donde está guardado mi secreto, las pocas cosas de entonces de las que no quiero ni puedo olvidarme [...]. Ahora, algunas veces, yo agradezco [...] el derecho a acordarme sin que lo sepa nadie, sin que lo pueda sospechar nunca mi mujer, que duerme a mi lado, en la oscuridad de nuestro dormitorio, de aquella amiga o cómplice de Ataúlfo Ramiro a la que vi desnuda durante un segundo en Madrid, hace diecinueve años [...]. (168)

And it is with his memory of this naked woman, and his regret at not having dared to enter her room in spite of thinking she would have let him, that the protagonist-narrator terminates his narrative. As it turns out, his supposed *Bildung* has had much less to do with politics or with changing society and revolution than he wants us to believe. As a consequence, it is not his own heroic role in history, or revolution itself that he longs for: he nostalgically pines for the time when the belief in such a revolution was still possible. "En definitiva, es la nostalgia de cuando se tenía un futuro" (167), Salvador Oropesa says.

Of course, it is possible to read the novel as a responsibly moralistic work that is critical of the past. In this novel, nostalgia for the way francoism could have ended painfully emphasises the disappointing way in which it actually did end, and a critical stance is the result. Yet to account for the contrast between cyclical and historical time in such a way is to miss a turn in the work's plot. The reliance on the narrator's evaluation which this type of reading implies may, it becomes plain, be mistaken – for there are clear clues planted in the text which suggest that his heroic pretensions rest on his misinterpretation of facts. As a result, the value hierarchy of the novel is undermined as the narrator's values and evaluations are deprived of their authority.

The protagonist-narrator's account contains plenty of elements that deconstruct his rather heroic image of Ataúlfo, of the conspiracy, and of his own part in it. Ataúlfo, for one, is admired greatly by the protagonist-narrator, though his marked predilection for the enjoyments of good food, good wine and seedy night clubs seems incompatible with his anarchist idealism. While the protagonist-narrator turns a blind eye to anything that is strange about him, the reader is induced to form a very different judgment of Ataúlfo. For example, when the protagonist first visits the man's family home, it strikes him as surprisingly shabby and poor. Ataúlfo's wife appears in an old bathrobe, and the office she introduces the young typist into is small and crammed. The boy, however, concludes quickly that this seeming shabbiness is really a sign of greatness: "yo había oído decir que los verdaderos multimillonarios [...] se vestían de cualquier modo [...]. Aquella señora debía de pertenecer al grupo más selecto de los multimillonarios, o de los grandes de España" (87). Even when the lady of the house disappears "arrastrando las zapatillas", the young protagonist is left with "una impresión de misterio y lujo" (88). The plastic office chair is, of course, "una nueva señal de extravagante riqueza y desdén hacia las convenciones" (88).

These comical mistakes, which arise out of youthful innocence and admiration, soon lead to a destabilisation of the *Bildungsroman* plot. Ataúlfo keeps up a decidedly hedonist lifestyle, and the narrator-protagonist admires him for this skilful "manera de moverse [...] disimulando magistralmente su militancia incansable bajo un disfraz de despreocupación y aun de libertinaje del que no se despojaba ni en presencia de su propia mujer" (117). The betrayal of the conspiracy does not lead to any violence, but to a domestic scene between Ataúlfo and his wife, which the protagonist involuntarily witnesses. As he is sent to a night club to hand a note to a young girl named Nati, the *Bildungsheld* still firmly believes that she must be in on the conspiracy. To the reader, however, a new way of reading the work suggests itself: the so-called conspiracy appears more like an invention of Ataúlfo's to cover up for his infidelity. Since we are at all times restricted to the narrator-protagonist's narration and focalisation, this possibility is never made explicit. It is suggested, however, by the odd contrast between Ataúlfo's claims and the evidence his actions provide, while the narrator-protagonist also undermines his own authority by admitting, on a number of occasions, that he is gullible: "cualquier comerciante me engaña" (119), he says, and "me lo creo todo" (153).

Though the narrator-protagonist's version of events is never abandoned, this second possible reading, which relies on the narratee's judgments and evaluations, is certainly a disrupting presence in the novel. It undermines the narrator's authority, and so, the value hierarchy that has rested until now on his evaluations is severely shaken. Andrés Soria Olmedo describes the narrator-protagonist as a sort of Don Quijote, whose hopes and dreams lead him to a misinterpretation of reality: "es obvio que el episodio vivido por el protagonista es un episodio ficticio [...], la imaginación [del protagonista] se confunde con su esperanza de asistir a un momento decisivo de la historia de España" (175). If this reading is admitted, of course, the novel's ethical, responsible positioning is disturbed, even though the lesson of resignation is once again reinforced. It now turns out, after all, that the narrator-protagonist is still the innocent and idealistic man he once was, and that no apprenticeship whatsoever has taken place. In other words, *El dueño del secreto* becomes a parody rather than a typical *Bildungsroman*.

This parody might then be said to reach its culmination in the final chapter of the novel, where the narrator looks back upon his past. Here, the narrator describes his longing for the woman he saw naked on his errand for Ataúlfo. In doing so, he shows that he was much more preoccupied with women and sexuality than with actual political change. As it turns out, the protagonist-narrator resembles Ataúlfo remarkably: he fakes a revolutionary interest that only covers up for much more down-to-earth impulses. This, then, is not what we would call a *Bildungsheld*: the protagonist-narrator is neither noble, nor clever, nor wisened-up.

As Linda Hutcheon has already warned us, though, parody nowadays comprises more than mere ridicule (*A Theory of Parody*). It is possible for a genre stereotype to be evoked and embraced while it is exposed, and it may be argued that such is the case in *El dueño del secreto*. There is one scene in particular in this work where an actual, real and serious *Bildung* is enacted, though the lesson is a very different one from the resigned cyclical take on things which dominates the rest of the narrative. Through a description that breathes heroism rather than resignation in one's fate, the protagonist narrates how he took part in a student protest and experienced true fear as he only just escaped from the hands of the police. This occurrence, we may note, is one of the most autobiographical events in a novel that Muñoz Molina has described as a mix of autobiography and fiction (*El dueño del secreto* 172); and it is the more remarkable, therefore, that it is the place where the collective 'we' replaces the individual 'I' most consistently. His sudden active membership of a collective surprises the protagonist. Whereas one part of himself just wants to take off, there is another part, "creo ahora que la más volátil, la que de verdad era menos mía" (111), that spurs him on; and it is thus that he finds himself screaming at the police, "y eso que me ha dado siempre mucha vergüenza unirme a cualquier celebración colectiva" (111), and throwing stones: "algunos de nosotros (yo, aunque parece mentira, entre ellos) cogimos piedras" (112). Here, the membership of the collective inspires a sudden bravery in the protagonist, and for a short while he rises above himself and his fears. The description of the police nearing the students is almost cinematic:

> Hay cosas que uno no puede inventar ni olvidar: el crujido de aquellos pares de botas negras, el callejón de altos muros rojos que se cerraba delante de nosotros, las voces de aquellos hombres que nos dirigían las palabras más sucias de la lengua española mientras se nos acercaban acompasadamente, bajándose las viseras de los cascos, levantando poco a poco las porras como en un ademán estatuario de carga de caballería. (113)

Of course, this student demonstration does not, in the end, serve any purpose, a fact that is underlined by the novel's motto, a Francisco de Ayala quote stating that times of tyranny awaken in the majority of people, "que no tenemos madera de héroes ni de santos, nuestras posibilidades más ruines" (67). Nevertheless, the heroism that this collective outburst awakened in the cowardly protagonist obviously surprises him still, and has clearly been a formative experience. While the novel parodies the *Bildungsroman*, then, it still contains a real *Bildung* as the hero learns about fear and courage.

It is perhaps because of the autobiographical nature of this section that the narrator gains in authority, and this might explain why many of the readers of *El dueño del secreto* stayed with the narrator's evaluations without paying attention to the many places in the novel where his unreliability is suggested. So, Bradu sticks to a view of the work as "la reconstrucción de esos años y de esos círculos [con] la ligereza de las educaciones sentimentales escritas con ironía y compasión" (221). Salvador Oropesa reads *El dueño del secreto* entirely according to the resigned stance of the original *Bildung*, as an expression of the *desencanto* with democracy. In his eyes, "la novela consta [...] [del] secreto colectivo del olvido de lo que supusieron el tardofranquismo y la transición democrática, a favor de una sublimación de ésta y un olvido total de aquél" (156). In a large section devoted to the likes of iconic stars of francoism like Lola Flores, Marisol and Rocío Durcal (159), he even proceeds to explain the importance of the naked woman, the "clímax de la novela" (158), in this vein: "La libertad democrática se simbolizó a partir de una serie de desnudos femeninos" (159). Georges Tyras shows firm belief in the narrator's version by claiming that "él sigue siendo dueño de un secreto, el de la memoria" (156). Indeed, it looks like only Soria Olmedo and Epicteto Díaz Navarro have recognised the undermining elements the work contains, and the consequent double reading it allows. In his commentary and guidelines for the study of *El dueño del secreto*, Epicteto Díaz Navarro hesitates between compassion and ridicule – he notes the narrator's longing for the beautiful, naked woman and asks readers whether "¿hay alguna prueba que verifique la realidad de esa conspiración?" (*El dueño del secreto* 194), but he still seems to feel for the protagonist-narrator:

> [El protagonista] recuerda dos aspectos que para él fueron fundamentales: la política y una mujer a la que vio fugazmente desnuda. [...] Ahora comprendemos que ese secreto alienta en medio de la monotonía y la grisura (política y erótica) de su vida presente. (*El dueño del secreto* 169)

It is safe to say that a concordant reading here means a great simplification. To read this work as a responsible critique of the *Transición* only, is to overlook the parodic layer of the work and to ignore the unreliability of the narrator. By virtue of the scholars' concordant reading, however, *El dueño del secreto* becomes a straightforwardly critical work, and as I mentioned before, such a reading would fit in remarkably well with Muñoz Molina's reputation as a responsible writer. This reputation is visible in the titles that studies of his work carry: Tyras's article appeared in a volume entitled *Ética y estética de Antonio Muñoz Molina*, and José Carlos Mainer deals with the author in "Antonio Muñoz Molina ou la prise de possession de la mémoire".

Nonetheless, a concordant reading is a very violent reading here. The novel is in fact open to a number of readings which, while they seem to exclude each other, can also be combined – the protagonist may be ridiculed, felt for, and exposed at the same time. It is interesting that nostalgia and autobiography seem to contribute to concordance (in chapters 4 and 5, their discordant potential will be discussed), and that it is precisely the use and subsequent parody of the *Bildungsroman* which is responsible for its fundamental discordance. Readers are tempted to feel empathy for the narrator precisely through his nostalgia, and they want to believe him as an autobiographical, and thus seemingly referential, authority. It is the parody of an apprenticeship that shakes this authority and makes nostalgia look ridiculous; and it is the generic stance turned upside down that provides the novel with these many possible readings.

Instead of providing a comfortable, easy read, then, this *Bildungsroman* does the opposite. It allows some readers to be touched and 'improved', and for others to enjoy a critical deconstruction that is introduced as a surprising plot twist. *El dueño del secreto* ends up adhering to the genre stereotype as well as breaking down its structure – so that we are left puzzling over what the actual lesson of this novel could possibly be.

Rafael Chirbes, *Los viejos amigos*

Los viejos amigos by Rafael Chirbes (2003) is a novel that does not entirely follow the average coming-of-age plot. Instead of revolving around one hero or heroine experiencing personal growth, it has a larger number of protagonists and is characterised by polyphony and a wide variety of perspectives. Still, it contains enough of the genre's usual ingredients to call up the image of a series of *Bildungen*. The novel's protagonists, who used to form a cell in the communist anti-dictatorial movement of the late 1960s and early 1970s, gather in a restaurant in Madrid to commemorate that past. More than twenty-five years have passed (the festive dinner takes place in 1996), and the former revolution fighters have now become older and wiser: they look back on their dreams and ideals in the knowledge of what has become of them. There is, then, the usual process of ageing through experience, there is the formative period, the late adolescence and early maturity of the protagonists, there is the move from a village (Denia) to the big city (Madrid) and there is, last but not least, the lesson learnt. All of these conventions together evoke the genre stereotype of the *Bildungsroman*.

The way in which this work is structured, though, differs from the typical coming-of-age novel: it contains a number of sections – fifteen, as López Bernasocchi and López de Abiada count – which "corresponden a seis voces narrativas y que a su vez constituyen quince monólogos interiores" (107). We witness, it appears, the *Bildung* of six different characters, the narrator-protagonists: that of Carlos, a frustrated writer; that of Demetrio, an unsuccessful painter whose boyfriend is dying of AIDS, and who also carries the virus; that of Rita, who has resigned herself to a tranquil life of hard work; that of Narciso, who has become a PSOE politician; that of Pedro or Pedrito, who constructs holiday homes in his native village; and that of Amalia, a faded beauty who suffers from depressions. Obviously, these narrators are all very different individuals, and it might be expected that the lessons they learn in the novel differ accordingly, in spite of the fact that they share the same formative experience. Masoliver Ródenas states:

> Los personajes pertenecen además a distintas clases sociales y tienen aspiraciones muy distintas, por lo que, unidos en principio por unos mismos ideales revolucionarios, dichos ideales se ven transformados por los marcados rasgos individuales. (433)

This view of the characters as real individuals who undergo personal learning processes starting from a shared experience is adjusted somewhat, however, by what other scholars and critics note. It is remarked in almost every publication on the work that the individuals portrayed here form a particular group, a generation, and that their individual lessons boil down to one and the same experience: that of disappointment and loss of ideals. *Los viejos amigos* deals with "personajes derrotados" ("Chirbes alerta"): "una generación, la [de Chirbes], que 'soñó con cambiar el mundo, pero aplazó el momento', lo que hizo que ya no sirviera para nada" (Intxausti). It is "la amarga constatación del fracaso generacional" (López Bernasocchi and López de Abiada 113). María-Teresa Ibáñez-Ehrlich goes as far as to say that the many viewpoints we are presented with are only a trick. The refraction of a single lesson into a variety of apprenticeships lends more authority to the message of a 'super-I' hiding behind them:

> Pero en esa yuxtaposición de diversos 'yo' se esconde igualmente el propio autor; se diría que Rafael Chirbes, autor implícito, fracciona su alma y sentimientos en un perspectivismo que tiende a objetivar lo expuesto por los personajes, a dar carácter de verdad a su versión de la Historia. (60)

This novel, then, can be read both as the narration of a multitude of smaller educations or, alternatively, as the *Bildung* of a group, a collective entity, that comes to represent a generation.

If we look closely at the individual narrations of the protagonists, we note that these characters' experiences are indeed remarkably similar. At first sight, of course, the differences are obvious: some of the characters come from simple village backgrounds, others are rich and worldly-wise. There are those who stayed in Madrid, the city that saw the birth of their communist cell, and those who returned to the coast. What is more, many of the old friends feel a great dislike for one another, most notably Pedro and Guzmán, who get into violent discussions during the dinner; and the divorced couples, Amalia and Narciso, Rita and Carlos, do not get along very well, either. Significantly, not all the characters, not even all narrators, have actually come to the dinner – Rita, for example, stayed away, and so did Narciso. Nonetheless, the dinner invitation has induced each and every one of them to look back upon their lives. And, as varied as these may have been – one has lost a son to drugs, another has contracted HIV, and a third has suffered a traumatic divorce – the overall tone is that of pessimism, the overall experience that of dreams lost and illusions forgotten. The difference in personalities merely serves to highlight different facets of one and the same message – often in exactly the same wording. Carlos stresses the importance of manual labour, of construction, and its superiority to art – finding "todo cuanto aprendió el niño que fui, una vieja retórica inútil, muerta, montones de ruinas" (186). Pedrito, too, claims on numerous occasions that he enjoys "el trabajo como forma de olvido" (94). The subject of social ranks is broached by different narrators in very similar terms: Demetrio feels that the 'winners' have tried to "ponerme en mi clase" (26), while Carlos concludes that the class distinction is part of cyclical time: "Hay una resistencia de la clase aún más allá de la muerte. [...] [H]ay una flexibilidad especial en los gestos, en la mirada, que sólo la gimnasia de la clase repetida durante generaciones transmite" (130). The narrators thus echo each other's preoccupations, and their narrations form a sort of network of recurrent themes.

The homogeneity of the *Bildungen* is reinforced by the narrators' and characters' frequent use of a collective 'we'. This is visible, for example, in the following remark of Pedro:

> A los cincuenta y nueve años puedo permitirme mandarlo todo a la mierda, ¿entiendes? Mandarlo todo a mamar. He pasado ya lo mejor. La borrachera buena ya la he pasado. El amor, la capacidad de enamorarme, de entontecerme, todo eso ya lo he pasado. ¿Qué me queda?, ¿qué nos queda?, ¿la resaca?, ¿la lucidez alucinada de la resaca? (126)

Here, Pedro speaks of his personal disillusionment, yet immediately turns it into the disillusionment of them all by repeating a sentence in which he replaces the singular personal pronoun with a plural. A similar procedure is frequently visible in the direct speech of the characters and the musings of the individual remembering narrators. Rita generalises, for instance: "somos nosotros los incidentes pasajeros de cuanto nos rodea" (147). Pedrito asks disappointedly: "¿Qúe hemos ganado? ¿Qué hemos perdido? [...] Nuestras ilusiones" (8). Guzmán complains: "Decíamos que queríamos cambiar el mundo y, cuando nos han dado esa oportunidad los votos de los ciudadanos, os habéis puesto a criticarlo todo" (198). Apparently, all protagonists find that their version of history is contested: they have to defend it against the 'winners', but also against the younger generation, whose exponents Lalo and Juanjo, the sons of Guzmán, dominate the political discussions at the table and are described by Pedrito as annoying know-it-alls.

In spite of the work's polyphony, then, one clear *Bildung* is achieved, so that *Los viejos amigos* has a very concordant, moralistic face. The various narrators end up conveying the same, or similar, values. Owing to the work's resigned stance and its focus on lost illusions, critics and scholars have read the novel as a work that is highly critical of transitional forgetting. "*Los viejos amigos* ofrece a través de la memoria la historia de España de los últimos treinta años que cuestiona y ataca la versión oficial de una Transición y una época democrática ejemplares" (60), Ibáñez-Ehrlrich claims. López Bernasocchi and López de Abiada state that "La obra de Chirbes versa [...] sobre la Transición política española desde una posición que rezuma desencanto e incluso frustración" (105). Masoliver Ródenas finds that the work "ofrece una visión crítica, demoledora, de nuestra realidad política" (432). Chirbes himself has often declared his critical intentions: to him, "[e]l arte por el arte es falta de escrúpulos", and in *Los viejos amigos*, he describes a generation that "prefirió curarse con la medicina del olvido en lugar de aprender con el purgante de la memoria" (Rodríguez Marcos). It seems, then, that the message of *Los viejos amigos* is plain, its structure concordant, and its polyphony no hindrance for a straightforward *Bildung* to be shared by narrators and empathising readers alike.

At the same time, it seems that the similarity of all the different narrations is a consequence of a second major deviation from the *Bildungsroman* stance: the focus on retrospection. Whereas in itself it is not impossible, as we have seen in the analysis of *El dueño del secreto*, for the *Bildung* to be narrated from the future, the very nature of the process of learning suggests a bridging of the gap between youthful innocence and mature judgment. Naturally, then, the narrator-protagonist of *El dueño del secreto* mostly focalises his account through his younger self, only to switch to full retrospection in the final chapter. In *Los viejos amigos*, however, there is no such focalisation through the younger self in order to show mental growth: focalisation is restricted to the narrators, who provide their descriptions with latter-day judgements. Thus, while they formulate the high ideals they once shared, they immediately stress their emptiness. Their ideals may best be summarised in two words: revolution and art – even the militant Pedrito, the leader of the group who initiated a number of violent actions and claimed that "la literatura está reñida con [...] la revolución" (9), was guided in his revolutionary spirit by the poetry of Baudelaire. Pedro is one of the first, though, to explain that these two words are empty words, that they are 'air'; and that as you get older, such words and such high ideals lose their lustre as time passes and death approaches.

Rather than a *Bildung* or process of maturation, these narrators turn out to describe how latter-day disappointment disfigures the memory of youth. "Los jóvenes tienen pocas ideas, pero claras [...]. Luego, toca matizar esas buenas frases" (207), Carlos muses, who finds that youthful ideals end up in a "túrmix, y se convierten en una pasta monocroma y confusa" (206). Sadly, "las emociones se gastan" (207); "el tiempo no cura, sino agrava" (73), Pedrito claims. Time has gone on, the ideals of art and revolution have proven to be illusions, artists and revolutionaries do nothing but "vender aire" (46). Because of its constant retrospection, *Los viejos amigos* is characterised by cyclical time. People are insignificant in the face of history, to hope for anything better is pointless, and abstract dreams and illusions will be sold and forgotten. In this cyclical time, the young are destined to make the same mistakes as their elders – which is underlined by the presence at the dinner table of Guzmán's twin sons, the successful protest singer Lalo and his equally anti-globalist brother Juanjo, who works for an NGO, and by the way their father tries to protect them from losing their ideals by going against one of Pedrito's bitter speeches: "Seguramente lo único que quiere [Guzmán] es que sus hijos no se enteren de que esto, todo esto, está sin control, a la deriva" (132).

The cyclical image of time thus emerges out of the very aspects of the novel that *deviate* from the *Bildungsroman*-stereotype: the group perspective and the focus on retrospection. The places where the *Bildungsroman* is called up in turn imply a very different chronotope, Bakhtin's fifth type, where biological and historical emergence go hand in hand. Here, the characters learn and experience, they undergo a transition; at the same time, Spain's historical transition to democracy is prepared and finally takes place. Of course, it comes too late, so that the lesson is one of disappointment; but still there is ample reason to connect the development of each of the *Bildungshelden* and link it to the often-described process of *desencanto* that took place in democratic Spain.

It is therefore understandable that scholars tend to read this work as a *Bildungsroman* of the fifth type, in spite of a strong undermining presence of cyclical time. This reading is certainly a very clear possibility due to the positioning of nearly all evaluating characters as victims of the dictatorship. López Bernasocchi and López de Abiada show that the characters can be divided into two groups: "los fracasados y los 'vencedores' (es decir, los tránsfugas o 'transformistas', los acomodaticios o camaleones), los que han sabido adaptarse a los tiempos y que [...] acaso nunca fueran verdaderos revolucionarios" (115). But in the hierarchy of characters, the 'losers' receive much more space and attention than the 'winners'. In fact, the only narrator who is part of that last group is Narciso, who is portrayed as a traitor and a coward and whose narration is the shortest by far, taking up as little as ten pages (62-71). On the whole, then, we get to see the remembered past and the group members through the eyes of the 'losers', who tend to resent the success and forgetfulness of the others. So, it certainly is possible to read this work as a critique of society, as an expression of *desencanto* and of anger at the forgetful attitude of transitional Spain. Yet this critical evaluation is overshadowed by the characters' reflections on ageing and dying – and these imprint the work with a far more general, human feeling of loss.

The cyclicality of time is thematised particularly in one central section of the novel where the *Bildung* is summarised. It is focalised through Carlos, it seems to be told by a sort of omniscient narrator, and it is printed in italics to further set it apart. In this section, all themes of the novel come together around the one group member, Elisa, who died young, of cancer. Incomprehensibly, López Bernasocchi and López de Abiada count Elisa as a 'loser' (116), while from her description it becomes quite clear that she had become a successful expert in baroque art, and enjoyed the luxuries of democratic life. She, if anyone, was a revolutionary who did not really care for political change, only interested in a "revolución bella y ordenada" (106), the revolution's aesthetic side. In this part of the novel, though, the antagonism of winners and losers is abandoned in the face of the ultimate cycle of life and death: as she lies dying, surrounded by tasteful and beautiful objects, the irrevocability of death is shown, as well as the value of time and the importance of making things happen instead of waiting for them. Elisa, though a 'winner', unites certain significant characteristics: she studies the baroque period, "el esplandor de la fruta y la podredumbre, cuestión de minutos" (116), and architecture, which Carlos and Pedrito value so highly for its being real and constructive. Her most important study on the subject bears a significant motto, quoted twice in *Los viejos amigos*: "eres lo que fui un día, soy lo que serás" (101). The cyclical repetition of life and death could hardly have been phrased better.

This passage, so remarkably different from what surrounds it, places an emphasis on death and time that is elaborated especially towards the end of the novel. Indeed, this is precisely the impression the reader is left with after the final interior monologue of *Los viejos amigos*, spoken by Pedrito:

> Pienso que abrazo cadáveres que han salido de fin de semana. […] Beso ahora bocas que pronto estarán muertas, y hoy están invadidas por las bacterias. […] Mi boca llena de bacterias dice, 'te quiero, Elisa', y la voz pone un hosco eco en el vacío de la habitación del hotel. Entre tanto, el mar rompe en los acantilados de Denia, lame las doradas playas que, desde hace veinte años, no tienen más arena que la que traen los camiones desde no se sabe dónde para reponer la que cada invierno el temporal engulle. Paisajes portátiles, dientes de quita y pon. (220-221)

Thus, the novel ends with a reminder of how life necessarily implies death, and always carries its destruction within itself.

Los viejos amigos indeed constructs a variety of perspectives that finally come down to one and the same message. The individual voices differ greatly, but in the end, they repeat the same insights and evaluations. Their authority, moreover, is strengthened by a generational 'we' that highlights the antagonistic nature of 'their' truth – the truth of the 'losers'. This, then, is a strong message, a clear lesson learnt: "eso es la vida" (199). But it is not the *Bildungsroman*-stereotype that allows this viewpoint to be carried across so clearly. Rather, it is precisely in the two aspects of the work where the *Bildungsroman*-stance is abandoned, the polyphonic setup and the retrospective narrative, where we find concordance most strongly imposed. The number of *Bildungen* reinforces the general validity of the lesson, whereas the retrospective focalisation stresses the outcome of the *Bildung* rather than the road towards it. The cyclical view of time comes to the foreground: it pervades the entire novel and is of great thematic interest. The smallness of man and the inevitability of life's cycles are at the core of this work.

We may conclude that if this novel manages to construct a convincing semblance of concordance at all, it does not necessarily do so thanks to the evocation of the *Bildungsroman*-stereotype. We may speak of a process of *Bildung*, but this learning process has already been completed right at the start of the work. Consequently, the nature of this *Bildung* is perhaps so general, and leads to such melancholy resignation in all the characters, that the work reads, more than as a critique of social circumstances, as an account of life itself. Even if scholars still read the work as such, it has become clear that the actual critical potential of the process of *Bildung* is undone to a great extent. The lesson here is stated by, rather than experienced through the eyes of one or more *Bildungshelden*; feelings of compassion are only awakened through the nostalgia that comes with retrospection. While it is still possible to read *Los viejos amigos* as a work that denounces Spanish forgetfulness, since francoist resistance emerges as a theme and the novel betrays a definite sense of *desencanto*, the overall concern of this work is the very process of getting older that its 'viejos amigos' experience, each in their individual way. So, two-conflicting-readings suggest themselves in the place of one.

Álvaro Pombo, *Aparición del eterno femenino contada por S.M. el Rey*

That *Aparición del eterno femenino contada por S.M. el Rey* (1993) calls up the *Bildungsroman* stereotype does not immediately become clear. The novel is set some time during the final years of the Second World War, in the small world of a child, that of protagonist-narrator Ceporro or Jorge, which Fernando Valls aptly describes as "un mundo cerrado, fosilizado" (206). Ceporro and his cousin, el Chino, live in the house of their grandmother, where they play on the terrace, receive boxing classes from don Rodolfo, and watch the comings and goings of maid Belinda and of doña Blanca, the grandmother's best and only friend. Ceporro states: "En esta casa se ha vivido siempre" (Pombo 10). The only change is brought by the seasons, and it is a very predictable change: Ceporro keeps an eye out for the swallows that build their nest above the terrace, returning every year with the summer heat. It seems that in this small universe, everything has its fixed time and place.

This peace is disturbed by the arrival of Elke, a German war orphan adopted by the grandmother's sister, Aunt Lola, who lives downstairs. At first, it seems that this interruption only briefly stirs things up, and that life resumes its quiet pace once Elke has become part of Ceporro's daily routine: "A su hora venía don Rodolfo. Belinda iba y venía por la casa. Elke subía por las tardes. A las cuatro llegaba doña Blanca, para quedarse ya la tarde entera" (217). That the disruption is more profound than that, however, becomes first apparent when el Chino confesses that he is in love with Elke. Gradually, the small world of Ceporro changes completely: Belinda and Rodolfo get married, el Chino is taken to Stockholm by his diplomat parents, and a private teacher is hired over summer to help Ceporro pass the tests he failed at the end of the previous school year. Finally, Ceporro becomes aware that he, too, is in love with Elke.

Whereas the beginning of the novel seems to offer a static situation, a sort of idyllic, cyclical time, the *Bildung* becomes more and more obvious after Elke's arrival. Narrator Ceporro has a tendency to reflect extensively and explicitly on his own development and that of his friends – and while he finds the process a difficult one, he ends up evaluating his own growth as positive. Halfway through the novel, the narrator says: "Y me daba cuenta de que nada había cambiado, ni en la casa, ni tampoco en la terraza: sólo nosotros tres" (126). The three friends, who earlier on liked to play noisy war games and destroyed part of the roof as they climbed Mount Everest, have now become quieter and like to spend the day reading. Further on, as el Chino leaves for Stockholm, Ceporro sighs: "Todo había cambiado para siempre y no se podía descambiar" (141). As he spends his time studying with Elke, he ponders on falling in love in the childlike language that determines the tone of *Aparición del eterno femenino*:

> [L]o que tenía que saber era qué era lo que hacía Elke, sin querer, que yo sintiera. Eso es lo que quería yo saber. ¡Y lo sabía, eso es lo bueno! Pero no sabía cómo decirlo de una vez, porque tenía que ver con demasiadas cosas a la vez. Tenía que ver, por ejemplo, con que Elke estaba ahora que el Chino estaba fuera. [...] Y también tenía que ver con don Rodolfo y con Belinda, que al casarse se habían vuelto muy distintos a como cada cual era antes de casarse. Y si todo esto lo sumaba, no acababa de salirme ningún número homogéneo con los sumandos de la suma. Salía un sentimiento que venía a ser como tener en casa un pájaro, un vencejo vivo. No se sabe qué hay que

hacer, ni si comerá pan o sólo alpiste o le gustará beber leche como a un gato o sólo agua o sólo pan en migas no muy grandes o qué, y qué pasará si le coges por las alas o si le acercas mucho al pico un dedo, o qué significa el que píe o el que no píe, o qué verán los dos ojillos, por lo regular de color negro, que unas veces parecen asustados y otras lo contrario de asustados. Pues eso, más o menos, venía a ser lo que yo sentía por Elke. Total: nada. Pero no nada por nada sino, al revés, por todo, porque al echar cuentas lo que salían eran demasiadas cosas a la vez. (155)

Aparición del eterno femenino is thus a coming-of-age novel which describes what Valls calls a "rito de paso" (204), a "proceso de maduración individual" (205) which "forma parte de una amplia tradición literaria en la que se cuenta el paso de la infancia a la adolescencia, los primeros amores" (204). Significantly, the title refers to the *Ewigweibliche* in *Faust* by the *Bildungsroman*'s founding father, Goethe.

Interestingly, the *Bildung* described is actually the process of trading in one chronotope for another. The fictional world is determined by the cyclical nature of time – in an even more idyllic and pure incarnation, it would seem, than in *El dueño del secreto* or *Los viejos amigos*, since historical time is almost absent in the novel. Masoliver Ródenas calls the work's static world "el reino de la infancia" (253): it is the world of a child, a sort of eternal present. Though Ceporro calls himself its king on account of his good memory: "Por eso soy el rey, porque soy el que mejor memoria tiene", he immediately adds: "Me acuerdo de todo, si me da la gana. Si no, no" (39). And where Elke is concerned, whose arrival had been known far in advance to himself and el Chino, he finds it natural that her coming ended up taking them completely by surprise: "Cuando quisimos recordar era verano y en verano todo se olvida. Así que también Elke se nos olvidó a mí y al Chino junto con todo lo demás" (29). In fact, one of his worst memories is of the time el Chino went away for a couple of days with his parents, and he assumed his friend would be gone forever; and when el Chino leaves again, for Stockholm, Ceporro worries because he hardly thinks of his friend while he is absent. Ceporro's innocence and childhood are marked by a cyclical chronotope, and, as a consequence, it appears that he will have to exchange this eternal present for a new chronotope in order to become part of the adult world.

This adult world is not actually entered by the young protagonist, but it is foreshadowed by the behaviour of the adults that surround Ceporro. In spite of the novel's emphasis on growing up, on *Bildung*, this world does not appear as something worth aspiring to: the grown-ups are rather shallow and ridiculous characters. As Masoliver Ródenas puts it: "el infantilismo de los adultos, con todo lo que tiene de paródico encuentra su contrapartida en la fértil pureza de los niños" (319). In fact, both Valls and Masoliver Ródenas note that the portrayal of the adults happens at a "nivel paródico" (Masoliver Ródenas 261) – not a parody of the *Bildungsroman* itself, but "la parodia de un vivir inmovilizado en el pasado, representado aquí por una familia bien, tradicional" (Valls 205). They find that the parodised text is the language of the adults: Valls discovers "un tufillo joseantoniano" (205), he detects "una determinada concepción de la mujer como especial depositaria y portadora de valores eternos", and a "melodrama con tintes nacionalcatólicos" (206), and Masoliver Ródenas finds that the novel "recrea un lenguaje muy específico: el de la telenovela y el de la España falangista de posguerra" (259). While these discourses are incorporated into the novel without narrator Ceporro's ever exposing or criticising the adults' behaviour, it could be said that the discourse of the adults stands out by its contrast to Ceporro's original voice. Ceporro does not understand the norms and values the adults live by, and his interpretations of events are often incorrect, which makes them both endearing and funny and questions the values that Ceporro has misunderstood – but that the real reader, an adult, *can* recognise. The value hierarchy, in other words, is determined by the narratee's democratic norms and values, and this narratee recognises that Ceporro's own ways of talking and thinking are to be preferred to the normative discourse of the humourless, francoist adults. A parodic reading is thus certainly a possibility.

Both the falangist and the telenovela discourses are most visibly present in the episode of don Rodolfo's engagement to Belinda. Rodolfo is a bachelor who likes his liquor and takes advantage of Belinda's adoration by borrowing money from her, without seriously planning to marry her. When the grandmother finds out they have been kissing, however, she practically forces them to get engaged, which she considers the only 'decent' thing to do: "¡Un caballero a una chica decente lo que no hace es darla un beso en vano!" (115). Ceporro does not understand why: "Pero, Belinda, ¿qué tiene que ver veros con casaros? ¿Estáis ahora casados? ¡Si ahora que aún no estáis casados ya te tiras media tarde nada más que viéndole y llorando, como os caséis lo que te vas, Belinda, tú es a desecar...!" (103). The drama lasts considerably longer because Rodolfo has no money or home to offer his Belinda, so that things are only settled when the grandmother allows them to live in her house. Valls qualifies this entire sequence as hilarious:

> La decidida y tajante intervención de la abuela para que el matrimonio entre Belinda y don Rodolfo se lleve a cabo, tras consumar la pareja el atrevido acto de besarse, produce hoy más hilaridad que indignación por lo moralista y metijona que se muestra la señora de la casa. (206)

Masoliver Ródenas goes further and reads this parody, not merely as a parody of a *telenovela* or of middle-class falangist language, but as a satire of post-war Spanish society as a whole. He finds that "la casa [...] que vive casi totalmente al margen [...] de la otra realidad franquista" is really "una representación o actuación en clave paródica de una farsa y una tragedia que el libro no menciona como tales porque el lector ya las conoce" (316). He goes on to insist:

> En *Aparición del eterno femenino* lo más singular es que, por una vez, el mundo exterior tiene una presencia decisiva y moldea a los personajes de la casa de tal manera que casi carecen de vida interior: desprovistos de sentimientos genuinos, todo lo que hacen, dicen y sienten se convierte en paródico. [...] Lo que ocurre aquí es que no hay un mundo exterior porque el mundo exterior está encerrado en la casa: la casa representa este mundo anclado en una utopía que es la utopía que vivió gran parte de la clase media y la clase alta española identificada con los valores ('valores', si se prefiere) del franquismo. (313-315)

In the eyes of Masoliver Ródenas, the portrayal of the adults in this work becomes a critique of a certain class, a certain background; and this parody is achieved *implicitly* by contrasting the adults' behaviour, the interpretations and confusion of Ceporro and the knowledge of the narratee.

While it is thus possible to read the adults' discourse as parodic, the adult world becomes an even darker prospective through other intrusions of historical time. The outside world is hardly referred to, but in this case, ellipsis draws attention to what is omitted, and makes the occasional hints stand out the more clearly. Explicitly, francoist society is only described in a superficial manner: the grown-ups have a tendency to start singing national hymns such as 'Cara al sol', and to celebrate Franco and Spain on festive occasions; and the Second World War is made a part of the children's war games – Ceporro and El Chino pretend to be fighting against Montgomery and helping Rommel, and on Elke's arrival, Ceporro imagines she is a Bolshevik spy and tries to get her to confess. But while the outside world does not otherwise intrude, its real impact on the lives of the children is suggested in a way so circumspect that it raises all kinds of questions. Elke is very skinny when she arrives at the house, "el puro hueso transparente por debajo del pellejo" (48). According to Ceporro, she suffers from amnesia due to the trauma of a bombardment: "la amnesia suya era un caso grave" (67). Ceporro himself does not talk about anything that happened prior to his life at his grandmother's, nor does he explain where his parents are or what happened to them. But there are moments where the novel suggests that Ceporro has consciously lived the Civil War, that he has seen people fleeing their homes and seeking shelter from bombings. He describes certain scenes with remarkably vivid detail: "Eso es lo que

hacen en las guerras lo que se llama la población civil: empeñarse en salir de los refugios y arrastrarse, con lo puesto, serpenteando lentamente, empujando bicis, coches y carritos, cargados por lo regular de cosas raras, a lo mejor un comedor entero" (87). When the children destroy the roof by pretending to climb Mount Everest, Ceporro describes the result as follows:

> Lo que más hay después de un bombardeo, después de que cae la última bomba, son incendios y mucho polvo a desplomarse los tabiques. Y al principio tampoco es que oigas nada, ni siquiera las sirenas de las ambulancias, nada. Sólo notas que te asfixias y algún que otro aullido de las víctimas. Igual nosotros tres. (87)

Ceporro's account implies that he knows from experience what war is like, but this is never openly stated anywhere.

The background of the Spanish Civil War, francoism and the Second World War is neglected almost entirely, but it is, hauntingly, present. The shadow of the outside world is felt not only in the children's world, but also in that of the adults. The grandmother and doña Blanca mention the Civil War when they criticise Lola for adopting a German orphan, "[p]orque a mí no me digas que en España después de una guerra de tres años no han quedado huérfanas ningunas" (28), and a couple of drinks at the wedding of Belinda and Rodolfo induce Blanca and Rodolfo to recollect the hardships and hunger they suffered then. But all in all, the War and the dictatorship are not often addressed. Again, however, it is subtly suggested that the War did have some consequences for the family. Ceporro mentions, for instance, that the house of the grandmother has been expanded to make room for the grandmother's sons, "porque mis tíos, los hermanos de mi madre, de jóvenes ocupaban mucho sitio" (10). The novel shows no trace of such a large family, though: Ceporro's uncles are not talked about in the novel, just as his parents are never referred to.

Within the space of the novel, history remains only a background threat, and the *Bildung* of Ceporro takes place against a static backdrop where time remains cyclical and changes occur almost imperceptibly. Ceporro's *Bildung* is often also characterised by his discovery of certain, apparently eternal truths. So, Elke's fundamentally different nature dawns on him only gradually. He sees her, in the words of don Rodolfo, as 'the eternal feminine'. Elke does seem to have something eternal and distinct about her. Her age, for example, is very unclear. "Para empezar se había quemado, con todos los muebles y la ropa y su casa, la partida también de nacimiento", Ceporro explains; and "Elke parecía algunos días muchísimo más vieja que nosotros y otros días al contrario muchísimo más joven" (67). Ceporro often describes her as a swallow, a bird, "medio pájaro" (98); and when he sees her dressed up for the first

time, he finds that "ahora lo que no cabía es ya duda es que había que añadir una Elke nunca vista a la Elke más vista que el tebeo" (171). Elke stands out the more because of her faulty Spanish, faithfully rendered by the narrator's transcription: "¡Qué karraja mirras!" (79), she shouts for instance. Altogether, Ceporro is experiencing "el descubrimiento del otro" (209), as Fernando Valls puts it. But while change thus does occur, it takes on a cyclical form, and the "espacio 'duradero' de la infancia" (Masoliver Ródenas 319) is maintained until the final sentence of the novel: "como si acabar fuese imposible y el final no fuese el fin de nada para ninguno de nosotros ocho…" (Pombo 191).

Aparición del eterno femenino can thus be said to have a complex structure due to the particular setup of the *Bildungsroman*-stereotype. The stereotype first follows the lines of the standard *Bildungsroman* plot as it describes young Ceporro's entrance into adolescence. However, it departs from the traditional stance by leaving off early: the *Bildung* is not completed, at the end of the novel, and Ceporro, the king, is still in possession of his childhood realm, so that his retrospective narration can retain its funny, and often touching, childish tone. The haunting of history and the parody of the Spanish middle class suggest that this is for the better, and they give the novel a double layer that supersedes the otherwise straightforward nature of a *Bildungsroman* plot. Even though the individual process of growth may seem like a positive development, the thought that Ceporro will trade in his childish language, full of mistakes, but also full of original comparisons and connections, for the grammatically correct, but rather bland and prescriptive language of the adults, is not a very happy one. What Ceporro has yet to learn are the rules and truths of an adult world that is implicitly violent and limiting. When Ceporro asks don Rodolfo for advice about the situation of el Chino and his crush on Elke, Rodolfo responds by reading more into the situation than necessary: "Elke es prima vuestra y se acabó, y además menor de edad, Ceporro, así que, para empezar, si está enamorado que se aguante" (69). It is clear that Ceporro's innocence and youth prevent him from understanding Rodolfo's reduction of this complicated strug-gle with friendship and love to sexual attraction.

Of course, the *Bildung* of Ceporro is still valued by the young narra-tor himself, who looks back on the years he describes from a time by all appearances immediately posterior to it, still firmly in possession of his childhood. He realises that he has changed and improved, that he has become quieter now and cleverer, and that he understands and sees more than he used to. But at the same time, the *Bildung* is denounced, and the road to adulthood portrayed as a departure from the 'eternal' paradise that is childhood. So the indirectly incorporated value system of the adult narratee in historical time comes to the foreground, precisely because of history's uncomfortable and disturbing ghost – though it does not repress Ceporro's reading altogether. The transition from eternity to historical time is a threat that overshadows the endearingly funny narration of Ceporro. Parody and haunting thus open up the novel to a complex double reading – which means, as a consequence, that the genre stereotype is once again no guarantee for an uncomplicated reading experience.

Félix de Azúa, *Momentos decisivos*

Momentos decisivos by Félix de Azúa (2000) begins with a quotation of Kierkegaard that reads: "No creceré por lo que me suceda, sólo me harán crecer mis propios actos" (9). The repetition of the word *crecer*, to grow, says it all: this must be yet another novel in which adulthood is reached, childhood left behind, and possibly a *Bildung* achieved. The first chapter of the novel also suggests as much. An anonymous narrator receives a letter from a childhood friend, Alberto, who asks him a special favour: since he has some success as an editor and occasionally writes articles for a newspaper, would the narrator consider writing the story of Alberto's life? Though in his letter, cited by the narrator, Alberto specifically requests the work to allow him "ver aquella vida mía en la lejanía" (17), it is immediately plain to the narrator that Alberto wants the work to centre around a formative time in his life: a decisive moment, as Alberto calls it, a moment which "tuerce el futuro con irreparable fatalidad y nos introduce por un camino para el cual no estábamos pertrechados" (11). Such a moment, which, Alberto stresses, may be trivial enough in itself, defines the rest of one's life. For him, Alberto, the decisive moment was in fact an "año decisivo" (16), beginning with the moment his friend and fellow aspiring artist Federico decided to leave for the United States, and ending with his own departure to America, months later. This period constitutes the time frame of *Momentos decisivos*.

The emphasis on early adulthood as the decisive time in Alberto's life strongly suggests that this is a *Bildungsroman*. It is unusual for the first-person narrator not to be the one undergoing the *Bildung*: a first clue that this novel may not adhere to the stereotypical plot throughout. Since the narrator immediately focuses on Alberto, though, and focalises his account mainly through him, it is clear who is the young protagonist who is doing the learning and growing here. The narrator seems bent on conveying that Alberto is on a quest, on what appears to be an identity search. He calls Alberto a person suffering from "desasosiego" (24), somebody who "todavía no tenía decidida la clase de paraíso o infierno que le correspondía. Y ¿era verdaderamente un *lugar*, lo que andaba buscando?" (179). Alberto describes himself as a "chercheur" (260).

The narrator thus accompanies Alberto on his search and portrays him in his surroundings. Alberto's family, the Ferrers, are a family of *vencidos*. The grandfather was an important figure during the Second Republic, who was executed at the end of the Civil War, and the family have slid into despair and poverty. The father is a man "con aire ido" (51), the mother is characterised by "la intranscendente, la trivial queja, más maniática que fundada" (203). The elder brother, Jordi, "lleva consigo esta tristeza negra que no puede explicarse" (354) and has inherited the feelings of defeat and depression that haunt his parents. It is no wonder, then, that Alberto wishes to escape the oppressive atmosphere of his home and seeks the company of Juan Labernia and Lena Marín, whose families and circumstances could hardly differ more from his own. Lena's family is *nouveau riche*, right-wing and opportunist. Significantly, a colleague of her father's tells Lena: "Tu padre me ha hecho muchas putadas, pero yo respeto a los hombres que muerden hasta que se les caen los dientes" (105); and it is remarked that the father "tras la entrada de las tropas franquistas en Barcelona, firmaba sentencias de muerte" (193). Lena's father is a businessman whose lack of a conscience has made him rich, who betrays his wife not very cleverly with the servants, who spoils his precious daughter and who has no scruples when it comes to earning money. Lena herself is presented as a cold and uptight, spoilt and authoritarian snob, who knows very well how to play off her parents against each other – which she shows when she convinces them to let her go on a weekend excursion with Juan and Alberto, a highly inappropriate undertaking for a member of an Opus Dei family. Juan's family, on the other hand, is a family in decline: they still conserve their important place in Catalan society, but this position is becoming weaker.

Alberto seeks the company of Lena and Juan even if it makes him unpopular with his former friends, who accuse him of "haberse vendido a las piscinas" (23). Alberto feels inferior to both the wealthy Lena and to Juan, who is looked upon by all as Lena's future husband (316). As it turns out, though, Juan and his family also suffer humiliation: in return for their aid to and mediations for *vencidos* after the Civil War, they have been obliged to hand over their country estate to Lena's family, the Maríns. We also read that the Labernia family have protected their old friends, the Ferrers, from imprisonment or even death – so that the fates of Juan, Lena and Alberto are strangely connected. Alberto only finds out part of this in the course of the novel, though, and chiefly seems to hang out with Juan and Lena because they are so different: "sólo buscaba la compañía de la gente distinguida", he explains in his letter to the narrator, "mi familia [...] estaba compuesta íntegramente por gente de lo más corriente" (13).

Meanwhile, Alberto learns about friendship and love, and in the process gets to know himself. He has what appears to be his first sexual encounter with Gloria, the pretty friend of his sister Eulalia, and in his turn takes Lena's virginity – a rather uncomfortable and painful experience which retrospectively makes Gloria appear in a very positive light as Alberto realises she "había abierto una puerta infrecuente a la que con mucha prudencia comenzó a llamar admiración y con voz casi inaudible para su conciencia, respeto. '¿Dignidad?' pensó aterrado" (316). He thus neatly consumes the two love affairs, one good, the other bad, that Buckley prescribed in his prototypical *Bildungsroman* plot. He also tries to seduce Juan's mother, but discovers as he kisses her that "ahora había dejado de interesarle. 'Es como matarla', pensó, pero ya la había matado. Aquella mujer iba a la deriva y él buscaba firmeza" (189). The typical link between sexuality and vocation is also established, and it is no coincidence that Alberto mostly acquires his knowledge about love, sex and women in the studio of a painter, Toti, who allows him the keys – both his private encounter with Juan's mother and his two dates with Gloria take place there.

All through *Momentos decisivos*, the young artist is trying to find his own artistic path: he attempts to paint in American Pop Art style, but destroys his work, unsatisfied. What he is really looking for is something like a piece of paper on a wall, without a picture on it: "lo difícil es que no se vea nada más que lo que hay, un papel y un muro, en la obra de arte del futuro no se verá nada en absoluto" (43). Luckily, Juan gets hold of some French and American magazines for his friend, who then understands that his idea of the piece of paper on the wall fits in with an international artistic current: "Vio […] una forma de dibujo en el borde de la inexistencia, pero sin ironía, sin crítica. Intuyó una semejanza entre aquella pieza mínima y la insignificancia que tanto le había emocionado cuando la esquina de papel se agitaba clavada contra el muro" (128). He decides to quit painting altogether, looking not for art but for actions against art; a chance meeting with Marcel Duchamp, the master of the ready-made who appears on a terrace in Calella, confirms his newly found personal aesthetic.

Altogether, this novel describes a process of growth: the development of an artistic vocation joined to a sentimental education. But Alberto points out in the letter which the novel's narrator quotes at the beginning that his has not been a very happy lesson. Alberto recognises that his 'decisive moment' (the precise occurrence of which remains vague) has been a moment of loss: "El caso es que guardo muy buena memoria de aquellos sucesos, de aquel momento que significó una pérdida tan indolora como irreparable y definitiva" (12). He himself provides the following explanation:

Fernando, por ejemplo, siempre ha defendido que todos los tiempos son iguales y que es una trivialidad no por repetida menos irrelevante considerar el nuestro como el peor de los tiempos. [...] Es cierto, no hay salvación ni para adelante ni para atrás, pero se tarda mucho en saberlo y cuando lo sabes ya no te sirve para nada. A pesar de todo, estoy persuadido de que el tiempo de mi juventud fue más oscuro y también más rico que otros tiempos, como cuando decimos de un alimento que es rico en vitaminas, o de un suelo que es rico en fertilizantes. El tiempo de mi juventud era más rico y más oscuro. El tiempo no siempre es el mismo. En aquellos años yo tenía una necesidad imperiosa de claridad y eso me llevó inexorablemente al momento decisivo. [...] Yo sí sé cuál fue mi momento, aquel que cambió mi columna vertebral de hueso y cartílago por otra de temor y remordimiento. (12-13)

What Alberto seems to be describing here is an example of Bakhtin's fifth and last kind of *Bildungsroman*, where man's emergence reflects historical emergence, and where the protagonist finds himself on the border between two epochs.

But Alberto's view on his *Bildung* is undermined by the narrator's version of things. Alberto may call the narrative's temporal and spatial settings rich and dark, but they are also remarkably stable and unchanging. No new time emerges during Alberto's student years, which are portrayed as years of standstill and passivity, as the narrator does not fail to make clear:

El remitente de la carta hacía referencia a unos años, hacia mediados de los sesenta, que habían ya perdido la tensión heroica de la posguerra. Sus figuras altivas, ensangrentadas y harapientas, vagaban por el Averno, pero aún no había amanecido el aura de las rebeliones que comenzaron a sacudir el mundo a partir de 1965 y que pusieron en circulación otras imágenes más delicadas, ornamentales, imágenes menguantes pero de una potencia insospechada. Aquéllos fueron años estancados, sin oxígeno, como pozas de aceite industrial en cuya superficie flotan grandes manchas irisadas que sugieren el relumbre de la muerte. Basta un mínimo suceso, el imperceptible roce de un insecto, para que espejeen todos los colores del arco con destellos de joyel. Sin embargo, nada puede vivir en ese lugar muerto. Así fueron aquellos años en los que la dictadura triunfaba sin resistencia, nadie alzaba la voz, la gente hábil medraba, e incluso los pobres, colmo del sarcasmo, se enriquecían. (18)

The narrator thus undermines Alberto's own evaluation and goes on to critically depict society's immobility. The novel limits itself strictly to Barcelona, with an excursion to Calella – and it stresses this Catalan background in numerous sections, particularly at the openings of the individual chapters, where the city or aspects of the landscape are described. *Momentos decisivos* focuses not on movement and historical decisions, but on a period of stagnation, both in the life of the indecisive Alberto and in the life of the country. "*Momentos decisivos* se sitúa en una época clave, 1963 ó 1964", Masoliver Ródenas says, "años neutros de la consolidación del franquismo, posteriores a la represión y anteriores a las grandes (¿e inocuas?) transformaciones" (158). The critical stance of this work, clearly expressed above by the narrator, is obvious. Alberto's education is a failure, and francoist Spain of the 1960s is to blame. The sheer weight of those years presses down upon society, and only if Alberto had left for America, he might have escaped the burden of living francoism in its most immobile form.

This criticism of francoism causes the novel to depart from the *Bildungsroman* genre's conventional structure – particularly when the narrator starts focusing increasingly on characters other than Alberto. The account of Alberto's individual growth, of his search, is constantly interrupted by the narrator's interest in others. The first character to gain importance is Alberto's brother, Jordi: there is a chapter where Jordi himself is the narrator, and there are numerous passages and even entire chapters that deal with Jordi's life, work, friends, and activities. As a part of anti-francoist resistance, Jordi and his friends cooperate with a dissident group of Catalan businessmen, and they plan to disturb an official meeting by reading an undermining speech. In order to acquire the necessary funds, Jordi is to sell a painting contributed by Picasso. He hands the work to Alberto, whose attempt to sell it to Sandra Labernia serves him as an excuse to meet her in private, away from her home and her family. The deal falls through, though, and Jordi, who is unsatisfied with the limited scope of action, decides to take matters into his own hands and shoot the local sergeant-general of the francoist army. He leaves home and starts living on the streets, spying on daily life in the barracks and hatching a plan. Just in time, he realises that he will be incapable of murdering another human being, and prefers to join the workers' front instead. This, then, is also the *Bildung* of Jordi; and the extensive references to his doings certainly take the attention away somewhat from Alberto's coming-of-age.

Whereas the attention for Jordi still turns this work into a double *Bildungsroman*, the narrator's descriptions of all manner of minor characters are more disturbing to the generic stance of the novel. The domestic struggles of Lena's family are awarded two separate chapters, and Alberto's father gets to narrate his life story towards the end of the novel. An entire chapter is focalised through Juan's mother Sandra, who is portrayed until then as a rather clichéd fallen *femme fatale*, an alcoholic who regrets her fading beauty and parades around rooms voluptuously with finely clicking heels, the ice cubes clinging against her glass, while she does not hesitate to display her "pecho abundante" (27) by feigning heat and opening a button of her blouse (28). In this chapter, we see how she regrets the ageing of her body and hides the process behind a layer of make-up and fine clothes, turning herself into "la mujer eternal resplandeciente y fuerte, la santa, la mártir, la virgen, la reina y la odalisca" (139).

The novel thus pays elaborate attention to characters other than Alberto, and the individual focus of the *Bildungsroman* stereotype makes way for the portrait the narrator paints of society. "[L]os personajes, incluso los más secundarios, no sólo pueden ser considerados como centrales, sino que, además, un momento decisivo de su vida los convierte en seres excepcionales" (158), Masoliver Ródenas argues. The work becomes the "expresión de los conflictos y los fracasos de una generación en un país, Cataluña, igualmente derrotado" (159). In order to become a critique of society, *Momentos decisivos* moves away from the *Bildungsroman*'s individualistic perspective. It has the freedom to do so, since it is not narrated by Alberto himself.

As a result, Azúa's novel turns out rather eclectic. It portrays Juan and his father as latent homosexuals, talks of the suicide of Jordi's friend, the poet Gabriel, and goes into the personality and the desires of Gloria. Also, it devotes a considerable amount of space to a parody of the Catalan bourgeoisie. The man who hands Jordi the painting of Picasso, "el hombre más importante de Cataluña" (88), is described as old-fashioned and peculiar. He lives in a house where "todo era minúsculo y brillante, como de miniatura flamenca" and where "el brillo sustituía a la luz y no sólo las cosas sino también las personas eran de visión indirecta" (88). The narrator describes this privileged and educated man's manner of speaking as "un catalán arcaico, melodioso y seductor, más literario que oral" (89), and tries to reproduce it as faithfully as possible – albeit in Spanish:

> Me alegro mucho verles en casa, a usted le tengo ya muy conocido, querido Jordi, pero el pequeño es toda una sorpresa, no se puede negar que son ustedes nietos del buen Francesc, pero yo diría (y excúsenme este ejercicio de psicólogo aficionado, más bien pueril) que el mayor ha heredado la pasión y el sentimiento que consumen y atormentan (como todos aquellos que vivieron las fechas heroicas y lamentables), mientras que el pequeño, ¿Alberto?, se ha quedado con el escepticismo, el fatalismo, la incredulidad de su abuelo tras la derrota, así es la teoría de las generaciones, una banalidad, sin duda. (89)

The length of the sentences, the dependent clauses and remarks between brackets, the slightly dramatic use of adverbs and nouns ("la pasión y el sentimiento", "las fechas heroicas y lamentables", "el escepticismo, el fatalismo, la incredulidad"): they all contrast with the much more colloquial and simple direct speech of the other characters in *Momentos decisivos*.

This parody is extended as the narrator critically describes how the Catalan entrepreneurs behave in their meetings with Jordi and his friends, refusing to go too far with their protests or to collaborate with either students or workers. Gabriel laughs at the odd and indirect phrasing of the pamphlet that is to be read at the meeting, particularly at the 'square sky' mentioned in the first sentence, which reads: "Fríamente y desde el fondo del fondo, bajo un cielo cuadriculado y raro, los que subscriben afirman que hay una juventud en ascenso y que no es una juventud vulgar" (115). And when, towards the end, the working class is portrayed as men who appreciate a Picasso much more than the bourgeoisie, and who show real camaraderie against a background that is positively idyllic (complete with dancing gypsy girls on a lonely beach), it becomes abundantly clear that the parody is a critical satire of the Catalan bourgeoisie, of men who, in contrast to grandfather Francesc, have done all in their power to remain comfortably settled at the cost of higher idealism.

In sections like these, the narrator takes over and diverts attention from Alberto's *Bildung*, undermining his evaluations and firmly imposing his own critical outlook. The narrator's identity is not completely disclosed, though it is revealed indirectly towards the end of *Momentos decisivos*. Upon receiving Alberto's letter, the narrator remarks that "años atrás, yo mismo lo había anunciado" (18). So, when we read that Alberto's despised acquaintance Lluch, a law student and soldier obsessed with films, exclaims: "un día me pedirás que cuente tu historia" (252), we realise that this, then, is the narrator, the main evaluator of *Momentos decisivos* and the one who imposes a view of francoism that is far more critical and outspoken than Alberto's.

The figure of Lluch immediately acquires an importance it did not have before. As it now turns out, Lluch plays an instrumental role in the novel. He gets hold of the weapon Jordi needs to shoot the sergeant-general, but he also tells Jordi about the officer's love life, so that Jordi starts seeing him as a human being and repents his murderous intentions. We also find out now that Lluch has a story of his own. As we accompany him on a trip to his native village (where the narrator mysteriously holds on to a third-person narration), we hear how his father was killed in front of him because he accidentally let slip in the local café that he and his fellow card players were into contrabanding. We are further told that Lluch received a scholarship during his first year at university, but that he lost it because he failed one exam. Ever since, he has been taking exams to hide this fact from his mother, passing them all with high grades which do not count because he is not officially enrolled. As this story unfolds, yet another character, Lluch, claims centre stage; and *his* apprenticeship reaches its culmination as he threatens fascist students with the very gun he procured for Jordi, openly showing his hatred for the regime for the first time, while he also wets himself out of fear when the first shots get fired.

Suddenly, the novel's setup, as well as its value hierarchy, changes: a character steps to the foreground who collaborates with the regime, working as a soldier, but who also feels a deep hatred towards francoism caused by a childhood trauma, which is why he helps Jordi with his plan to assassinate his superior officer. As it turns out, Lluch himself grows considerably during the length of the novel. He develops from a slightly ridiculous young man whose attempts at befriending Alberto fail constantly, and who is looked upon as a loser by all those who surround him, into somebody who openly shows where his real sympathies lie, standing up against francoist youths in the cafeteria of his faculty. Is this, perhaps, a novel that describes the apprenticeship of Lluch rather than that of Alberto, the apprenticeship of that hidden narrator who haunts the novel for a considerable while before showing himself? His judgments, norms and values structure the novel, and the development of this narrator, who ends up overcoming his fear and opportunism in order to show his true self, places Alberto's struggles with Spain's standstill culture and Jordi's *vencido* desperation in a new light. Apparently, it *is* possible to grow, to change, during the years described; but only Lluch manages to do so, liberating himself from his subordinate role and protesting openly, not silently.

The novel thus gains in complexity due to its choice of narrative instance. The *Bildung* of Alberto remains important in the final part of the novel, especially when it describes his visit to Calella with Juan and Lena. In a number of lengthy chapters, we read how he tries to seduce Lena, finds out about Juan's homosexuality, and meets with his hero, Duchamp. Juan crashes the car and has to be transported to a hospital. Also, Alberto finds out that the holiday home of the Maríns is actually the former estate of the Labernias. But another reading is now possible, one that focuses on narrator Lluch; and this reading is reinforced when in the final chapter, Lluch assumes the role of a film director who provides the work with Hollywood-style film credits on what the lives of his story's protagonists Alberto, Juan, and Lena have been like since. Of Alberto, he says that "a pesar de sus palabras, dudo mucho de que conozca cuál fue su momento verdadero" (360), and: "No le guardo rencor [...]. No me cuesta reconocerlo, le desprecio, pero era uno de los mejores" (361). As he concludes the narration, he talks of himself, not of Alberto, and repeats his critical view of Catalonia under Franco:

> En aquellos años indefinidos, opacos, hacía ya mucho que había concluido la tragedia con la derrota de todos los héroes, pero también el drama carecía de grandeza y los personajes vegetaban pasmados, inanes, esperando eternamente sobre un escenario escuálido la llegada de un visitante desconocido, entonces, en aquellos años, sólo quedaba la comedia. Hombres y mujeres quietos, detenidos. Fue una época extraña, un tiempo muerto. (358)

Meanwhile, though, he also sheds a new light on Alberto's *Bildung*: "casi todos decidieron, pero él no. Y cuando también, por fin, se decidió, era ya demasiado tarde, imagino. Le decidieron desde fuera y cuando emprendió la *recherche*, ya era tarde, su momento había pasado y él se apuntó a una imitación de momento" (359). Apparently, the year described here has not really been decisive for Alberto, and it is the simulacrum of a *Bildung* rather than an actual coming-of-age that is portrayed in the novel.

All in all, the fact that Lluch is the narrator, not Alberto, leads to great complexity here. While the *Bildungsroman* stereotype is called up once more, this novel itself is not a typical *Bildungsroman*, and a number of readings becomes possible. This could be the *Bildung* of Alberto, which has failed, according to the narrator, but it is also the *Bildung* of his brother Jordi and particularly that of narrator Lluch himself. The novel is directed by this narrator, and the characters are portrayed and evaluated by him. Accordingly, Alberto's role is judged severely, as is his tendency to let the standstill epoch paralyse him. In Lluch's normative system, the decision to fight the system openly, individually, *can* be taken, but it needs to be taken at the right moment, and Alberto never arrives at this moment while Jordi lets it escape. At least, though, they have had their moments – which is perhaps why Lluch calls Alberto 'one of the best'.

Here, then, the *Bildungsroman* actually gives way to a complicated network of relationships between characters, most notably between Lluch, Alberto and Jordi. The importance of Alberto that characterises the novel initially, and the surprising turn the work takes afterwards, when Lluch turns out to be the narrator, cast the year described into a complex light. It becomes rather unclear what power this period really had over Spaniards, whether all resistance was necessarily smothered or whether it was still possible and meaningful to rebel against francoism, if only to save oneself. Judging by Lluch's final account, this latter vision seems to acquire importance. Yet at the same time, Jordi's struggles point towards the opposite, and the centrality of Alberto's disappointment also allows a different reading. Needless to say, the work becomes discordant to quite a high degree, and the calling-up of the *Bildungsroman* genre without resorting to it entirely aids considerably in constructing this discordance.

Conclusion

The very connotation of predictability which the term 'stereotype' carries with it implies that genre, which I have called a 'macro-stereotype' earlier, can make a novel seem highly concordant. Yet this concordance is easily threatened. A *Bildungsroman* stereotype can be called up throughout the novel, while it can be parodied or exposed at the same time. In such a case, the apprenticeship stance does not necessarily lose its validity – it merely becomes one of multiple readings. In *El dueño del secreto* by Antonio Muñoz Molina, the narrator experiences disappointment as his revolutionary ideals prove to be in vain. He resigns himself to his fate, but not without longing for what could have been, and in this role he manages to awaken empathy in many of his readers and critics. At the same time, of course, it is suggested that his take on events is all wrong, and that he is still innocent, foolish and a tad self-important. The *Bildungsheld* is deconstructed and the process of coming-of-age ridiculed, but the work is still readable as a *Bildungsroman*, particularly because it contains moments where *Bildung* escapes parody. In due course, the work becomes discordant and allows different readings and interpretations.

In Rafael Chirbes's *Los viejos amigos*, the *Bildungsroman* stereotype is not parodied. At the same time, though, the novel departs from the genre's usual conventions in two important respects. First of all, it unorthodoxly portrays a number of parallel comings-of-age, which come down to one general, collective *Bildung*, that of the group of old friends (and, by extension, their generation). The lesson learnt is a bitter one: with democracy, the youthful ideals are lost and exchanged for the shallow enjoyment of capitalism and democracy, and it is clear that the novel is meant as a critique of Spanish society of, and after, the *Transición*. Secondly, the work is narrated in retrospect, another significant departure from the stance of the *Bildungsroman*. Because of this, it seems to speak much more of a process that repeats itself in all human lives than of the historical moment of the end of francoism: the loss of ideals and lustre as man gets older, sadder and wiser. A double reading is thus suggested, where social critique is undercut by resignation and temporal cyclicality. We are not witnessing the learning of a lesson, but we are told retrospectively what that lesson was, and the social critique that emanates from the novel is at the same time countered by a suggestion that the lapse in morals is unavoidable in the face of life's disappointments.

The *Bildungsroman*-structure of *Aparición del eterno femenino* by Álvaro Pombo is not interrupted as such, but the coming-of-age is not completed. The young protagonist happily remains on the threshold of the adult world with its historical time, still in possession of his childish, eternal realm. Historical time does become a haunting force in the work, though. History is conspicuously absent, but slight remarks and occasional references to the recent past and to the present outside the house of Ceporro's grandmother make this absence a haunting one. It is possible to read this work, also, as a parody of the grown-ups and their world, and this only serves to make growing up seem more grotesque and tragic. Here, growing up is as inevitable as it is sad: the child's eternal present is a paradise doomed to be lost. Though the main evaluator of the novel, narrator Ceporro, may be unaware of this even if he senses some of it, the dominant value system is the implied one of the narratee in historical time – and this narratee is sensitive of history's haunting force.

Momentos decisivos also contains a removal from the stereotypical conventions of the *Bildungsroman*: its narrator differs from its protagonist. As a result, the narration, while it contains many passages that focus on protagonist Alberto's personal growth, deviates frequently from this *Bildung* and ends up centring not only around Alberto's brother Jordi's experiences, but above all around those of narrator Lluch himself. The portrayal of the Spanish 1950s becomes confusing because of this: the year described is called one of standstill, and it is not surprising that Alberto is smothered by it and Jordi driven to despair. At the same time, Lluch's own development shows a different road, a path towards individual liberation, no matter how insignificant in the face of history. This novel can be read in many ways: as a *Bildungsroman* about either Lluch, Jordi, or Alberto, and as a work critical of francoist society and its impact on their generation. The use of the *Bildungsroman* stereotype does nothing to lessen this complexity.

All in all, then, the *Bildungsroman* as a genre stereotype provides the reader with a handy frame of reference, but it is certainly no guarantee for a concordant reading. In *El dueño del secreto*, it is openly parodied, and in the other three works, it is abandoned or its conventions are left behind in a significant way. In all these works, in fact, the *Bildungsroman* stance actually heightens the discordance in the novels. While it opens up certain expectations, these expectations are frustrated either because of parody or because the typical plot is not maintained. On another level, though, these expectations are also fulfilled to a certain extent: there is always a *Bildungsheld* involved, and a process of growth to be isolated, even if the only result is disillusionment.

The consequences of this use of the generic stance for the portrayal of memory discourses is equally confusing. In itself, the *Bildungsroman* is quite a normative scheme to impose upon a memory narrative. The growth and development it implies suggest a positivistic stance, which can either be linked to historical or cyclical time or related inversely to it, for instance when a character becomes disappointed, sadder and wiser. The character then moves forward, but the times in which he lives are portrayed negatively. But when parody is involved, the positive and the negative conflate: Muñoz Molina's narrator both longs for his past and criticises it, and he has both become wiser and remained idealistic. When the *Bildungsroman* is called up through its conventions, but the novel itself is not a standard *Bildungsroman*, the normativity and the chronotopic nature of the generic stance can stand in contrast to those of their surroundings. Thus, the *Bildungsroman*'s historical time collides with the narrators' cyclical time in *Los viejos amigos*, and the work can both be said to be critical of the *Transición* and the *desencanto* and consumerism of democratic Spain, and utterly resigned to the way history has repeated itself. Alvaro Pombo's narrator Ceporro grows up and becomes cleverer and wiser, only to have to leave his childhood realm behind and become a part of the unpleasant adult world with its historical time. Here, francoism is only a ghost, a shadow in the novel, and this conspicuous near-absence of memory makes francoism loom in the background all the more threateningly. In *Momentos decisivos*, the past is quite negatively portrayed, and the struggles of the many protagonists show that its standstill nature makes it difficult, but not impossible, to actively escape its laming nature. In the value hierarchies of these novels, the normativity of the *Bildungsroman* and its chronotope is complicated and sometimes even undone.

CHAPTER 4

Nostalgia's Emotional Weight

On Nostalgia

Many Spanish memory novels, which revolve around processes of reminiscence and looking back, are set up according to a wholly or partially maintained *Bildungsroman* stance. In itself, this genre stereotype can give way to quite a degree of discordance, as the previous chapter made clear. But there is yet another aspect that a large number of these novels share: they manage to evoke sadness and longing as they deal with memory. The novels, in other words, frequently call up the emotion of nostalgia. As we have seen, emotions are highly suspect when it comes to maintaining concordance of plots, but they are also indispensable in plot construction. This raises the question, in the context of Spanish memory novels, what type of emotion nostalgia really is. Can it be contained and rational, leading only to 'fear' and 'pity', to empathy? Or is the empathic longing it evokes not that easily containable?

Where nostalgia is concerned, one thing is clear: it has been struggling with a bad image. David Lowenthal states that there exists a strong "antipathy to nostalgia" (20); John Su mentions that "a diagnosis of nostalgia typically earns a writer or scholar condemnation" (2); and Michael Pickering and Emily Keightley point out that "nostalgia has been viewed as the conceptual opposite of progress" (919). Nostalgia is often seen as "a form of amnesia" (Su 2) that is reactionary, xenophobic, and thus revisionist. Susan Stewart defines it as "a sadness without an object, a sadness which creates a longing that of necessity is inauthentic" (23). Chris Ferns, too, calls nostalgia "a compensatory fantasy of returning to the past, in the face of one's inability to deal with the present" (43) as he contrasts it to utopia, which, reactionary as it may be, at least offers radically new alternatives and has a clearly defined object: "a more perfect society [...] created by the unaided use of human reason" (32). In short, nostalgia has been portrayed as an "'inauthentic' form of memory" (Cook 4).

At the same time, scholars agree that nostalgia is omnipresent in contemporary (postmodern) culture, especially since the 1990s. Lowenthal suggests that it is precisely this omnipresence, combined with its increasingly commercial nature and its tendency to be reactionary, which "engender[s] special ire" (21). Whether this is the case or not, it is obvious that, as Linda Hutcheon puts it, "a lot of contemporary culture [is] indeed nostalgic" ("Irony, Nostalgia and the Postmodern" 190). Gilles Lipovetsky notes, in discussing our current, 'hypermodern' culture: "[W]e now have the emotional-memorial value associated with feelings of nostalgia. This is a phenomenon that is indissociably post-modern and hypermodern" (60). Nostalgia's importance in contemporary culture becomes apparent in works like *On Longing* by Susan Stewart, which deals with such cultural phenomena as souvenirs or collections, and in more recent studies like those of John Su and Pam Cook, which analyse nostalgic novels, and films, respectively.

Such analyses of cultural objects have resulted in a new definition of nostalgia. Nostalgia's bad image, it becomes clear, is caused by a particular perception of what nostalgia is, exactly. According to Pickering and Keightley, nostalgia "became associated with a defeatist attitude to present and future" (920): it was assumed to uncritically prefer an idealised past to the present. Also, nostalgia in its typically postmodern incarnation had the bad luck of emerging together with irony. Hutcheon, referring to Stewart, points out that of these two modes, nostalgia lacks "the knowingness of irony" ("Irony, Nostalgia and the Postmodern" 197). This difference caused a sort of hierarchy, where "[i]rony is superior to nostalgia by its quality of knowing detachment, while nostalgia – if unleavened by irony – remains simply naïve and unaware" (96). Recently, however, things have started to change. As Linda Hutcheon puts it, "[i]n the 1980s, it was irony that captured our attention most; in the 1990s, it appears to be nostalgia to be holding sway" (192).

Scholars thus agree nowadays that nostalgia can no longer be seen as the uncritical acceptance of a perfected image of the past. They argue for a better appreciation of the phenomenon by arguing that nostalgia is not the subjective opposite of an objective history: history is certainly no more objective than nostalgia. Pam Cook describes the relation of nostalgia and history as "a continuum, with history at one end, nostalgia at the other and memory as a bridge or transition between them" (3). In this continuum, Cook admits, history *suppresses* the fictional elements of reconstruction of the past whereas nostalgia foregrounds them. Nevertheless, both are a form of memory in the sense that they reconstruct the past from a present viewpoint. Linda Hutcheon concludes: "The aesthetics of nostalgia might, therefore, be less a matter of simple memory than of complex projection" ("Irony, Nostalgia and the Postmodern" 195).

Another aspect of nostalgia to have gained recognition is that it connects the past to the present in a meaningful way. Nostalgia represents a dissatisfaction with the present that causes the nostalgic to project his frustrations onto a supposedly better past, and the past is reconstructed in such a way that it reflects what is felt to be missing or wrong in the present. John Su points out: "Nostalgics pine for very specific and concrete objects" (5), and so, Stewart's "sadness without an object" becomes firmly rooted in history. The idea that nostalgia says something about the present certainly counteracts the supposed 'revisionism' traditionally connected with the phenomenon. As Su puts it: "To the extent that it enables individuals or literary characters to articulate in clearer and more precise terms unacknowledged disappointments and frustration with present circumstances, nostalgia does provide useful knowledge about the world" (9).

John Su takes this line of thought furthest. His study is perhaps the best example of renewed appreciation for nostalgia: it reads as an ardent defence of nostalgia, particularly in literature. Unlike Hutcheon, Su does not turn his attention to nostalgia merely because it is apparently omnipresent in contemporary culture and cannot be overlooked for that reason only. In Su's view, nostalgia is a way not only to *remember* the past – or perhaps *reshape* is a better word – but to deal with it. Su thus adds a distinctly ethical dimension to nostalgia:

> [L]iterature can contribute to ethics by virtue of acquainting readers with different worlds and providing alternative ways of perceiving familiar ones. Narratives of "inauthentic" experiences like nostalgia can offer a unique contribution in this regard, encouraging readers to perceive present social arrangements with respect to idealized images of what could have been. (56)

Su proceeds to argue that critics who see nostalgia as a form of amnesia are not all wrong. Amnesia, especially in the case of a traumatic history, is certainly a dangerous possibility. It is up to the writer of the narrative to take up an ethical standpoint by facing the challenge of "locat[ing] and recover[ing] experiences that a community has failed to understand and assimilate" (148). Interestingly, Pam Cook, though she does not take as firm a stand as Su in this respect, also argues that "a more interesting and challenging dimension [to nostalgia is] [...] [that] it can be perceived as a way of coming to terms with the past, as enabling it to be exorcised in order that society, and individuals, can move on" (4).

Both Cook and Su, then, are interested in nostalgia's potential of being put to ethical use. Writers who make use of nostalgia's powerfully emotional effect have a task: to create contrasting and alternative histories through their nostalgic idealisation of the past. This is done, for example, in Jean Rhys's *Wide Sargasso Sea*, where nostalgic Jane Eyre-style versions of the past define the present "in terms of its failure to satisfy past longings" (Su 56), and also help "foregrounding memories of suffering, alternative histories, lost possibilities, and uncertainty"

(56). The responsible nostalgic writer shows an awareness of how unrealistic the idealised version of the past is, and plays with that knowledge by opposing it to versions of the past *and* present that have not undergone such idealisation. The nostalgic writer as Su would like to see him is a writer who evokes the feeling of nostalgia in a reader by making past and present meet, by making the gap between the two palpable, and by recognising and showing that the ideal past is irrecoverable simply because it was never perfect to begin with.

Su finds the ethical potential of nostalgia to be of particular importance in those instances where a traumatic past is nostalgically recalled: he argues that literature has the power to "undo traumatic history to some degree by redescribing the past" (149). Nostalgia can provide a framework in which the traumatic past can be placed, so that it is made manageable. Su sees the potential danger of nostalgia in such texts, but states: "The longing for a lost or imagined homeland certainly *can* reinforce trauma [...] by oversimplifying the past and repressing uncomfortable events, but it *need* not do so" (149).

Clearly, John Su sees nostalgia as a phenomenon that can create a hierarchy of values within a novel because of the comparative structure it necessarily carries with it. Nostalgia becomes a highly concordant element that can open up a literary work to an ethical reading – an ethical reading in the Aristotelian sense, that is. This is only possible, though, if nostalgia is accompanied by the necessary criticism, so that its idealising and sentimental qualities are put at the service of the hierarchy it constructs. Indeed, almost all nostalgia carries with it some autocritique, because the feeling of longing is only truly experienced through the urgent awareness of the unbridgeable gap of time separating the present from the past. Nostalgia which is completely uncritical of itself might only be possible in what Svetlana Boym calls "restorative nostalgia", which evokes a *national* past and future; on a more individual level, however, "reflective nostalgia" is operative, revealing "that longing and critical thinking are not opposed to one another" (49-50).

While nostalgia is thus accompanied by critique, that does not necessarily mean that its force is contained. In an influential essay, Linda Hutcheon elaborates on the idea of nostalgia as a form of remembering that can both contain and criticise longing. Hutcheon defines nostalgia as "the invocation of a partial, idealized history merge[d] with a dissatisfaction with the present" ("Irony, Nostalgia and the Postmodern" 195). She points out:

> I want to argue that to call something [...] nostalgic is, in fact, less a *description* of the ENTITY ITSELF than an *attribution* of a quality of RESPONSE. [...] [N]ostalgia is not something you "perceive" *in* an object: it is what you "feel" when two different temporal moments, past and present,

come together for you and, often, carry considerable emotional weight. (199)

According to Hutcheon, nostalgia is the evocation of a *feeling*. It can come to be joined to critique or irony, but it is not ironic or critical in itself, as Boym and others would have it. Rather, it is the mere feeling of longing, the sadness Stewart described, that cultural objects may call up. Naturally, the objects may use strategies to evoke nostalgia – usually, as Hutcheon points out, by confronting past and present. As a result, the object – in our case, a contemporary Spanish memory novel – is charged with "considerable emotional weight".

If nostalgia is to function ethically in the Aristotelian way, as Su suggests it may, this emotion has to be containable and rational: it needs to be reduced to one of the tragic emotions. Indeed, it is possible to conceive of nostalgia as one of the most effective ways for a memory novel to call up pity and fear in the reader. Pity and fear are the empathy, the compassion that a work awakens in a reader, who starts to feel for, and with, the characters. Nostalgic longing does just that: it is at once recognisable to every reader, so that its inherent sadness may stir the reader into pity. In this sense, nostalgia can become largely equivalent to a tragic emotion, and since it simultaneously establishes a hierarchical structure and contributes to plot construction, concordance seems guaranteed. Carefully embedded in a critical frame, nostalgia may easily perform the ethical task John Su designs for it. The question is, though, whether the nostalgic emotion is really as controllable and rational as it seems. Linda Hutcheon's use of the adjective "considerable" suggests a vehemence that is hardly compatible with Aristotle's tragic emotions.

Hutcheon goes on to problematise nostalgia's concordant capacities even more. She stresses that nostalgia cannot be critical of itself: it is the feeling of longing being evoked, and not the awareness that such a thing is happening. While nostalgia is criticised, therefore, it is still called up at the same time, and not wiped out entirely by the critique that it is paired with. To complicate matters even more, Hutcheon remarks that nostalgia functions in rather the same way as irony, which is also something that is evoked: "two meanings come together, usually with a certain critical edge" ("Irony, Nostalgia and the Postmodern" 199) – so that it should be possible for objects to be ironic *and* nostalgic. According to Hutcheon, this simultaneous evocation of irony and nostalgia occurs especially often in postmodern culture: "In the postmodern [...] nostalgia itself gets both called up, exploited, *and* ironized" (205). It follows that a text containing nostalgia can be open to the emotion of longing, while still allowing a critical or even ironic reading at the same time; and this, of course, would allow not one, but multiple readings of one and the same text, so that it gains in discordance.

All things considered, the idea that nostalgia can give way to a con-cordant reading appears to rest on a misconception as to how nostalgia can be defined. It is assumed that nostalgia's emotionality can somehow be controlled if it is held within a critical framework. Nostalgia is en-dowed with a critical quality that puts it at a distance as soon as it is evoked. This misconception is widespread, even among scholars who are familiar with Hutcheon's article. Confusingly, for instance, John Lyons elaborates on Hutcheon's idea of nostalgia and irony being called up at the same time, but by calling this ironic nostalgia, he suggests that irony here is a quality of nostalgia, which is exactly what Hutcheon does not say. To her, ironic nostalgia is really the evocation of both irony and nostalgia in the same instant. According to Lyons, "truly ironic nostalgia is already a perfect awareness of distance – in fact, because distance is a *requirement* of nostalgia, irony and nostalgia are, at the highest intellec-tual level of the latter, entirely fused and interdependent" (97). Lyons also appears to confuse irony and criticism: "One may use one's irony […] against one's own sincerely felt nostalgia (a kind of *autocritique* or self-medication)" (96). Lyons thus reads Hutcheon's article on irony and nostalgia as if it were advocating John Su's critical nostalgia, and in this way, he does not do justice to the complexity of either irony and nostal-gia or their combination.

Instead, we would do better to look upon nostalgia as an emotion that a text calls up by confronting a past and a present, and which can be called up *at the same time* as irony – Lyons's ironic nostalgia – or, as happens in many other cases, evoked in a non-ironic way and then *afterwards* criticised. This is what we may call critical nostalgia. It is a form of remembering where the rememberer comments on the nostalgia he has just evoked: Lyons's "self-medication". Nostalgia is thus not a process of remembering where longing is evoked, but it is the evocation of such longing. It can be combined with irony and followed by critique, so that even when it betrays a dissatisfaction with the present and ideal-ises the past, it may criticise this process while or after executing it.

Altogether, then, John Su's belief in putting nostalgia to what he considers to be ethical use is not entirely justifiable, not only because his conception of what is ethical may be questioned, but also because he relies on a concordance that is not necessarily achieved by nostalgia. On the one hand, nostalgia in a novel creates a clear hierarchy of value systems, because it constitutes, essentially, a comparison. Not only is the present compared to the past, but also, different versions of that past are contrasted: the not-so-perfect remembered past may be compared to a longed-for ideal version. On the other hand, however, nostalgia is a separate emotion that can still impact a work even when it is criticised immediately or combined with irony as it is evoked. Problematically, too, nostalgia is the sort of emotion that, as Linda Hutcheon already remarked, carries with it an intensity which cannot do concordance much good. Since it refers to an idealised past, it has a definite seductive quality. Is it really true that this seductiveness can be kept fully under control? Or does it at times escape the comparative framework it helps create, to even end up, occasionally, undermining it? This question becomes the more urgent because nostalgia can occur paired with irony or criticism, but also accompanied by haunting. The contrast of a present with a non-existing past, the confrontation with a temporal distance: these are situations of repetition, of vanished originals and their simulacra, and of ghosts of the past that haunt a present. It seems that this aspect of nostalgia may prove particularly disturbing in memory narratives where trauma is thematised – precisely the places, then, where John Su found the ethical use of nostalgia the most fruitful.

Reading a nostalgic novel could therefore prove to be a much less straightforward activity than John Su suggests. If we pay attention not only to the hierarchies imposed and the concordance suggested, but also to the disturbing sides of the emotion itself and the double reading that ensues, the nostalgic memory novel may turn out to be discordant to a greater degree than Su suggests. Criticism of certain versions of the past or ironic representations of these do not prevent these romanticised narratives from being included simultaneously into the narrative. What is more, their very impact and the pity they may arouse in the reader may make them strongly undermining forces within such a critical framework. The value hierarchy could then actually become highly unstable: seductive and critical versions fight for a place within one and the same work. In these memory novels, nostalgia may lead to difficult struggles of different value systems. Perhaps, a reading less focused on concordance and more interested in such struggles does more justice to these novels' complexities.

Manuel Vicent, *Tranvía a la Malvarrosa*

Tranvía a la Malvarrosa by Manuel Vicent (1994) is a thoroughly nostalgic novel: it employs a number of strategies to evoke an emotional image of the recent, dictatorial, Spanish past. In the novel, the activation of all five senses is attempted in order to imbue the reader with it: street noises, Mediterranean colour schemes, local bands and the smell of paella set the scene. Indeed, even Valencia's red-light district smells like "flor de alcantarilla" (76) and has the flavour of "flujo de cebolla que llegaba junto con el viento sur" (77). A particularly clear example of the importance of sensorial images in the novel is the following description, where a sound image is created of a local Valencian fair:

> La feria de diciembre en la Alameda. Sonaba la melodía Corazón de Violín dentro del aroma de almendra garrapiñada y el estruendo de las sirenas y los

> cochecitos de choque se unían a la canción ay Lilí, ay Lilí, ay Lo... y un
> vientecillo húmedo discurría por el cauce seco del Turia, levantaba los
> papeles, se llevaba la música junto con los gritos de los feriantes. (101)

The nostalgia of sensory elements in the novel is perhaps best summarised by the narrator himself: "Todos los placeres pertenecían a los sentidos y parecían eternos" (183). The idealised past is gone, and what seemed to last forever at the time, is now nothing more than a – sensorial – memory.

Tranvía a la Malvarrosa deals with the adolescence of young Manuel as told by a first-person narrator looking back on his youth from present, democratic times. He describes his move from a village to the city of Valencia, his discovery of women and literature, his changing attitude towards religion – in short, his coming of age in the 1950s of francoist Spain. For this reason, it is once again mainly the narrator's voice that determines the novel's ideology.

The first impression we get of this narrator's evaluation of the francoist past is a positive one, and this impression is caused most of all by his nostalgic descriptions. Clearly, Valencia in those days was a marvellous place to live. Added to the romantic, sensorial image of the past is a touch of humour and colour by way of a great number of anecdotes where remarkable secondary characters, who remain largely undeveloped, enter into the story. Prime example of this is the series of anecdotes concerning Vicentico Bola, the immensely fat godfather of the narrator, who enjoys riding around on a small motorcycle and takes his godchildren to the big city to have them deflowered in the local brothel. Its prostitutes hold Bola to be the secretary of the governor, who has promised "colocar en sindicatos y en el gobierno civil a algunas de las chicas si la cosa se pone mal" (35), instead of a melon salesman at the local market. Particularly the story of Bola's narrow escape from a forced marriage shows clearly the anecdotic way this character is described: the pregnant bride, and the complete wedding party, vainly knock on Vicentico's door while the groom-to-be quietly sleeps and his mother and aunt tell everybody to keep quiet lest they wake the sleeping boy. There are other anecdotes, too, interrupting the storyline for no other reason than to add *couleur locale* to the novel: the mention, for example, of a Valencian girl who, upon being groped in the tram, exclaims in juicy Valencian: "Ja té vosté la mà en la figa. I ara qué fem? Ya tiene usted la mano en el coño. ¿Y ahora qué hacemos?" (150).

Tranvía a la Malvarrosa's romantic stance and its setup as a *Bildungsroman* also contribute to the nostalgic atmosphere. Manuel, the protagonist, grows up in this novel: the period described shapes him personally. He has his first encounters with love, sex, and literature. The pure and innocent love he feels for a girl he knows from her holiday stays in his coastal village structures *Tranvía a la Malvarrosa* and adds an element of a romantic quest. Young Manuel, on coming to Valencia for his studies, is perpetually looking for pretty blonde Marisa, whom he knows to be living somewhere in the city. The two have never actually talked, but shared a great deal of timid looks during her visits to the coast. The feelings of Manuel for Marisa are, therefore, highly innocent and represent an ideal of romantic love.

This ideal, as any nostalgic image, is perfect by virtue of its very un-attainability. Manuel never gets to know Marisa, and so their love can remain unspoiled by reality. He does, however, spot her twice as she is riding the tramway towards the Malvarrosa beach (hence the novel's title). The image of the girl dressed in pink, always riding away from her admirer, strikes Manuel as poetic: "Podía afrontar algo lírico: la pasión por aquella niña que huía en un tranvía sin que yo pudiera conseguirla jamás" (138). She even serves him as a muse for his first attempts in the field of literature. The pure and nostalgic nature of this first love is foregrounded by Manuel's more down-to-earth relations with girls: his platonic relationship with the tragic and worldly-wise prostitute called La China, and, especially, his liaison with a modern, liberal French girl whose free spirit and daring behaviour contrast with Marisa's shyness and her bourgeois reclusion. Marisa stands for nostalgic love, an image of perfection that can never be reached but to which other, later loves may be compared. Significantly, Manuel is thinking of Marisa when he is taken to a brothel by his godfather Bola, and later on, insists on calling French Juliette by the name of Marisa.

Where love is concerned, then, the narrator describes a loss of inno-cence. In many places, it becomes clear that both the narrator and the protagonist experience a nostalgic sense of time passing. As a child, Manuel was in a state of blissful innocence, which gets more and more corrupted by his experiences of life. Young Manuel typically wants to hold on to that innocence, as his picturing of his sexy French girlfriend as "una Marisa que se llama Juliette" (193) demonstrates. Similarly futile attempts at maintaining his innocence are visible where religion is concerned. As a young boy, he wants to become a missionary, and his father insists he be sent to a seminary. In Valencia, however, he soon falls from faith. He spends a long time trying to hold on to it, though: "Yo no creía en Dios, pero lo necesitaba todavía" (115). He even signs up for Jesuit classes where a remarkably socialist view on Christianity is taught, agrees to serve as a spy to a vicar and infiltrates another Chris-tian course of a rather unusual nature, which results in his being fol-lowed around town for a considerable time by a spiritual keeper named Arsenio.

The protagonist struggles with certain value systems that are not compatible with his own experiences. He loses faith in the doctrines of the church, and his romantic idea of love is replaced by a much more carnal one. He hangs out with prostitutes and even gets arrested by a soldier for making out with his girlfriend in the dunes. Their time spent in prison perhaps signifies the very end of his innocence: "hasta esa noche siempre había pensado que no tenía ningún motivo para la rebelión [...]. A partir de ahí me hice un resistente" (188-189). It is with the values of the francoist dictatorship, and especially catholic morals, that Manuel's discovery of life's pleasures collides, which causes him, as he himself puts it, to rebel.

In the story, then, there is a protagonist who starts out blissfully innocent, and whose blind belief in the values and norms of his time collapses as they stand in the way of his increasingly liberal and hedonist preferences. He has trouble throwing off the yoke of this value system, afraid that nothing will replace it, suffering from a "terror de encontrarme solo conmigo mismo" (126). He tries to hang on to it, while at the same searching for alternative value systems by, for example, attempting to become a member of Ortega y Gasset's select minority: "Ahora yo solo quería ser guapo, atlético, sano, inteligente, tomar yogur batido, fumar Pall Mall lentamente, leer a Camus, a Gide, a Sartre" (113).

The narrator, the older Manuel, looks back on his younger self critically. In describing his loss of innocence, he often points out the bad sides of that innocence. He sees his younger self as still so inscribed in the dictatorial value system that he was quite unaware of what was really going on. He recalls, for instance, the day he first came to Valencia, which happened to be the day of San Donís, a local holiday. Coincidentally, Franco also visited Valencia just that day, and as a consequence, anyone suspected of opposing the regime was put in prison by way of precaution. Young Manuel, however, had no idea of all this: "Las sirenas de la policía que sonaban por todas partes yo no las asociaba entonces al terror sino a la fiesta [...]. Ignoraba que ese día había tantos pasteles en las pastelerías como demócratas en la cárcel" (60).

In another place, the narrator gives a clear view of his current opinions on Franco, and of how they contrast with his youthful blindness to the regime's bad sides: "El enano sangriento del Pardo seguía metiendo en la cárcel a los esforzados luchadores por la libertad y el pueblo hambriento... Yo no comprendía nada" (144). That the narrator describes Franco as a bloodthirsty dwarf contrasts with the earlier description of young Manuel's image of him: "Franco para mí no era un dictador sino un gordito anodino al que parecían gustarle mucho los pasteles, con aquellas mejillas tan blandas, el bigotito, la barriguita bajo el cincho, las polainas de gallo con la voz meliflua, el gorro cuartelero, la borlita bailando en la frente" (102). Clearly, the narrator's democratic value system clashes with that of his younger self. At the end of the novel, when Manuel finally breaks with that value system and starts rebelling against it, he comes nearer to the adult version of himself that the narrator represents.

However, innocence is still bliss to the narrator. He still longs for the time when he could hold on to bits of that a priori innocence that comes with youth. The past that he experienced as a young man, and that started disappearing precisely *through* being experienced, is an idealised society full of colourful characters, smells, sounds, and colours. An increasing consciousness of the oppressive regime dominating that beautiful world 'ruins' it for Manuel. What the narrator really longs for is an experience of youth, a discovery of the world, in an environment that is both exactly the same as the one in his childhood and (paradoxically) different, because it would not be a dictatorship. His awareness that what he longs for never really existed, or existed only as long as he, a child, still unquestioningly accepted the francoist value system, is the source of his nostalgia.

And yet, the narrator in a way also betrays a pleasure in the darker sides of his childhood. In a remarkable chapter of *Tranvía a la Malvarrosa*, young Manuel becomes so fascinated by a criminal law case that he decides to turn it into fiction, thus performing his first act as a writer. After stating that his young alter ego "recreaba el crimen como un acto más de la agricultura" (90), the narrator goes on to reproduce the result of that recreation. The story deals with retarded *El Semo*, who rapes and kills his pretty young neighbour Amelita, a deed which sparks off debates on whether he is capable of distinguishing good and evil, inevitably leading to his execution. In the story as it is told in *Tranvía a la Malvarrosa*, the murderer does not repent his crime, since to him, Amelita was, just as all other fruits and vegetables in his agricultural surroundings, ripe and ready to be consumed. The description of the murder is highly lyrical and once again, sensory perception dominates. Surrounded by fragrant flowers,

> [e]l Semo le puso la zarpa en el cuello y aún gruñó su vulgar deseo con cierta timidez, pero Amelita se revolvió bruscamente y la lucha continuó sobre la hierba en una extensión de margaritas. Los dorados insectos celebraban mínimas cópulas de amor muy puro en los árboles. La luz de la tarde iluminaba la lucha de los cuerpos envueltos en voces de auxilio y blasfemias. (90-91)

The crime takes place in beautiful, intoxicating, erotic surroundings, complete with copulating insects, that suggest strongly how natural an urge the violent rape really is. Even though the narrator does not try to disguise the brutal nature of the act, he accords it a primitive beauty. Also, the ending of the story suggests that the deed was not really evil: to the simple mind of *El Semo*, it was, indeed, 'just another act of agriculture'.

Interestingly, the portraying of this evil deed in paradisiacal settings is developed in a way similar to the acknowledging of the less pleasant aspects of francoism in an overwhelmingly nostalgic and romantic rendering of the past. In both cases, the narrator points out that morally, francoism or the raping and killing of a young girl are to be rejected. And yet, since the boy who accepts the dictatorship and the killer are, both in their own way, innocent, they can be rebuked, but they cannot be considered evil. Young Manuel has grown up in beautiful surroundings (as they are nostalgically portrayed) and of these surroundings, the francoist dictatorship has formed a natural part. Similarly, Amelita is completely integrated into *El Semo*'s equally idyllic surroundings and has the same status as any ripened orange. The story of *El Semo*, then, can be read as a sort of *mise en abyme* of the novel as a whole. The narrator's account of the brutal killing does nothing to undermine the beauty of the scene. If anything, this touch of decadence heightens it.

The narrator of *Tranvía a la Malvarrosa* is a critical nostalgic who knows and points out that the past he pines for is not as perfect as he likes to remember it. Still, he is seduced all the same by nostalgia and its emotional impact, preferring to focus on its beauty and to forget about its traumatic aspects. He lets himself be overcome by nostalgia while at the same time keeping a critical distance. Yet, the nostalgic narrator also seems to derive a certain form of pleasure from the realisation that the past was not perfect, but putrid. The beauty of the sounds and colours, the deliciousness of the smells – they all gain extra clarity because they disguise something rotten just below the surface.

Nostalgia's emotive force escapes the hierarchical structuring of value systems of which it is also a part. It undermines the apparent dominance that the democratic value system has over the prior, dictatorial one. Still, that dominance might remain intact if what was longed for was an idealised version of the francoist past where francoism itself does not have a place. In *Tranvía a la Malvarrosa*, the value hierarchy is shaken. Most of all, this is visible in the importance of sensory perception and eroticism in the narrative. While they induce Manuel to break out of the values and norms of Catholicism and the Spanish 1950s, they also cause the narrator to add a sense of perversion to his nostalgic longing. Decay is *inherent* in the longed-for past. What the narrator really longs for is not a childish state of innocence, but the exact moment where that perfection culminated and started its decline.

It is clear, then, that the sheer emotional force of nostalgia undermines concordance, and that the discordance it provides is not a temporary one, serving to emotionally involve the reader, but one that remains vibrant throughout the work. Although the narrator explicitly speaks out against the dictatorship, the past's darker sides that putrefy the otherwise perfect nature of it have a seductive, not a repelling effect. Indeed, it is often the presence of the forbidden, or the contrast between warm passion and the cruelty associated with the regime, that heightens the erotic charge of a scene. Such is the case, for example, when Manuel and his girlfriend Juliette make love in an empty house. Actually, this is the former house of writer Blasco Ibáñez, which was confiscated by the fascist Falange and later abandoned completely:

> Fuimos a refugiarnos en la casa de Blasco Ibáñez. Subimos al primer piso donde había una terraza cerrada con unas cariátides en cada ángulo y columnas estriadas. Una gran mesa de mármol sostenida por cuatro leones alados que había allí sirvió para que Julieta se tumbara y entonces comencé a acariciarla. De pronto ella sintió miedo, pero aquella casa era deshabitada. Fuimos al tercer piso. [...] En un lado habían hecho un nido las golondrinas que entraban y salían a través de las ventanas rotas. En el primer piso había habitaciones con estanterías metálicas llenas de libros del Movimiento Nacional, periódicos viejos, folletos, la colección de la revista Jerarquía. Contra una de aquellas estanterías Julieta se abandonó al ver que en la casa no había nadie y el sol en ese momento se había ido dejando la tarde llena de fruta. (205-206)

In this typical scene, where lust (again associated with fruit) is not only not diminished but heightened by references to the Civil War and francoism, the two lovers use the magazines they find as an improvised mattress, and end up "abrazados bajo un montón de periódicos de la Falange destrozados al final del combate" (207).

Here, we see how the darker side of the past is made part of the evocation of nostalgic sentiments. Discordance openly disrupts the comparison of the past and present value systems on numerous occasions. While the novel obviously places the present one at the top of the hierarchy, and the narrator shows that in spite of his nostalgia, he is not blind to the bad sides of the past, the version of it that eventually speaks most from *Tranvía a la Malvarrosa* is a much more revisionist one, which is aware of francoism's less pleasant aspects but treats them rather like an attractively obscure side effect. As a result, the plot's concordant structure makes way for multiple readings, and the reading according to which Manuel rejects his past through a critical evaluation of his own nostalgia is certainly not the strongest one. Rather, we are left with the image of the dictatorial past as a forbidden fruit: nostalgia's emotionality is heightened by the very hint of rottenness that the work is simultaneously exploiting and criticising.

Julio Llamazares, *Escenas de cine mudo*

No such pleasure in the bad sides of the past is allowed in Julio Llamazares's *Escenas de cine mudo* (1994), even if at first sight, this work appears to be affected by nostalgia in a way very similar to *Tranvía a la Malvarrosa*. Its narrator cannot help experiencing a sense of longing for the past when he flicks through a family photo album, telling the story of his youth (set in the late 1950s and early 1960s) in a mining town called Olleros, where the miners' lives were extremely hard and often quite short due to poverty and an unhealthy working environment. The narrator starts from the "fotografías [...] que resumen en treinta imágenes los primeros doce años de mi vida" (13). Every chapter contains both the description of a picture and that of memories evoked by the picture. There are no actual photographs to be viewed in the book: we are dealing here with what Marianne Hirsch calls "prose pictures" (3), represented by narrative only. The effect of this technique is, according to Hirsch, the hiding of the actual picture by "a verbal overlay", thereby highlighting its structure and the impact it has on the viewer, while undoing the static character of a photograph (3-4). It combines photography and narrative and is open to a visual and a verbal reading (121).

While the "verbal overlay" allows for multiple readings, though, it reduces the photograph's effect at the same time. When we look at a picture, we may experience what Roland Barthes has called *punctum* (49): a shock of recognition. Hirsch suggests that "[u]ltimately, the puncture of the *punctum* is not the detail of the picture but time itself" (5), as the viewer is confronted with a sudden awareness of the temporal distance separating him or her from the depicted. Photographs are thus privileged sites for haunting. Llamazares's narrator clearly undergoes this puncture, as Caridad Ravenet Kenna also notices (198), given his many musings on life, death, and ultimately, the passing of time. The photographs make him aware of the presence of ghosts:

> Desde cada fotografía, nos miran siempre los ojos de un fantasma. A veces, ese fantasma tiene nuestros mismos ojos, nuestro mismo rostro, incluso nuestros mismos nombres y apellidos. Pero, a pesar de ello, los dos somos para el otro dos absolutos desconocidos. (27)

A picture can establish a connection between past and present, and in a way, bring back the dead:

> Aunque ya no los reconozca [a los amigos en la foto] y no sepa quiénes eran o qué hicieron, ni siquiera si se han muerto, mientras la fotografía exista, ellos seguirán viviendo. Porque las fotografías son como estrellas: siguen brillando durante años aunque haga siglos que ya se han muerto. (206)

To the narrator, life and death are combined in a picture, making him feel "el paso del tiempo y la impotencia y la angustia de no poderlo parar" (51). The reader, though, does not get to see the photograph and merely reads its description. Therefore, the picture does not impact him as much as it does the narrator. But since this awareness of time passing and the dead never returning may be familiar to the real reader, the narrator's experience may heighten the sympathy or pity the reader feels for him.

The use of prose pictures gives the narrator the opportunity of constructing the novel as a film and, more particularly, a silent film. The title *Escenas de cine mudo* is in itself significant enough, and the conception of the work as a sort of film made of narrative is reinforced by the title of the introduction: "Mientras pasan los títulos de crédito" (13). The prose pictures do not just come to life: they are scenes that flow together to form the movie of the narrator's life. The narrator realises, though, that a film like that cannot recover the past – it can only create the illusion of doing so. "Aunque los recuerdos fluyan con precisión, aunque las fotografías se suceden y encadenen", he states, "en el fondo no son más que carteleras" (181). This failed attempt at recollecting the past produces sadness and longing in the narrator, who realises that the traces of the ghost exclude the possibility of this ghost ever coming to life again.

Escenas de cine mudo is, clearly, a deeply nostalgic novel. As we have seen, Linda Hutcheon defines nostalgia as the feeling that arises when past and present come together; and this is precisely the experience that the narrator is trying to convey. Nostalgia is evoked through photographs. The narrator knows that the past can never be reclaimed, as the ghost's *punctum* tells him, yet he longs for those days gone by. At the same time, the narrator is critical of his own nostalgia: he points out repeatedly that what is longed for is unattainable. He also criticises his own longing by constantly mentioning that the past he pines for was not ideal at all.

At first sight, the memories of the narrator are beautiful ones. We hear about the narrator's family, about his friends, about the games they played, and so on. In these memories, usually focalised through young Julio, the dictatorship is a given – it is merely the backdrop against which Julio's youth plays out. The young protagonist's knowledge of the dictator, Francisco Franco, is determined by school book photographs and cinema news bulletins (157), overheard conversations of grown-ups (160) and a class excursion with the aim of cheering on the *caudillo* on his passing through the area. On this last occasion, it is not so much Franco who impresses him – the dictator goes by the crowd without even stopping – but the trip itself: he is away from his native village for only the second time in his life, and the memory of that day remains fixed in "la visión de la *Chivata*: esa vieja DKW azul y negra a cuyas ventanillas sigo asomado [...] agitando una bandera y mirando hacia la cámara" (146).

Frequently, the narrator abandons the child perspective in order to construct a sort of collective memory of Olleros. Significantly, the novel does not begin with a prose picture, but with an account of the village's history and its development into a mining town. The narrator obviously intends to remember not only his own childhood, but above all "Olleros, el poblado minero perdido entre montañas y olvidado de todos [...] donde yo aprendí, entre otras cosas, que la vida y la muerte a veces son lo mismo" (13). We thus read about the introduction of television in the village (115), about the rivalry between Olleros and the neighbouring town of Sabero (149), about the tragic fate of Tango, a charming wom-aniser pretending to be an Argentinian cowboy (173-178). In this manner, the narrator creates a fictional universe which he describes as "la vida en blanco y negro" (121): "En Olleros, los únicos colores que existían fuera del cine – cuando el color llegó al cine – y, antes, de mi imaginación eran el blanco de los tendales y la nieve y el negro omnipresente e irrespirable del carbón" (126).

Since he constructs a memory of the village, the narrator often puts his happy childhood into perspective. Such is the case in the above episode, where Franco passes by without stopping because, it is said, he is in a big hurry to go fishing. The real reason for Franco's hurry becomes apparent to the narrator at a later time: "Ignoraba todavía que los *mineros* éramos un peligro, el mayor de todo el viaje, para los encargados de velar por la seguridad de Franco" (144). The narrator points out that, as a child, he did not realise how much the miners of his village had to suffer under francoism, or that they were considered subversive and a potential danger. Tellingly, the chapter on the 1964 miners' strike is called "La huelga (película para mayores)" (155). Little Julio, it is implied, was simply too young to understand what went on. The narrator (not a miner's son) also mentions that he never really saw how bad the circumstances were for the miners; in fact, he believed for a long time that "era el tabaco el que los hacía toser y respirar de aquel modo" (101). In chapter 12 ("Pulmones de piedra"), the narrator de-scribes the heavy breathing and early death of the neighbour who suf-fered from black lung disease, and, looking at a group portrait of miners from the village, concludes:

> Como Luis, había muchos hombres en Olleros aquellos primeros años. Mineros todavía jóvenes [...] que parecían ya viejos a los cuarenta años. La mayoría de ellos había entrado en la mina siendo niños todavía y a los treinta o treinta y cinco ya se habían jubilado. Pero, aún así, ya era tarde. Cuando los retiraban [...] tenían ya los pulmones llenos de polvo y la muerte grabada en la mirada. (101)

The narrator, however, makes it very clear that, due to his young age, he saw all those things as natural facts of life.

Time and again, the narrator confronts his childish innocence with later knowledge. A description of the hill behind his parents' house where the village children used to play ends in the assertion that in those days, they did not realise they were playing on top of the graves of the many miners who had died in accidents, sites quickly covered in litter by the villagers "como si así [la gente] quisiera olvidarlos" (37). Though his tender age may serve as an excuse for his complete obliviousness to the dark sides of life in Olleros, the narrator himself feels it is an insufficient excuse. The contrast between his beautiful, happy memories and his later knowledge of events tortures the narrator. When he looks at a picture of retired, ill mine workers in which he happened to appear, he laments his outsider's position in the mining town: "[Y]o, como en la foto, pasaba simplemente por delante. Tengo la sensación, ahora que pienso en ello, de que eso fue lo único que hice durante todos aquellos años" (103). Although he realises that his innocence was the cause of this, he still appears to feel guilty:

> Si, durante los doce años que viví en Olleros [...] yo no llegué a comprender del todo lo que ocurría a mi alrededor y no compartí, por tanto, la vida de aquella gente más que de modo circunstancial, no fue por desinterés, ni por insensibilidad, sino por desconocimiento. (107)

The narrator's apparent need to apologise for his limited knowledge of what went on around him as a child is indicative of this feeling of guilt. The guilt, then, arises from the discrepancy between the morally mature narrator and his careless and happy former self. He cannot avoid condemning the child for something it cannot be blamed for.

This is where we see the difference between the ideological structure of Manuel Vicent's *Tranvía a la Malvarrosa* and that of *Escenas de cine mudo*. In both novels, nostalgia is called up – in the one, through sensorial images, in the other, through prose pictures. In either novel, there is a narrator whose value system differs greatly from that of the younger self. And in both novels, there is a nostalgia for the innocence of the child, as well as a critical awareness that what is longed for is unattainable. But whereas in *Tranvía a la Malvarrosa*, the narrator indulged in the aesthetically pleasing image of perfection containing its own ruin, the narrator of *Escenas de cine mudo* appears stuck in a moral dilemma, a feeling of guilt for longing for a lost world that, in hindsight, contained so much evil.

It is clear, then, that the ideological structure of *Escenas de cine mudo* is determined by the narrator's values – the narrator's voice and evaluations dominate the novel. He subordinates the values of his younger self to the value system he has acquired since. This narrator undergoes an experience of his past coming back to haunt him: ghosts are called up through pictures and they awaken a strong feeling of longing in him, a nostalgia for a lost past. Both the narrator's extensive musings on the passing of time and on life and death, and his incorporation into the narrative of a sort of collective memory – the voice of the NODO-news bulletins, for example – invite the reader (and especially the contemporary Spanish reader) to be affected by the soothing version of the past that this nostalgia constitutes.

At the same time, however, we see that the narrator is acutely *aware* of nostalgia's emotive force. Repeatedly, the narrator tries to correct his own tendency to be swept away by nostalgia's force. He longs for an imperfect past, and he cannot help it. His awareness of the fact that what causes such nostalgia in him is really something *bad* makes him feel deeply guilty. The narrator knows that his longing is wrong somehow in the light of democratic values, and yet, the ideal of innocent youth is irresistible. The narrator cannot approve of what he longs for.

Escenas de cine mudo is a novel in which nostalgia's seduction is acknowledged, and the difficulty of its ethical use is demonstrated. Clearly, the hierarchy of value systems, the dominant of which supports the democratic, non-revisionist version of the past, is confronted with a discordant, revisionist force which it does not manage to contain or neutralise. The conflict between both of these value systems and both of these discourses is addressed rather than resolved in favour of one or the other. The longing gets in the way of the narrator's idea that the dictatorial past was devastating, most of all in the village of Olleros, and makes him cede to the intensity of more individual and happy memories. The narrator's moral conflict remains unresolved; his ideology is at odds with his nostalgia, and he knows it.

Enrique Vila-Matas, *París no se acaba nunca*

The two previous analyses have shown that in novels where nostalgia and a traumatic past are combined, nostalgia's emotive force leads to heightened discordance. The sense of guilt that Llamazares's narrator experiences because of this is also traceable in Vicent's novel, even if the 'immoral' turn also allows pleasure to be heightened. Neither of these works' narrators succeed in neutralising and controlling the force of nostalgia by criticising it after evoking it. In Enrique Vila-Matas's *París no se acaba nunca* (2003), nostalgia's revisionism is also recognised. As he narrates his past, the novel's narrator tries to combat it by resorting not only to criticism, but above all to irony.

The narrator delivers a lecture at a congress on irony whose objective, he tells his audience, will be to "revisar irónicamente mi pasado en París". He intends to use an irony which he defines as compassionate rather than harsh: an irony "que se mueve entre la desilusión y la esperanza" (11). Looking back upon his young self, he cannot help but feel sorry for that poor boy from Barcelona who went to Paris in 1974, and whose extreme lack of self-confidence was caused precisely by his lack of irony – he could not yet see himself from a distance and took himself completely seriously (96). The narrator intends to benevolently revise his Parisian years with the ironic vision he has since acquired.

The result is an account of the period that tellingly starts with the following remark: "Fui a París a mediados de los años setenta y fui allí muy pobre y muy infeliz. Me gustaría poder decir que fui feliz como Hemingway" (12). The narrator here quotes Hemingway's 1964 work *A moveable feast*, or *París era una fiesta* as the Spanish title reads, in which Hemingway describes his own Parisian years, which he claims to have been very poor but very happy. Inspired by the autobiographical work of his idol, the young protagonist goes to Paris in order to "tratar de llevar una vida de escritor como la de Hemingway" (12). Sadly, the boy's days in Paris are not nearly as happy or as colourful as those described in *A moveable feast*. Paris is a grey and dark city to him: "En París siempre llovía y hacía frío y había poca luz y mucha niebla" (233). Also, he lives in a "cochambrosa buhardilla" (12) and lacks money, friends, and self esteem.

Above all, the protagonist has come to Paris to live the life of a writer, the best way he knows how:

Sin lectores, sin ideas concretas sobre el amor ni la muerte, y para colmo escritor pedante que escondía su fragilidad de principiante, yo era un horror ambulante. Identificaba juventud con desesperación y a ésta con el color negro. Vestía con ropa negra de la cabeza a los pies. Me compré dos pares de gafas, dos pares idénticos, que no necesitaba para nada, me las compré para parecer más intelectual. Y me puse a fumar una pipa. (30)

Unhindered by any experience, he clumsily tries to begin his writing career. Sat in his attic, in front of his huge desk and typewriter, he embarks upon what is to become his first novel, *La asesina ilustrada*. In it, he nihilistically proposes to kill the reader. Meanwhile, he has great trouble understanding the leaflet of literary instructions his landlady, the writer and filmmaker Marguerite Duras, has given him: "No podía estar dando muchas vueltas al asunto *problemas de estructura* cuando aún quedaban pendientes otros que parecían más complicados, como, por ejemplo, *unidad y armonía* o *técnica narrativa*. Así pues, en lo referente a la estructura, no convenía tener demasiados escrúpulos" (41-42). The monotony of his life is interrupted by cinema visits, drinks with acquaintances, and the unwanted appearance of Petra, a girl he was seeing in Barcelona and whom he treats horribly. On the whole, however, his two Parisian years are lonely and hard. The narrator therefore states that he is not nostalgic of those years, though they constituted his youth: "vivo sin nostalgia" (136). Throughout the novel, he claims that he sees his younger self with irony, not with nostalgia.

It is true that *París no se acaba nunca* is principally an ironic novel. As a matter of fact, it contains a number of different types of irony. One of those is the type that can be called romantic (Schoentjes 26) or meta-fictional (Adriaensen 37). It is called up through the figure of parabasis, where the reader is addressed directly: "Un procedimiento corriente de la parábasis en literatura consiste en la intervención activa del autor en el relato, que interpela directamente al lector con comentarios sobre el proceso mismo de escritura o de lectura" (42). Since the narration is structured as a lecture, this type of irony is very present in the novel, where it thematises the relation between the author and his creation. The narrator directs himself openly at an audience, and at a certain point, he even manages to offend a specific audience member by addressing her personally and 'dedicating' the lecture to her: "Desde luego usted, que no se llama Clara, es la mujer nueva de esta conferencia [...]. Está bien, márchese, nadie se lo impide" (156). Also, by ironically addressing the subject of irony, *París no se acaba nunca* can be called auto-ironical (Adriaensen 42). And the revision of the narrator-protagonist's Parisian years is ironic in its humorous descriptions of the young and innocent boy taking himself very seriously, like the above quote on Duras's stylistic tips.

Yet the descriptions of the Parisian years are not merely ironic – for what the narrator fails to admit is that irony and nostalgia are not mutually exclusive. The narrator 'benevolently' and 'compassionately' ponders over his own youthful innocence and foolishness. If there is not an explicit sense of longing, there is at least an obvious sense of something lost: "París, que no se acaba nunca, me acompaña siempre, me persigue, significa mi juventud" (15). What the narrator refers to as compassionate irony is in fact ironic nostalgia: irony and nostalgia are called up simultaneously. As he describes his past, it is obvious that the narrator is affected by a feeling of nostalgia. It is quite probable that though he denies this, he is aware of it, as the following passage suggests:

> Salto para confesarles ahora a todos ustedes que me siento afortunado de no añorar mis años de aprendizaje como escritor. Porque si yo, por ejemplo, pudiera decirles ahora a ustedes que recuerdo de aquellos años la intensidad, las horas consumidas escribiendo en la buhardilla, consumido yo también a lo largo de todo un día y luego, por la noche, inclinado sobre mi mesa mientras el mundo dormía, sin sentir cansancio, electrizado, trabajando hasta la madrugada, y aún después... Si yo pudiera decirles algo de todo esto, pero es que no puedo hacerlo, no hay mucha grandeza, belleza o intensidad en los minutos de mi juventud dedicados a la escritura. Lo sé, es

deplorable. Pero ésa es mi suerte, vivo sin nostalgia. No añoro mi pureza, ni mi entusiasmo estimulante, ni la intensidad. (136)

The narrator here pretends there was nothing extraordinary about his first experiences as a writer. This, however, might very well be meant ironically: from the emotional force of the description of his writing activity, and from the narrator's subsequent admission that he *has* actually known such enthusiasm and intensity, it may be deduced that he *does* remember it with nostalgia. The narrator says one thing, but by the, highly emotional, way he says it, it becomes quite likely that he also means the opposite.

That the work is nostalgic becomes clear enough when it turns out that the Paris described is sometimes referred to as a place where the protagonist is profoundly miserable, but that it is portrayed at the same time as a sort of idealised version of itself. Paris in *París no se acaba nunca* is populated with famous Parisians: not only does the protagonist live in Marguerite Duras's attic, he also moves in her leftist intellectual circles. It is thus that he comes to meet a famous actress like Isabelle Adjani (87) and other people who are a part of the lively Parisian film scene. There is the protagonist's chance encounter with writer Georges Perec, who, annoyed that the boy is staring at him from a rather small distance, comments, "El mundo es grande, joven" (40); there is the appearance of a painter's servant who, the narrator suggests, is none other than Lenin himself (203); there is the young millionaire from the Canary Islands who wastes his family fortune on a huge novel project dealing with the question of how one can live in Paris without acting like Pío Baroja, the Spanish author of the twentieth century (164). Paris acquires an almost mythological character, filled as it is with the *fine fleur* of the 1974 art scene.

On top of this, the novel is vastly intertextual and thus firmly grounded in literary tradition. It describes a city central to many of the great French, American and Spanish authors, and citations range from Rimbaud to Borges to Greene. The majority of authors quoted have at one point in their life lived in Paris, and many of them received their literary education there, just like the protagonist of *París no se acaba nunca*: Hemingway, of course, but also Henry Miller, F. Scott Fitzgerald or Pío Baroja. The narrator frequently refers to the experiences of these other writers in the French capital, usually in a humorous way:

Baroja solo dejaba atrás su cuarto de hotel en París para *dar la cena* – como vulgarmente se dice – a los amigos que le visitaban y a los que, como contara Ramón Gómez de la Serna en un *retrato* de Baroja, se empeñaba en ensombrecerles la vida con largas monsergas sobre la importancia de la ciencia [...]. (166)

Paris acquires an atemporal dimension through the works of all writers who ever wrote about it, and the narrator suggests that he, by going there to write his debut, inscribed himself into this literary universe.

The characterisation of Paris as a fictional space is reinforced by the introduction into the story of some obviously fictional elements. The narrator explains, for example, how he imagines a monster that lives in a bar in Paris, a mythic monster that has taken the shape of an *odradek*, "esa criatura kafkiana que es un especie de armatoste en forma de carrete, formado por una serie de hilos viejos y rotos" (52). Of course, the narrator does admit that this monster only exists in his imagination. Later, he meets a woman called Gilberta Lobo, who "se vanaglorió de llamarse de forma parecida a Gilberta de Saint-Loup, un personaje de Proust" (153) and a young man called Alfonso, who, upon being told by the main character that he looks like Hemingway, maintains that he really is Hemingway (159). Instances such as these contribute to the 'literariness' of Vila-Matas's Paris.

This fictional Paris is as alluring to the young protagonist as it is to the latter-day narrator, who seems to have lost none of his enthusiasm for the city. Nostalgia appears in a much less ironic guise when the narrator describes in his lecture how he takes a new trip to Paris. Upon returning to Paris with his wife in 2003, the narrator approaches the city in much the same way as his younger self did: he looks for his own ideal world through relating present-day Paris both to literary persons or places and to his own Parisian period. Thus, he is reminded of W.G. Sebald's description of the National Library upon visiting it, as well as of Duras's friend Mitterand, who initiated its construction, and who used to live in her attic (the very attic which the young protagonist inhabited himself) back in 1943 (146). This same longing for an ideal Paris is visible in the narrator's ongoing idolisation of Hemingway. He still ardently admires his literary hero, though he does so in a much more ironic way than before. He describes how his wife and friends laugh at him for believing he resembles the great writer, and relates humoristically how he entered, and lost, a Hemingway look-alike contest in Florida. At the same time, though, he still pays homage to the American author. On numerous occasions, the narrator reproduces episodes from Hemingway's life, usually in the form of an anecdote. At one point, moreover, the complete plotline of a short story of Hemingway's is summarised (21). The narrator thus pines for exactly the same thing he was pining for as a boy. He is still active in literature, and still longs to achieve some state of bliss through becoming part of Literature – and of literary Paris.

In spite of the narrator's ironic account of his past, then, he cannot help longing nostalgically for his ideal Paris. Clearly, irony cannot control nostalgia any more than criticism can. What is more, it allows two in principle exclusive readings to be possible at the same time. What is ironised is also allowed, and what is remembered nostalgically is also inverted. So, it seems that irony and nostalgia do not lend themselves particularly well for a concordant reading: we are faced here with a playful alternation of nostalgia and irony, so that the novel becomes open to many readings. Nostalgia and irony together give this novel its complexity.

The novel retains its playful nature, above all, because exceptionally in the corpus of texts I study here, it is set exclusively in Paris, and the Spanish past is only grudgingly referred to. There are only few paragraphs in the novel that refer to Spanish reality during the years, decisive as they were for Spain, that the protagonist spent in France. The first reference to the dictatorship occurs when the protagonist, on his first holiday in Paris, sits in a café and tries to write a story. There is a young girl sitting alone at a table close by, which surprises him, since "en la Barcelona mojigata y franquista de la que yo venía era impensable ver a una mujer sola en un bar, y ya no digamos leyendo un libro" (Vila-Matas 13-14). Small-minded, dictatorial Barcelona serves as a contrast to intellectual, vibrant Paris: the narrator qualifies the atmosphere in Barcelona as "irrespirable" (50). In Paris, the protagonist avoids Spanish *exiliados* that have fled the dictatorship: they only make him feel "deprimido por las obsesivas [...] conversaciones en torno a qué sucedería cuando muriera Franco, agotado por la plúmbea rigidez de sus planteamientos políticos, y, en fin, sobre todo desalentado por lo machacados que andaban [...] por la heroína o por el más rancio vino español" (50). He himself does not share their interest in politics, though he does declare himself a 'situationist' and dedicates himself to "*sentirme* de extrema izquierda" (49).

When Franco dies, he is glad, but not impressed. He receives the news twice – once, as a mistake, the second time, for real –, each time from his tall, black neighbour who calls him *tubab*, a fact which *does* leave a lasting impression. After the second time, "[e]staba sintiendo que las circunstancias de aquel momento eran pavorosamente trascendentes cuando de pronto [...] me alejé del trance solemne y fui a parar directamente a una nadería" (144). He cannot concentrate on the importance of the moment and, after an initial pang of guilt, asks himself whether that really matters. A couple of days later, he travels to Barcelona for the first time in almost two years. The narrator claims, however, that this has nothing to do with Franco's death: "no sé para qué [hice un breve viaje a Barcelona], tal vez para que mis padres vieran mi tobillo vendado" (173). Not a single comment on the political situation he encountered there finds its way into the narration.

Obviously, this 'careless', or rather ludic, treatment of the Spanish dictatorship and the death of the dictator, this lack of interest for exiled Spaniards or for anything that occurs outside of the Parisian, fictional realm, is quite surprising. That the hungry, poor young boy who dreams of becoming a writer would be too much absorbed by his own dreams and worries to pay much attention to what happens in his home country is perhaps understandable, but that the older and supposedly wiser narrator who ironises the preoccupations of that young boy has still not gained any perspective is remarkable. It seems like an odd oversight precisely because the work is set in the highly significant years of 1974 and 1975. *París no se acaba nunca* seems bent on retaining the literary, nostalgic ideal of Paris and not allowing harsher realities to enter onto its pages. From an ethical point of view, this might seen as questionable, as we are reminded of the critique of post-structuralist playfulness in the face of difficult realities. Of course, *París no se acaba nunca* could be blamed for this lack of morality and responsibility. Yet this is not the case at all: Vila-Matas's work has been very well received. Juan Antonio Masoliver Ródenas states admiringly: "Leo ahora *París nunca se acaba* [sic] y para mí se confirma lo que hace tiempo sabía: que con Enrique Vila-Matas estamos ante uno de los escritores más extraordinarios de la narrativa contemporánea europea" (391). And Leandro Pérez Miguel summarises: "La crítica elogia su nueva novela".

Perhaps it is precisely *because* the playful approach is not combined with the historical reality of the francoist dictatorship, that the novel is so well received. After all, the experimental in combination with the difficult and the painful can lead to a perceived unethical form of literature. This postmodern work could then become one of those cases where playfulness in the face of 'trauma' would feel revisionist and wrong to many a reader, as if the gravity of historical events were relativised to an extreme. Here, then, the choice for a narrative with a ludic tone and setup, if it does not want to become 'immoral', has no choice but to steer clear of a discussion of the dictatorial Spanish past. In this sense, the exclusion of Spain in favour of Paris is perhaps the condition for the very discordant way in which this novel is to be read.

Andrés Trapiello, *El buque fantasma*

The last novel I want to discuss in this chapter, *El buque fantasma* by Andrés Trapiello (1992), seems out of place in a discussion of nostalgia. It differs greatly from the works of Vicent, Vila-Matas and Llamazares in wanting to describe a youth very far from romantic: it was unhappy, and governed by ideals that led to disillusionment only. The novel has a narrator called Martín, who recounts his student years in order to do away with what he considers to be the myth of those years. The ghost ship of the title is "un mito que todo el mundo cree y que nadie ha visto" (Mora). This myth, as the narrator does not fail to make understood, is that of student resistance. In spite of everybody later claiming to have been a part of it and to have lived some sort of revolution, the message of *El buque fantasma* is clear: the students putting themselves in danger during the last years of the francoist dictatorship did so for absolutely nothing. *El buque fantasma* intends to combat a revisionism that is, for once, part of the left wing transitional memory discourse: a false belief in their own influence in the democratisation of Spain. In doing so, the work has been criticised severely for wanting to teach its readers, "desde la orilla de un escepticismo ligeramente jactancioso" (Echevarría 98), a lesson of what it was really like – while raising all kinds of doubts as to "la legitimidad de buena parte de sus propósitos" (99). Clearly, something must be undermining or complicating the moralistic stance here.

El buque fantasma deals with the emotional development of its narrator-protagonist, Martín Benavente. In 1972, Martín goes to study at the university of the provincial town of V., where he makes friends, loses his virginity to his older lover Dolly, falls in love, and discovers his vocation as a journalist while working for a local newspaper. The narrator tells us how he meets a fellow student and active communist called José Rei; how José convinces him to join his anti-francoist group; how he takes part in manifestations and distributes illegal flyers; but also how he falls in love with José's girlfriend Celeste. When a member of their communist group gets arrested and denounces the others, Martín narrowly escapes going to jail as his innocent flatmate Floro is mistakenly arrested in his place. José does get caught, and when he is eventually released, the hardships and torture he endured have left their traces. When he fails to find a job and Celeste breaks up with him, he starts drinking heavily and eventually commits suicide.

This plot is clearly in line with the narrator's attempt at revising the myth of resistance. José Rei's suicide indicates that there was nothing beautiful or romantic about student resistance. The narrator explicitly re-evaluates its memory, arguing that the way it is seen nowadays has little to do with what it was really like. For example, the murder of Franco's intended successor, Carrero Blanco, by Basque terrorist group ETA is now sometimes conceived as the beginning of the end of francoism. The narrator claims that

> Ahora es posible que salga alguien sosteniendo lo contrario, pero entonces aquel atentado no cayó bien a nadie: venía a desbaratar los planes que todo el mundo tenía en relación a un proceso contra diez sindicalistas […]. Luego, pasados unos meses, puede que el hecho hiciera prosélitos y simpatizantes. Puede. En los primeros días, no. (11)

Also, the narrator accuses many members of his generation of claiming a part in student resistance that they did not play. He even compares those he criticises to the Frenchmen who, during the Nazi occupation, collaborated out of fear, and who, after the liberation, all "habían cantado en alguna occasion delante de algún alemán, con vibrante patriotismo, la *Marsellesa*" (126). This rather harsh comparison is a good example of the vehemence with which the narrator, who was, of course, one of the persons who *did* offer resistance, expresses himself on the subject.

The narrator's attempts at myth-wrecking continue in his portrayal of the different groups in which the students organised themselves. These groups are described in a rather condescending and ironic way, to the point of satire. The narrator starts with his own group, the *Juventud Comunista*, all of whose members use ridiculous aliases: Martín is called Olegario, and others are named Segundo, Arsenio, Sagrario, etcetera. The group's mental leader Gabriel is a stereotypical 'rigorist': "No le gustaba nada de lo que nos gustaba a los demás. [...] Sólo le gustaba tocar el violín. [...] Usaba el violín únicamente para interpretar en él unas versiones inquietantes y poco humanas de la *Internacional* [...]. Tampoco se reía nunca" (32). Gabriel delivers lengthy monologues on Marxist and Leninist theory, and he takes the underground work of the group much more seriously than the protagonist, who, on his first secret mission, gravely offends Gabriel by making jokes.

Then, there is the hardly more favourable description of the other student groups and the way they relate to each other. For example, the narrator points out that under no circumstances the *Juventud Comunista* may be mistaken for the *Juventudes Comunistas*, since the first is Maoist as well as Marxist, whereas the second is more orthodox, and besides, much less action-oriented – "Cosas de la gramática tanto como de la semántica, si se quiere, pero serias, muy serias" (46), the narrator explains. Unsurprisingly, when these and other groups assemble to convoke a manifestation, rivalries between them threaten the common cause. It is in the description of one of those assemblies that the narrator ridicules the students downright. Only by yelling out the 'magic words' "Compañeros: ¡Unidad! ¡Unidad!" (109), a student manages to stop the quarrelling between members of different ideological groups and provoke the necessary catharsis that unites all participants. Nevertheless, after the vote for a manifestation has come through, there is still some dissent:

El vasco exaltado conminó:
– Todos! ¡A la manifestación vamos todos! Nada de rajarse ahora. Se ha votado, ha salido mayoría y tenemos que ir todos. ¡Todos! El que se raje, maricón.

132

Protestaron algunas feministas, porque les pareció discriminatorio:
– De acuerdo – se enmendó Txiqui –. El que se raje, maricón o puta. (111)

The protest of the feminists is a prime example of how the students are portrayed as young, innocent, exaggeratedly idealistic and highly unprofessional.

The narrator thus firmly imprints his own values on the novel by continuously judging those who romanticise student revolts of the early 1970s, pointing out that the students were no heroes and that no one should remember them as such. There are many places in the novel where the narrator shows a disillusionment as to how the past has been narrativised. In his eyes, resistance took great risks to achieve what the narrator deems to be very little: "Comisarías, procesos, expedientes académicos y una vida echada a perder o torcida para siempre. Para siempre. Para nada" (128). After all, Franco died in his bed and nothing the students did made any difference. The narrator explains,

Hoy puede parecer ridículo que se padeciera tanto por tan poco, justamente porque el riesgo que se corría en una manifestación no era proporcional a la amenaza de los años de cárcel que le sobrevenían a uno si era detenido en ella. No. Hoy se pensará: '¿Una manifestación? Bien poca cosa'... De acuerdo. [...] Una manifestación en términos absolutos no es nada. En términos relativos lo era todo [...], de manera que mi miedo, el de Celeste, el de todos, era el tumor que a unos afectaba y a otros no, sin que se supiera la causa. (116)

The contrast between the mocking description of the students, who take themselves ridiculously seriously in actively yet unsuccessfully trying to awaken the working class, and the treatment they receive from the government, is considerable – and this contrast reinforces the concordantly pursued message of the work. In spite of their innocence and their incapacity to cause any real damage, they are arrested, locked up for months or years, and sometimes even tortured: "con Tejero se emplearon a fondo, le golpearon en las plantas de los pies, le dejaron dos días esposado a un radiador, le cubrieron con una manta mojada y le apalearon" (241). Tejero attempts to kill himself twice; José Rei commits suicide after his release. What seems like an exciting game at first ends very gravely.

So far, then, the novel suggests a reading that is both concordant and moralistic. Yet Rosa Mora remarked, on *El buque fantasma*'s appearance, that this was "una novela [...] que puede ser muy polémica". That she was right becomes clear when we look at the reception it got from a critic like Echevarría, who positively butchers the work and finds that Trapiello "tropie[za] como novelista" (101). Just how violently the novel was criticised is visible in its 1997 epilogue, added to all reprints from July of that year onwards. This epilogue is signed by Andrés

Trapiello, and wants to convey the actual authorial intention. Trapiello feels the need to direct himself at "algunos lectores de la novela" who "se enfrentaron furiosos a su autor diciendo en su día que éste había mentido y empequeñecido la realidad histórica de la España de los años setenta, lo cual es ridículo" (284).

Interestingly enough, this last remark is grounded precisely in the novel's 'ethical' use of nostalgia. For in spite of the fact that this work does not appear all that nostalgic, it does call up the emotion in certain instances. In these places, the purpose is quite obviously to contrast the past's bad sides to a beautiful, idealised version of how it could have been. The narrator feels a nostalgia for an idealised version of the past that he is aware never existed in that way:

> Así quiero recordarla [a la ciudad] ahora. Con aquellas pocas calles viejas que seguramente habrán desaparecido, desde aquella lejanía, en aquella serena panorámica digna de un aplicado Canaletto. Nada de la ciudad levítica llena de militares, curas y policías, fachas y señoritos matones, obreros jactanciosos y estudiantes seráficos, sino la ciudad que un día contuvo cien sueños descabellados y verdaderos, aquella ciudad elevada, ofrendada a la luz más tenue y hermosa de Castilla. (95)

Here, the narrator becomes the ethical nostalgic John Su envisaged. He confronts his actual past with an idealised version, highlighting what was wrong and bad about the real past. In a couple of 'interlude' chapters, his longing for lost youth is made most explicit: in these chapters, events are interrupted by reflections of the author on how young he was then, how little they knew, and how distant it all seems: "A veces me he acordado de ellos" (125), he writes nostalgically about his former comrades. In another interlude, he describes that period in V. as a fog they were all lost inside: "A todos, por igual, nos mantenía unidos, ligados, aquella niebla" (171). Echevarría remarks scornfully: "[El narrador] encuentra la ocasión de redimir con un esteticismo de postal a una ciudad que él considera ominosa", and speaks of "un oficioso liricismo" (100).

Nostalgia is thus put into play by the narrator to reinforce the ideological structure of *El buque fantasma*. It is used to effectuate the conflictive demythification the author has in mind. But nostalgia immediately expands beyond these limits, and invades the entire novel. The older narrator is disappointed in life, and has turned away from revolutionary ideals after realising that he wasted his youth for no specific reason. However, when he tries to show how terrible his youth was compared to how it could have been without the 'revolution', he is swept away by nostalgia's emotional weight: he is distracted from the memory discourse he defends, and starts indulging in personal memories of his student life. The narrator, rather surprisingly after all his provocative statements on how much he and his generation suffered, proceeds to reconstruct events from a deeply individualistic perspective, in what could be called an attempt at reconstructing something of a youth. The strong ideological current is still there, but it is at times wholly overshadowed by the love life and mental growth of the protagonist. First and foremost, *El buque fantasma* is a nostalgically coloured *Bildungsroman* (which shows how the genre is bound up with the emotion of nostalgia), and it is centered around young Martín. So, for example, there is the moment Martín loses his virginity to Dolly. A whole chapter builds up to the moment, and then, the lovers are interrupted as Martín has to go for condoms. After this cliff-hanger, there follows a chapter called "Primer interludio: la ciudad", in which the narrator remembers the city and his life as a member of the *Juventud Comunista*. Then, the narration continues and the reader finds out how Martín lost his virginity.

This nostalgic focus on Martín's individual experiences becomes rather painful when things take a turn for the worse. When José Rei goes to prison and everybody thinks Martín is a traitor, he is mostly worried whether Celeste will believe him innocent (185-186). The day José gets out of prison, Martín is more concerned with other things, such as Celeste's calling him from Vitoria, and his boss at the local newspaper offering him a contract (219-220). And when José Rei explains to Martín that it was Tejero who, enduring torture, betrayed all their names, and then gladly supported the theory that Martín was the traitor, Martín does not feel particularly sorry for Tejero and all he has suffered. Instead, he even asks: "¿Quién va a reparar el daño que se me ha hecho? ¿Tejero?" (242).

The narrator-protagonist is more than a little self-absorbed. Clearly, he is seduced by the feeling of nostalgia that comes with looking back upon his younger years; and it is this nostalgia which entices him to abandon his revision of collective memory and replace it with a romantic wallowing in what has been. Indeed, romance dominates the novel. In spite of all the manifestations, all the suffering and all the fear, much of the novel is dedicated to Martín's love affair with bourgeois Dolly, his flirt with Lola, and finally, with his 'impossible' love for her sister, the beautiful, reactionary and mysterious Celeste. Even the suicide of José Rei is not a direct consequence of his time in prison and his problems adapting to his new life as an ex-convict, but follows just as much from his break-up with Celeste.

The narrator's focus on individual growth and romance that arises out of the uncontained emotionality of nostalgia plainly vexed *El buque fantasma*'s readers, who found that the novel reduced Spanish reality of the 1970s. Ignacio Echevarría concludes:

la novela, a partir de su ecuador, avanza por dos caminos divergentes: el de la crónica mordaz de la época, y el de la aleccionadora 'educación sentimental' del protagonista [...]. Da la impresión de que, sin un propósito claro, a mal traer con su vocación de novelista y su irresistible inclinación por la epifanía lírica y la estampa autobiográfica, el autor termina por perder el control [...]. (100-101)

In the epilogue, Trapiello defends his protagonist against real readers' complaints about his selfishness:

Martín Benavente es un hombre individualista y sentimental, que recuerda con vago humor todo lo que un día vivió con solemnidad, y con sencillez mucho de lo que nació impostado. A él ese desajuste, entre lo que es y lo que fue, no deja de mortificarle un poco, al contrario que a algunos que buscan en lo que fueron una justificación para lo que quieren ser y no son. Por eso Martín es un individualista. [...] Martín no [...] quiso hacer la novela de toda la generación. [...] No es un redentor, no es un predicador, no cree en más revolución que en la de ser libre cada día. (284-285)

El buque fantasma tries to perform a revision of memory that is to speak of a whole generation, but the nostalgia it wants to use as an ethical force that will support this undertaking turns against such an intention, as it distracts the narrator from opposing memory discourses and makes him focus, above all, on the youth of Martín Benavente – which, to make things more complicated, was not quite as bad as that of others. It is odd, to say the least, that the epilogue both claims that the novel is certainly no 'reduced version of historical reality' and defends it as the account of an individual who does not stand for a generation.

In the end, Trapiello's novel shows how the emotion of nostalgia can become such a strong force in a novel that the text starts contradicting itself. The moralistic stance is not maintained, because even though nostalgia is used in an ethical way and provides a framework that places memory narratives in a clear and firm hierarchy, this morality is counteracted by the nostalgic description of the protagonist's younger years. Instead of showing its readers an account of the student revolts without false lustre, nostalgia provides the novel with another type of revisionist lustre that understandably angers the real readers. The novel differs from *Tranvía a la Malvarrosa* in its pedantic tone and in its stated intention of setting things right, which is probably why it is much less palatable than Vicent's novel, which seems to *enjoy* the discrepancies between criticism and nostalgia, the complex readings that these allow and the feeling of touching on the forbidden it revels in. Here, then, nostalgia is a force that heightens discordance and that causes an open conflict between it and the work's proclaimed value system.

Conclusion

Nostalgia is an emotion everyone recognises, experienced by readers, writers, and fictional characters alike – for all have known the passing of time and the loss of what was before. Nostalgia in a novel may make the work bathe in a mist of sadness and longing that may affect the reader highly. Of course, its recognisable and sad nature can be said to evoke pity in the reader, so that nostalgia inspires one of Aristotle's tragic emotions. According to Ricœur, such rational emotions lead only to temporary plot discordance, which means that nostalgia may have an 'ethical' potential in the sense that it can educate its readers – a potential also recognised by John Su, particularly because nostalgia can organise a text hierarchically. The question is, though, whether nostalgia is ever rational enough: it brings with it a great potential for disturbance, not only because it may be linked to haunting processes, but also because it is, ultimately, a feeling. Thus, criticising or ironising it within the ethical framework may not suffice to dominate its emotional force.

In the four Spanish memory novels discussed here, nostalgia is indeed a factor that can heighten disturbance in a novel – not just to the point of suggesting an alternative, uncritical reading, but to the point of letting this reading overthrow the one suggested by the value hierarchy. The quality that Linda Hutcheon calls its emotional weight affects novels and allows undermining forces to enter into their structures. In *Tranvía a la Malvarrosa*, for one, the narrator's judgment of the dictatorship seems to determine the novel's value hierarchy, and to put into words its preferred memory narrative. Yet the nostalgia that is relished on every page of the novel suggests a reading which is diametrically opposed to this. The narrator of *Escenas de cine mudo* is aware of the two contradictory forces in his narration, that of his conscience and that of nostalgia, and sees himself forced to admit that he cannot overcome this duality. Irony might seem to be a forceful antidote in *París no se acaba nunca*, but the intertwining of irony and nostalgia makes the work playful and discordant to quite a high degree. And in *El buque fantasma*, nostalgia is so disturbing that the author adds a defensive epilogue, where he describes his intentions in a confused and contradictory way.

Clearly, nostalgia does not function in the way an Aristotelian tragic emotion would. It may, in fact, turn the reader against the novel instead of allowing him or her to empathise with its characters. The remarks of Trapiello's readers betray a strong sensitivity when it comes to the revisionist nature which his novel's focus on the youth of its protagonist carries with it. The concordant reading nostalgia sets out to achieve here is hindered by the overflowing of that very nostalgia, so that the entire narration is cast in an individualistic and perhaps revisionist light. Remarkably, it is actually quite tragic that this is a fate that would befall precisely this work, which conscientiously attempts to put nostalgia to what Su would call an 'ethical' use.

The other three novels managed to avoid such criticism: no such discussion was raised by Vicent's novel or that of Llamazares or Vila-Matas. This is immediately understandable with respect to the work of Llamazares, which thematises the problematic nature of the revisionism that nostalgia seems to imply, and offers a critical perspective which does not solve this problem, but which does serve to lessen it. Indeed, the reader may experience all the more sympathy for the narrator as he tries to balance his knowledge of the past as it was and his wish for how it could have been. In the case of Vicent's *Tranvía a la Malvarrosa*, this structure is much weaker: nostalgia is so strong that the occasional remarks of the narrator on the obscure sides of the past have little impact. What is more, the bad sides of that past really only increase the pleasure of nostalgia: the duality of the use and criticism of nostalgia serves to turn the emotion into something that is 'forbidden', and therefore all the more attractive. Vila-Matas's *París no se acaba nunca* finally, is highly discordant because of its literary way of openly combining the apparently exclusive phenomena of nostalgia and irony. It seems odd that this work has not been called on to take responsibility by any of the critics or scholars who like to act as judges, and that it is allowed to ignore the past when it is still necessarily present in its pages. But in fact, its point of departure is a postmodern playfulness that would have been difficult to combine with the portrayal of a painful past. Now, its lack of interest for francoist Spain prevents its playfulness from becoming problematic.

Altogether, we may conclude that nostalgia certainly does not function as a mere rational emotion in Spanish memory novels. Even if it is distanced through criticism or irony, and even if it is consciously used ethically, it still gains an intensity that destabilises any hierarchies that may stem from it. Nostalgia is not a merely *temporarily* discordant emotion. The consequence of this conclusion for Spanish memory narratives, is this: that the presence of nostalgia is always a complicating factor – and that it may undermine even its 'responsibility' at the very moment of imposing it. A memory novel banking on critical nostalgia will always need to incorporate the values of the nostalgic discourse, and these can come to dominate the critical stance rather easily. So, the francoist past is both positively and negatively portrayed, and the conflict between these opposing memory narratives makes the novels complicated and discordant rather than 'responsible'.

CHAPTER 5

Autobiography's Aura of Authenticity

The Power of Autobiography

Besides pity and fear, Aristotle lists surprise as one of the tragic emotions that introduce, in Paul Ricœur's terms, 'temporary discordance' into an otherwise concordant plot. That a surprise effect need not stand in the way of a literary work's being read concordantly, as a work with a clear meaning and message, is hardly surprising: it is a technique so common in narrative that it has become part of all kinds of stereotypical plots. What is more, surprise experienced by protagonist and reader alike can heighten the reader's empathy, so that pity is called up. It seems that surprise, fear and pity are thus very much connected in Aristotle, since surprise must lead to identification. At the same time, though, a surprise effect can be seen as a confrontation between the reading which the reader expects and that which the novel ends up providing him or her with. Even though the first reading is discarded, its presence in the novel next to another one is still a fact. It is imaginable that such duality, even if it is resolved within the novel, leads to more complexity, a higher level of discordance, and a much less 'readable' novel, than the Aristotelian model allows for. In this chapter, I will look into one strategy used frequently in memory novels to introduce surprise and to confront the reader with his expectations: the idea of referentiality, and particularly the referentiality of autobiography.

From the above, it may be deduced that in my view, autobiography is not a genre, but rather, an occurrence within a text. This is certainly not an idea shared by all, which is mostly due to the success and the enduring influence of Philippe Lejeune's theory of the autobiographical pact. Eakin calls this theory one of the "most successful attempts to date to establish a poetics of the genre [of autobiography]" (29), and Del Prado *et al.* go as far as to say that "[l]a noción del pacto autobiográfico es, a nuestro juicio, el criterio más válido, al no decir el único, para definir el género autobiográfico" (121). Lejeune conceives of autobiography as a genre and defines it as a "récit rétrospectif en prose qu'une personne réelle fait de sa propre existence, lorsqu'elle met l'accent sur sa vie individuelle, en particulier sur l'histoire de sa personnalité" (14). The reader knows that he or she is dealing with autobiography because of the title and information given on the cover, or because of explicit remarks of the narrator at the beginning of the text (27), but fundamentally, he or she must willingly decide to go along with these clues and accept the autobiographical pact between narrator, author and protagonist (15) that is a condition *sine qua non* of autobiography. The reader agrees to see the author, protagonist and narrator as identical.

The idea of autobiography as a genre has been criticised strongly, however. Although life-writing is of all times, and we can distinguish a tradition starting around the year 400 with the *Confessions* of Saint Augustine and reaching all the way to the testimonies of Holocaust survivors (Anderson 121), definitions of autobiography are "by no means stable" (7). According to Paul de Man, "autobiography lends itself poorly to generic definition" (68). Attempts at defining such a genre seem to "founder in questions that are both pointless and unanswerable" since "the works always seem to shade off into neighbouring or even incompatible genres" (68). Besides, autobiography "[does] not [...] reveal reliable self-knowledge" (71), since it is impossible to distinguish between fact and fiction when both the autobiographical and the non-autobiographical are narrativised.

Lejeune's autobiographical pact has been criticised, accordingly. His approach handily avoids lengthy discussions about the impossibility of identifying the real author with his fictional constructs of narrator and protagonist. Of course we know that the author, the narrator and the character are not really identical. Lejeune, however, simply points out that this does not matter as long as the reader accepts the impossible situation as possible. Naturally, this means that Lejeune attributes an "extraordinaria importancia a la figura del lector" (Del Prado Biezma *et al.* 213): it is the reader who has to decide to accept the pact. If he does, he will also assume that the autobiographer "at least [...] aspire[s] to some version of absolute and inclusive truth" (Evans 2). Paul de Man finds that this lends the reader a "transcendental authority that allows him to pass judgment" (72). The reader is now burdened with the task, formerly belonging to the author, of verifying autobiography's authenticity. De Man criticises Lejeune for trying to exchange one system of tropes, that of the author, for another, that of the reader. He accuses Lejeune of searching for "resolution and [...] action" (71), whereas in his opinion, autobiography's ambivalence remains unresolved. De Man is so critical of Lejeune because in his eyes,

> [a]utobiography is not a genre or a mode, but a figure of reading or of understanding that occurs, to some degree, in all texts. [...] Which amounts to saying that any book with a readable title page is, to some extent, autobiographical. But [...] by the same token, none of them is or can be. (70)

To de Man, autobiography is impossible. As soon as life-writing has taken place, it has become narritivised and, thus, fictionalised.

Manuel Alberca points out that this "nihilismo narrativo" seems to conduct to "un artimaña más para no comprometerse"; after all, "¿qué sentido tendría corregir o dar la versión verdadera de lo sucedido si todo en realidad es ficción?" (67). He rejects Paul de Man's ideas on autobiography: "En mi opinión, subyace aquí un principio equivocado [...]. La creencia de que la verdad absoluta es inasequible puede ser respetable, pero no parece que sea suficiente para igualar autobiografía y ficción" (66). Bringing to mind Wolfgang Iser's distinction between the fictional and the imaginary (*Das Fiktive und das Imaginäre*), Alberca does see a difference between fiction and autobiography: "Es verdad, como nos ha enseñado Paul Ricœur, que la forma de ordenar y explicar lo vivido es narrativo [...] pero esto no significa necesariamente inventar" (68). In fiction, the author is at liberty to invent; in autobiography, he is not. Understandably, Alberca finds de Man's depiction of autobiography as fiction rather restrictive. If properly applied, de Man's view on autobiography would seem to render any study of it useless.

Alberca thus concludes that there is a referentiality to autobiography that forces it to avoid invention. Apparently, it is the referential aspect of autobiography that sets it apart from fiction, as Eakin also suggests (29). It is also this referentiality that brings with it the confusing nature of autobiography, which causes Martha Pérez to name as the two most important characteristics of autobiography its mythical condition, since it 'writes' a world, and its tragic nature, since it is only a myth (93). In other words: it refers to reality, but is not 'real' itself – it is a story about reality. It is clear that autobiographical writing only *seems* to tell the truth. Really, it combines certain elements of reality, taken from "the two parallel streams of referential fact, biographical and historical" (Eakin 141) in a narrativised total. The "fictionalising of life" (Ballesteros 180), however, is not an invention of life: it intends to approach 'truth' as much as possible.

The apparent 'truthfulness' that its referentiality suggests, as well as the fictional nature of its narrative material, complicate the status of autobiography. Even if we assume that it cannot be considered anything other than fiction, the suggestion of autobiography does make a difference to the reader, not as a genre, but as a figure of reading, a "moment" that "happens as an alignment between the two subjects involved in the process of reading" (de Man 70), i.e., the author and the reader. Autobiography thus becomes an extratextual affair: Lejeune's pact between author and reader. Unlike Lejeune, however, de Man does not find that the problem of autobiography is 'resolved' by having the reader decide what he will believe. In the eyes of de Man, neither the author nor the reader can ultimately decide on the authenticity of a text. Instead of avoiding this ambiguity by the means of a practical solution like the one suggested by Lejeune, he wants to leave it intact.

Nonetheless, it is possible precisely with the help of de Man's conception of autobiography as a moment in the text to overcome his 'narrative nihilism'. If we see the autobiographical as a textual effect, we automatically assume that there are other moments in the text where it does not occur. In this way, the autobiographical *is* distinguished from the rest of the text: moments of 'invention' and of 'referential' autobiography alternate. Consequently, if we look at a work of literature where autobiography is suggested, its fictional status does not mean that we have to pass over this suggested referentiality. Instead, we can look at autobiographical moments in a plot as places where the reader may be affected or convinced of a certain 'truth': we can see it as a means the author can use for emplotment.

It would seem that autobiography is a very concordant force, then: it is apparently truthful and reinforces a text's authority. And in a more or less traditional autobiography, where the autobiographical moment lasts all through the work, this may be the case. The autobiography uses the prolonged autobiographical moment to support its claims to authenticity and referentiality – without ever actually being referential. Though the author of a 'generic' autobiography only *suggests* authority and a departure from fiction, the lack of places in the work where invention counterbalances such apparent referentiality may easily make the work pass for something other than fiction.

Yet in less traditional works, where autobiography is contrasted to clearly non-autobiographical, 'invented' sequences, autobiographical moments may come to provide surprise that does not lead to an uncomplicated reading experience. In their novels, authors of such works investigate what happens when the autobiographical Self creates a fictional Other. For such literature, Serge Doubrovsky coined the term "autofiction" as early as 1988: "Ni autobiographie, ni roman, [...] il fonctionne dans l'entre-deux" (69-70), is as close as he comes to a definition. I will refer to it as autobiographical fiction, a term which in my view avoids the impression that autofiction is a hybrid which melts together autobiography and fiction. The term can be used for any work that openly combines fiction (invention) and autobiography, thus raising questions on the status of either. Autobiographical fiction is both inspired and characterised by innovative impulses such as autotextuality and metanarrativity, and plays with fictionality and the narrator's status (den Toonder 202).

On the whole, autobiographical fiction tends to betray its nature by strewing around contradictory textual and paratextual clues. On the cover of a work, the word 'novel' may be printed; but the writer's biography on the back suggests strong similarities between the narrator and the author, and the author may even admit in interviews that it is based on his own experiences, though he may also insist that most of it, of course, is complete fiction. The autobiographical novel thus causes ambiguity: the reader cannot determine whether what he reads is invention or not. Autobiographical novels "are not bound by an autobiographical pact", Alexis Grohmann states (142). The autobiographical nature of parts of it must be deduced "not [from] what forms part of the text, but [from] what is outside it [...] and also in the actual book, but preceding or outside the text constituting the content, on the cover page, the title page, or the preface [...]. These marks determine how a text is received" (142). Alicia Molero de la Iglesia gives similar pointers as to how autobiographical fiction may be distinguished from other fiction. First of all, readers have to look for information on the cover or in the presentation of the book. Then, they can check the similarities and differences between the book and the author's life. And finally, they can look for parallels and hints in other works of the author or in interviews (201-203).

The function of the confrontation of autobiographical and fictional moments can differ from one work to the next. It is possible, really, to speak of a sort of sliding scale of autobiographical fiction. On one side, we find novels of a strongly experimental, metafictional and (post)modern nature, which use autobiographical moments and their alternation with moments where the autobiographical pact is disrupted to confront the reader with the fictional nature of the text he is reading. Through the surprise that comes with a disruption of the reader's expectations, the text becomes self-reflexive and purposefully causes the reader to experience indeterminacy. On the other side, we find novels which claim to be works of fiction, but which otherwise strongly suggest, for example, through including a narrator, author and protagonist that are strikingly similar, that they are really autobiographies. Here, fiction seems to work as a disguise for autobiography, as the writer escapes the truth claims of the autobiographical pact. The autobiographical moment here is not accompanied by any surprise effect, since it lasts all through the narrative. The novel suggests a reading that almost allows an autobiographical pact, and that provides the reader with more comfort and less doubt. Between these two extremes, a whole range of gradations can be distinguished of the extent to which autobiography and fiction are contrasted in a novel.

It is clear, then, that autobiography or the disruption of it can be used to effectuate surprise in the reader, the tragic emotion which serves as a temporary cause of discordance in Ricœur's eyes. The confrontation of two readings inherent in the surprise effect already implies a degree of discordance, and the question is whether this really is as temporary as Ricœur believes. Then again, the question may be asked whether auto-biography is capable of creating even greater discordance; perhaps, there is room for investigation here. It seems that there is some sort of added attraction to the suggestion of referentiality, an attraction that makes it surpass other literary surprise effects. The label 'based on a true story' that advertises works of fiction, and the ongoing popularity of historical fiction, autobiography and other works that imply referentiality, point in this direction, as does, in Spain, the sudden popularity of autobiographi-cal fiction (Molero de la Iglesia 201-203). Sidra DeKoven Ezrahi intro-duces the term "aura of authenticity" ("Representing Auschwitz" 128) that a text can assume. Ezrahi is talking, here, about Holocaust fiction, and she speaks of survivor testimonies and memoirs, problematising their claim to a sort of truth – the memoirs hide their fictionality by making use of a "documentary-*style*-writing" (128). As such, she is concerned with an illusion of referentiality that is made explicit and thus broken in autobiographical fiction. Nevertheless, her choice of the word 'aura' suggests that referentiality in a text, and as a consequence, auto-biography, may have a strong emotional impact. The term, of course, brings to mind Walter Benjamin's influential essay, "The Work of Art in the Age of Mechanical Reproduction" (1936), where he describes how the experience of a work of art is changed considerably when it is produced on a massive scale. In the era of mass reproduction, the work of art loses its "aura", the essence of originality that makes the 'real' artwork unique.

It is imaginable that the autobiographical moment has an aura: it suggests a real-world essence, and though it does not actually rise above being fiction, it seductively implies doing so. Perhaps, autobiography's referential effect might be compared to the *punctum* Roland Barthes attributed to photographs. In the case of the *punctum*, after all, the viewer of a photograph suddenly becomes aware of the passing of time, of the fact that the person or thing depicted has once existed, that "Ça-a-été" (Barthes 120); he suddenly sees the original in the copy. In an analogous way, autobiography's 'sting' could be the *punctum* that comes with the realisation that what is described in a novel *has actually happened*. Somehow, the autobiographical moment could cause a sort of identification of the real world with the fictional world, combining an awareness of their difference and at the same time stressing their over-laps. When we are suddenly confronted with autobiography, we may be struck by the awareness that we are reading a fictionalised, narrativised version of the 'real world'.

The shock effect is a tragic emotion in Aristotle, and as I suggested earlier, these kinds of emotions may be less rational than they seem in complex fictional environments, leading to a discordance so great that it could be more than just temporary. The aura of authenticity may enhance surprise and bring with it an even greater risk to a novel's concordant appearance, making it difficult to read it concordantly at all. What is more, if this *punctum* is actually an effect of autobiography, this suggests that the aura of authenticity could open up the novel to a process of haunting. The fictional world becomes a simulacrum or doubling of the real world; the traces of reality, it ghostly presence, are felt in the novel as it momentarily suggests referentiality. Naturally, if this was the case, then disturbance and discordance would be great, so that, rather than lending more concordance to a work in providing it with a firm authority, autobiography might just do the very opposite.

Javier Marías, *Tu rostro mañana*

In her study of the novels of Javier Marías, Isabel Cuñado points out that there are "numerosas manifestaciones de lo espectral que habitan la obra mariense" (2) – a remark which suggests a degree of discordance in these novels due to the elusive and far from straightforward nature of ghosts. Javier Marías, in fact, is familiar with the concept of the spectral: in *Mañana en la batalla piensa en mí*, the narrator speaks of "un verbo inglés, *to haunt*, [...] un verbo francés, *hanter*", which

> no es otra cosa que la condenación del recuerdo, de que los hechos y las personas recurran y se aparezcan indefinidamente y no cesen del todo ni pasen del todo ni nos abandonen del todo nunca [...] queriendo encarnarse en lo único que les resta para conservar la vigencia y el trato, la repetición o reverberación infinita de lo que una vez hicieron o de lo que tuviera lugar un día. (91)

Isabel Cuñado states that *all* of Marías's novels are haunted; she assumes that the ghost which haunts them is the traumatic Spanish past. Even the first novels, which are not set in Spain and have contributed to Marías's reputation as a decidedly un-Spanish writer, contain traces of this particular ghost, but, as Cuñado points out, the past is dealt with more and more explicitly in every consecutive novel: "[Marías] ha tratado y sigue tratando cada vez más de la realidad española" (9). As I mentioned in chapter 2, Cuñado's insistence on Marías's incorporation of the Spanish past in his novels reads like a defence against those who accuse him of a lack of 'responsibility'. Marías has never neglected the past, Cuñado claims, but it has become an increasingly important theme in his works – a development which reaches its culmination in *Tu rostro mañana* (2002-2007), where "se produce una aperture significativa al contexto histórico de la guerra civil española y la dictadura de Franco". In *Tu rostro mañana*, at last, the ghost is named explicitly.

Cuñado approaches *Fiebre y lanza*, the first part of this novel's three volumes to have appeared, looking for places where the traumatic past haunts. According to her, this haunting occurs in a number of ways. First of all, writing *in itself* is open to haunting. Cuñado cites from an essay of the author, "La huella del animal", in which he compares writing to a "huella, la cristalización de una experiencia que ignoraremos siempre fuera de su cristalización y en la que sin embargo podemos reconocernos" (35). To Marías, Cuñado states, literature is situated in "el 'espacio espectral'" (36) between reality and fiction. This certainly seems to be the case in *Tu rostro mañana*, where haunting is a central theme. Narrator Deza often returns to the subjects of silence and speech: silence can be a saviour, since to speak is sometimes to betray, but it may also lead to forgetting. The dead are condemned to silence – and whereas the writer can provide them with a voice, this is not their real voice, but a simulacrum only. *Tu rostro mañana* is thus principally open to haunting: it acknowledges that haunting is incorporated into its structure, and it thematises this functioning of literature as a 'spectral space' in which the dead cannot be called to life, but where they can return as undead. It is, one might say, the author's specific intention for his novel to be haunted. Nevertheless, Cuñado's assumption that it is the traumatic past that haunts here is not necessarily correct: it may just as well be the present that makes itself felt in literature as a simulacrum of reality. The question, too, is whether these spectres actually succeed in making the real reader experience true horror; this species of haunting is, as Derrida mentioned, typical of all literature and may not appear all too disruptive.

Haunting does not only occur because of the spectrality of writing itself. Holding on to her idea that in Marías's novel, it is always the traumatic past that does the haunting, Cuñado claims that it also returns through the strange and inexplicable: "[a] través de lo inexplicable y lo extraño, *Tu rostro mañana* llama la atención sobre las víctimas ausentes de las diversas narrativas de la memoria" (141). Cuñado points out that objects often play such an estranging part (5). Indeed, objects have a structuring role in Marías's works: they link "situaciones que, por la diferencia de los contextos respectivos, no tienen nada en común" (Pittarello 23). Moreover, the objects are important since they are open to haunting: "son la huella de quien ya no existe" (21). This goes, specifically, for objects that have an "aura", a term which Cuñado takes from Walter Benjamin but which she defines as the "experiencia del fantasma" objects cause (69): antique books, photographs, and other objects that can somehow confront those living in the present with what once was. An example of such an object is a terrifyingly strange antique sword used as a threatening weapon. Further sites of haunting are, still according to Cuñado, your typical ghostly motifs – the double, for example (117), and other elements of the novels that cause a sense of estrangement.

146

At the time Cuñado's study appeared, the second and third parts of Marías's novel had not yet been published. Her discussion of the spectral in the first part of *Tu rostro mañana* must therefore remain provisional. In it, she points to the estranging motif of a mysterious drop of blood that the novel's protagonist Jaime Deza discovers after a party on the stairs of his friend Sir Peter Wheeler's home, which he cleans up and the presence of which is doubted and denied later by Wheeler. Cuñado links this incomprehensible drop to the frequent mention of blood in relation to the Civil War – Deza describes it as "[d]ías de sangre" (Marías, *Tu rostro mañana I* 223) – and concludes: "la sangre es una imagen de la violencia que sufrieron las víctimas de la guerra y la dictadura" (141). Of course, Cuñado had no way of knowing that in the third and final volume of *Tu rostro mañana*, the nature of the drop is explained: it has been coughed up by Wheeler himself, a symptom of his developing lung cancer. Still, Cuñado is right in pointing out that "la gota [es] *incomprensible* y *extraña*" (146), not only because it suggests that Wheeler, who ages progressively in the work, is dying (and thus in a way no longer entirely part of the world of the living), but also because it appears on the same part of the stairs as did the blood of Wheeler's wife, on similar stairs, shortly after the Second World War, when she committed suicide. In this case, though, it certainly would be odd to assume that it is necessarily the *Spanish* past that does the haunting[1].

Cuñado's discovery of processes of haunting in *Tu rostro mañana* is certainly not mistaken: the dead *do* reappear in the literary space, and the text *does* contain strange motifs and auratic objects. It would seem that this novel is therefore discordant to quite a degree. But in a text that is of itself open to haunting, that even thematises it, this type of ghostly appearance cannot be considered very discordant. The reader *expects* haunting, and that is what the novel provides, so that while a degree of uncertainty destabilises the text, discordance is quite limited. Yet there are places in the text where the haunting past *does* lead to rather severe discordance, and these are the very places where the particularly Spanish past, above all the Civil War, is referred to most directly, causing actual shock and horror to be called up. This occurs not in the passages which talk of auratic objects or which develop estranging motifs, but

---

[1] Antonio Gómez López-Quiñones makes similar assumptions when he considers, also upon reading only the first part of Marías's novel, that the drop of blood "crea una atmósfera fantasmagórica e inquietante" which "casi exige que se haga cargo [el protagonista] de una Guerra Civil en tanto que debate, problema y conflicto moral que exige ser discutido incluso en un tiempo (especialmente en un tiempo) que parece haberse enroscado en el descreimiento y el olvido" (92).

rather, in a number of autobiographical moments where the painful past is talked about.

These moments' aura of authenticity, their seeming referentiality, comes as a surprise in a novel that otherwise seems bent on playing with the authority of autobiography and that, in the process, attributes a certain authority to *invention*. The mix of autobiography and fiction has been a recurrent theme in Marías's œuvre ever since he published *Todas las almas* in 1989: "Días antes de publicar *Todas las almas* [...] Javier Marías expuso [...] que cada vez estaba más interesado en utilizar materiales autobiográficos en sus novelas, 'no en tanto que testimonio, sino en tanto que ficción'" (Pittarello 48). Marías's novels, then, exploit the fictional nature of autobiography and play with the reader's expectations. They suggest autobiography, but they counterbalance it with a strong undercurrent of fictivity. In *Tu rostro mañana*, this procedure is also followed, but at the same time we find a small number of passages where autobiography is suddenly dominant – and where the playful tone recedes behind the cruel 'reality' they describe.

The autobiographical nature of these passages stands out the more because even if, all through the novel, an autobiographical pact is playfully suggested and sometimes highlighted, their surroundings in *Tu rostro mañana* are clearly a product of invention. At the beginning of the first volume, *Fiebre y lanza*, its narrator-protagonist, Jaime Deza (also known as Jacques, Jacobo, Giacomo, Santiago, Jago, Jack, Jacopo, and Diego Deza) has just left his wife Luisa and their children, and has moved to London for a dull job at BBC radio. Soon, however, Sir Peter Wheeler, Professor of Spanish at the University of Oxford and friend and mentor of the narrator, incorporates him into British international intelligence service MI6. Part of a select group of interpreters, he works under a man known by the kafkaesque name of Bertram Tupra from now on. At first, he really only interprets; soon, however, he is asked to interpret persons as well as languages. He has to determine whether they speak the truth, what they are like, and what they are capable of doing; in short, he is to use his gift, "el raro don de ver en las personas lo que ni siquiera ellos son capaces de ver en sí mismas, o no suelen" (*Tu rostro mañana I* 313), or, in other words, the ability to know today "sus rostros mañana" (465). Gradually, Deza becomes aware that his judgments decide the fate of the people he studies – possibly, with lethal consequences. This realisation finally induces Deza to quit his job and return to Spain.

It is the employment of the narrator as a sort of MI6 spy (the mention of a James Bond novel in this context heightens the effect) that first imbues the novel with the sense that this narrative is an invention, and its action scenes in particular may remind the reader of this stereotypical sequence that is so very much part of the fictional. In *Fiebre y lanza*, Deza witnesses how his boss, Bertram Tupra, threatens to kill a Spanish diplomat with as extravagant a weapon as a sword. In the third volume, *Veneno y sombra y adiós*, Deza purposefully sets out to intimidate the new boyfriend of his ex-wife Luisa. As he discovers that this Custardoy batters Luisa, he does not hesitate to pay the man a visit, beat him up, hold him at gunpoint, and fracture his hand repeatedly. Other elements also suggest fictionality and invention: the fact that Deza's name is highlighted by its variety of forms indicates that he is not to be confused unthinkingly with the author, and when, towards the end of the work's third volume, Custardoy is introduced, the novel is definitively inscribed into Marías's fictional world – this Custardoy, after all, had already appeared in other works of the author, most notably in *Corazón tan blanco* (1992). The narrator's of this novel and that of *Tu rostro mañana* are not only distinguished clearly from each other, in spite of their similarities (they both have a wife named Luisa), but also from the real author: "Juan es intérprete en las Naciones Unidas y su mujer también se llama Luisa, por cierto".

In the face of these obviously fictional surroundings, the parts where the Spanish Civil War and its aftermath are addressed stand out all the more. At first sight, they seem to provide the fictional plot with continuity: they lean on the same non-autobiographical narrator who still resembles the real author, and are used as a further elaboration of the 'true face'-theme. A war, after all, provides the circumstances *par excellence* for people to show what they are really capable of. Narrator Deza has not lived to see a war himself, but he recounts a number of occasions where his father told him of his own experiences in the Civil War. What makes these passages seem so different from the inventions that surround them, is that they take on a particularly referential semblance without highlighting this in a metafictional way. Deza himself is reminiscent of the author, but it is also known that the story of his father's betrayal has been taken from real life: "Deza tiene algo del autor [...]. A la evidente asunción de la historia de su propio padre hay que añadir alguna de sus características" (Valls 300-301). In the acknowledgements, Marías's father Julián is one of those mentioned "sin cuyas vidas prestadas este libro no habría existido" (Marías, *Tu rostro mañana III* 707). Even more importantly, though, as the subject of the Civil War is broached in *Fiebre y lanza*, photographs are included to accompany the narration; these photographs lend these sections a decidedly autobiographical feel.

In *Fiebre y lanza*, two past events in particular are described. Both stories become recurrent motifs in *Tu rostro mañana*. One of them is the early death of Alfonso, the younger brother of Deza's mother, who was shot in the streets of Madrid during the first months of the war. Deza's uncle, who was only seventeen years old at the time of his death, comes to represent "todo horror y [...] toda guerra" (*Tu rostro mañana I* 90) – the way in which wars inspire people to behave ruthlessly and violently against innocent others. The narrator has found two pictures of this Alfonso among his mother's inheritance. One of them is the photo that was taken after his death, and which Deza's mother found in a police station when looking for her little brother; it was taken for bureaucratic reasons. The other photograph shows Alfonso, alive, and is reproduced on the pages of *Fiebre y lanza*. Deza describes his reaction to the first photograph, which he finds particularly shocking because of its contrast to the other one accompanying it:

> Mi impulso fue cubrirla de nuevo con el pedacito de raso, como quien guarece de cualquier ojo vivo el semblante de un cadáver, o como si hubiera tenido repentina conciencia de que uno no es responsable de lo que ve pero sí de lo que mira, de que lo segundo puede rehuirse siempre – puede elegirse – tras la visión inevitable primera, la que es traicionera, involuntaria, fugaz, la llegada por sorpresa. (208)

Here, the narrator describes how the photograph of the murdered uncle inspires a *punctum* of horror and aversion in him, and that the experience of his first look at the picture is so horrific precisely because he was not prepared for, and thus highly surprised by it.

The second story is that of Deza's father, who was betrayed by a friend at the beginning of the Civil War and consequently imprisoned and nearly sentenced to death. In *Fiebre y lanza*, the son recounts an occasion when he asked his father about this experience, and it is represented as a dialogue between father and son. Therefore, we see not only the father's, but also the son's (largely equivalent) evaluation of the story. The father, Juan Deza, admits that he had no idea of the true nature of his traitor: he had never suspected his friend Del Real of being capable of denouncing him for feigned reasons. It still appears "incomprensible, inexplicable" (203) to him. Though the traitor has gone on to make a successful career both under Franco and in the new democracy, while Juan Deza struggled for years to overcome poverty, the latter has always kept his mouth shut about what happened. Son Jaime expresses his surprise at the silence of his father, which he cannot understand in his wish to see some kind of justice done; but on the whole, father and son agree in their evaluation of past events.

In *Baile y sueño*, there is a third story, so terrible that Deza's father has never told it to anyone before telling it to his son. This story is not accompanied by photographs. In it, Juan Deza enters a café with a publisher who has just given him a translation job. Here, they encounter an acquaintance who starts bragging about his experiences during the war. He explains how he and some friends decided to kill a republican boy as if he were a bull in a bullfight. Once again, a seemingly civilised man turns out to have been capable of extreme and random cruelty with the war as an excuse. Not only was the deed extremely cruel, it was also performed upon a friend of Juan Deza's. The father of the narrator, then, had reason enough to make the story public when democracy arrived and the acquaintance had become a successful writer – and yet, he did not tell out of respect for the man's wife and daughter. Again, Juan Deza kept silent.

At a glance, then, these autobiographical passages serve to underline the dominant value system which the narrator maintains throughout the text, and which can be summarised in a question asked by Tupra, echoing a human rights discourse: "Por qué no se puede ir por ahí pegando, matando" (*Tu rostro mañana II* 408). The narrator uses his father's stories to elaborate on the question of violence and justice, carefully choosing a general perspective that does not privilege one side over another. Juan Deza explicitly points out that during and immediately after the war, there reigned "un descontrol absoluto, mucha gente [...] iba llena de ira. [...] Lo mismo en las dos zonas" (*Tu rostro mañana II* 300). Cruelty is not limited to political sides; it is present in certain humans. In fact, everyone, narrator Deza included, can have a cruel and violent 'true face'. In this context of what can essentially be considered the development of an ethical standpoint, the Spanish Civil War is mentioned often and extensively. The fact that the narrator connects it to his more general reflections on the nature of man, however, appears to lessen its importance. It is as if the mention of this war, just like the mention of a number of other ones, serves as an illustration of the narrator's general reflections only.

To see these autobiographical passages as mere illustrations of the general theme, or perhaps of the value system, of the novel, is to underestimate the force with which they interrupt the inventive flow of the novel. This force is caused first of all by the inclusion of the photograph of young Alberto, in *Fiebre y lanza*. There are more reproductions of posters, photographs, and pictures in *Tu rostro mañana*: in the first part, Second World War posters are reproduced, in the final part, paintings that Deza studies as he spies on his rival, art forger Custardoy. Yet the picture of Alberto as a young man accompanies the narration of his death – and this is what causes the *punctum* through which the dead haunt. The portrait of a now dead person is particularly unsettling when, as in this case, the photographed subject looks into the lens: Roland Barthes describes the "regard photographique" (172), a look which does not see, as paradoxical due to its mixture of intelligence and absent-mindedness, as it seems to be looking both at the spectator and inwards. There are more places in Marías's novel where a person's death is narrated, a photograph of that person alive included, and thus, haunting introduced onto the pages. In the third part, we read about the death of Jayne Mansfield, and her picture, which gave way to this narration, is shown (30). At the end, Sir Peter Wheeler's death is recounted, and his picture included (686) – the book's acknowledgements leave little doubt as to the identification of Wheeler with 'real' Sir Peter Russell, "que nació Peter Wheeler" (707). In both of these cases, the dead person is allowed to haunt the narrative through the picture, causing the viewer to feel the *punctum* as he or she realises that the person on the picture was alive once.

Such haunting through referentiality, which is accomplished by the use of pictures, turns the novel into a complex work to begin with. Reality is destabilised and a straightforward reading of the work may be hindered by a sense of ambiguity. The haunting process that is liberated by the Spanish Civil War fragments creates even more discordance, because of the shock and surprise that accompanies it. Alberto's photograph, together with the earliest reference to Deza's family history, is the first place where the fictional is abandoned to make way for the autobiographical, and for an aura of authenticity. Here, the surprise effect is stronger than in the cases of Jayne Mansfield's and Peter Wheeler's photographs. In due course, the other places where Deza's family's war experience is mentioned are also provided with an aura of authenticity.

The surprise of autobiography, of referentiality, is the more shocking here because of the cruelty of the events described. The connection of this shock to a painful past makes it possible that in a short, sudden moment, some of the horror of that past is transmitted. The past, as it were, intrudes on the novel through the *punctum*, first of a photograph, and then of the extended referentiality and autobiography connected to the photograph. Though autobiography is suggested all through the novel, it is counterbalanced by a strong undercurrent of fictivity. In the passages where autobiography is suddenly dominant, and where the effect of referentiality is heightened by, for example, the introduction of a photograph into a narrative, the reader may realise with a shock that the clearly fictional nature of the narration has made way for a seeming referentiality, and that the cruelties described *have happened*.

Here, then, autobiography and its connection, through photographs, with haunting, manages to turn *Tu rostro mañana* into a work that is far from concordant. The work is not only provided with an extra layer because of the appearance of the ghosts of some of the characters in its very fictional world, thus allowing for a reading that constantly hesitates between the possibility of autobiography and that of invention. It is also haunted by a painful past, and the reality of the cruelties described comes as a shock precisely because of their autobiographical nature. In other places in the novel, after all, cruel deeds are also described and thematised, but there, a 'protective' fictional layer lessens their impact. The James Bond-like background is a lot less terrifying, a lot less real, than the background of the Spanish Civil War. In the case of the Civil War fragments, the *punctum* is thus accompanied by a sense of horror at the nature of what is described.

As we have seen, Marías's narrator himself described the strong effect and emotion that surprise may cause as he talked of Alfonso's photograph and his unwitting discovery of it. The importance of surprise in the experience of horror is also thematised when Deza's father explains how he, quite by accident, overheard a fellow passenger in a tram. The woman pointed out a house to her companion, saying, for other passengers to hear: "Mira, ahí vivían unos ricos [...] y [...] un crío pequeño que tenían, lo saqué de la cuna, lo agarré por los pies, di unas cuantas vueltas y lo estampé allí mismo contra la pared" (300). Juan Deza explains that the remark impressed him deeply: "Me quedé helado y asqueado y me bajé en cuanto pude, para no seguir viéndola ni correr el riesgo de oírle contar más hazañas" (301). In fact, he mentions that he has still not been able to forget the terrible crime she proudly confessed to:

> al cabo de tantísimos años, cada vez que paso por la esquina de Alcalá con Velázquez no puedo evitar mirar hacia arriba, un cuarto piso, hacia aquella casa que la mujer señaló con el dedo una mañana de 1936 desde el tranvía, y acordarme de aquel niño pequeño muerto, aunque para mí no tenga rostro ni nombre y nunca haya sabido de él más que eso, un par de frases siniestras que el azar trajo a mi oído. (303)

The shocking impact an unexpected 'sinister phrase' can have on an accidental listener, which is further thematised when Deza's boss Tupra makes him watch all kinds of violent acts on video, is also experienced by the innocent reader of *Tu rostro mañana* who comes across such real cruelty by surprise in the middle of a fictional story.

At the same time that these passages on war crimes, precisely because of their surprising referentiality, can express the horror and the fundamentally incomprehensible nature of the violence of the Spanish Civil War, they also allow a reading that is much less in line with the norms and values of *Tu rostro mañana*. The focus on Alberto and on Jaime Deza's father Juan, and also that on the mother and the college friend who was killed in a pretended bullfight, suggest a reading where empathy is experienced towards these victims and where the reader may be tempted to put him- or herself in the place of the victim. Even if this is not always the same victim – Alberto was shot by Republicans, the father and his friend suffered at the hands of Nationalists –, these characters are the ones on whom violence is performed. While in the fictional parts of the novel, such identification is avoided (Deza's victim Custardoy is portrayed so negatively by the narrator, and Deza himself evokes so much sympathy, that the reader can easily side with the perpetrator), it is difficult to avoid it here. So, autobiography's referentiality both enables haunting and an empathic, 'simple', reading.

In *Tu rostro mañana*, autobiography's role is thus far from simple. It lets the painful Spanish past haunt the novel thoroughly, and its combination with a photograph's *punctum* maximises the shocking surprise effect. The cruelties described become real, historical cruelties, and this lends the novel much weight while at the same time allowing the past not just to be talked about, but also, to be felt in a highly disturbing way. Simultaneously, however, in a novel where the possibility of being a perpetrator as well as a victim is thematised and investigated, and where the boundaries of Self and Other are thus blurred and highlighted, the autobiographical moments undermine such a stance by allowing straightforward, moralistic identification with the victim. Thus, these moments' aura of authenticity both lets the past enter and allows the reader to make it his or her 'own'. Paradoxical as it may sound: the possibility of a simple reading besides a more complex one increases the work's discordance

Luis Goytisolo, *Estatua con palomas*

Unlike Javier Marías's *Tu rostro mañana*, Luis Goytisolo's 1992 novel *Estatua con palomas* does not appear to be a work of autobiographical fiction. Rather, it comes across as a quite traditional autobiography. Luis Goytisolo, the first-person narrator, remembers his past, and the reader is invited to accept an autobiographical pact as he describes scenes from his childhood against the background of his bourgeois family's struggle with the arrival of new times during the early years of the francoist dictatorship. He talks of his adolescence, of how he discovered literature, of his first loves. All the while, the similarities between the narrator and the author are striking, and their lives run parallel – which is particularly underlined by the appearance in the novel of Goytisolo's real-life brothers, fellow writers Juan and José Antonio.

This pact, however, does not hold: as it turns out, *Estatua con palomas* uses autobiography to lure its readers into a comfortably predictable reading, only to startle them out of it by making the plot turn 180 degrees. Suddenly, the autobiographical narration is interrupted by that of Junius Cornelius Scipio, a young Roman soldier and contemporary of Tacitus. A third-person narrative tells of his life in Rome and Alexandria, of the times he lives in – the first and second centuries –, and of the moral corruption of high society. From this point onwards, Junius's narrative and that of 'Luis Goytisolo' start alternating. At the end of the novel, it turns out that Junius's story is a fictional one that has actually been written by Tacitus. Tacitus is the second first-person narrator, whose voice takes the place of that of Junius, his creation. Then, another first-person narrator is introduced: David, a journalist, who has been interviewing Luis Goytisolo. It appears that Goytisolo's whole autobiographical narration has been a monologue told to David – who, in his own narration, mentions that he believes himself to be Luis Goytisolo's son.

Estatua con palomas's most striking quality, then, is the way in which it sets out to confuse the reader, making him accept the autobiographical pact and then violently breaking it. Its critics and the scholars that studied it have, therefore, stressed the importance of the reader. Ignacio Echevarría states that "[c]onviene [...] soslayar la perplejidad que, muy previsiblemente, ha de apoderarse del lector cuando [...] atraviesa las primeras cien páginas de este libro con la convicción de estar leyendo unas memorias" (87), and Wesley Weaver mentions that "[l]a lectura de *Estatua con palomas* lleva implícita una constante frustración de las espectativas del lector" (769). Rosa María Garrido concludes: "*Estatua con palomas* será [...] una obra con un referente histórico verdadero que cuestiona y subvierte tanto la historia como la ficción dejando que sea el lector el que decida si lo que está leyendo es verdadero o imaginado" (177). As if to demonstrate the importance of the reader, Garrido then goes on to discuss her *own* reading experience at length.

The confusion of the reader does not lessen after the moment the autobiographical pact is broken. Both scholars and critics point to the complex structure of the novel as the reason for ongoing and, indeed, increasing uncertainty as to how the different sections of the novel are related and by whom they are narrated. Weaver calls the novel a "rompecabezas" (763), a brain teaser; Garrido states that it is

> una obra de estructura complicada con referentes externos e internos a veces difíciles de dilucidar, y en la que la polifonía múltiple y confusa que constantemente subvierte el uso del yo y de las demás personas verbales exige una colaboración y dedicación que muchos lectores no estarán dispuestos a acordarle [...]. (177)

Indeed, the novel becomes increasingly fragmentary, and the reader often has to search for clues in each section in order to determine the identity of its narrator. Some sections are excerpts from letters, others are fragments from books that we may assume to be Tacitus's, and at one point, we are simply informed of the prediction of an oracle, a fragment which ends in mid-sentence (202-203).

However, as Fernando Valls points out, the structure of *Estatua con palomas* is really not all that complicated. It is simply "de una minuciosidad extrema y responde a un orden simétrico perfectamente establecido, pues las secuencias que componen los capítulos se organizan en un orden impar creciente hasta el nueve, para continuar en un orden par decreciente, 1/3/5/7/8/6/4/2" (120). One of the narrators of *Estatua con palomas*, Luis Goytisolo, reveals that he tends to organise his novels by numeric principles, and especially the number nine "no tardó en revelárseme como excepcionalmente útil" (262). Nor is the novel very complicated as far as narration or characters go. There is virtually no direct speech, there are only few characters, and the number of narrators is restricted to four. There is the 'autobiographical' narrator, Luis Goytisolo, who looks back on his youth; there is Tacitus, who narrates the story of Junius and reflects on his own life and works; there is Junius, who, in letters to friends, also has a voice; and there is David, who narrates the final chapter. The 'brainteaser'-like nature of the novel merely lies in the tardy revelation of who is narrating, precisely, and how that narrator relates to the others.

The novel is further made manageable by the parallels that can be established between the different narrations. The two stories, that of Luis Goytisolo interviewed by his natural son David and that of Junius and his creator Tacitus, develop in separate times and spaces. Though they seem wholly unconnected, their very juxtaposition suggests that there has to be a link between them. Fernando Valls notes that Tacitus is "utilizado – en cierta forma – como *alter ego* del autor" (121), an analogy that is supported by the parts of the novel where Tacitus and Goytisolo express their theories on literary and history writing. They both appear to be looking for their own voice, a different way of writing. Tacitus wants to find a way to make his narrative autonomous, to turn it into "una obra literaria, que, ni reseña histórica, ni discurso, ni poesía, ni intriga mundana, sea capaz de constituir un ámbito a la vez autónomo y superpuesto a la realidad" (339). Goytisolo describes a similar search for an own voice: "la formación del estilo, que es como decir de mi propia voz, fue mucho más paulatina" (261).

Both narrators struggle because they want to use fiction, as Valls puts it, "como vía de conocimiento" (120). Narrator Goytisolo makes clear that even when his writing is at its most autobiographical, it is still not intended as something individual and anecdotic. What he describes are "experiencias colectivas" (259), and his purpose in describing them "no es contar una experiencia personal, sino utilizar esa experiencia aparentemente personal para contar otra cosa" (260). In his view, literature is autonomous, but since it refers to certain shared, general experiences, it can contain a sort of higher truth and knowledge about the world or the collective to which one belongs. Tacitus, the historian, shares this outlook on literature: he wants to create "unos seres de ficción tan expresivos de lo que ha sido la vida romana desde los años de Domiciano hasta hoy, que el oyente llegue a tener la impresión de haberles conocido personalmente" (312). Both authors want to find a form to match this goal, and both find a solution by which they can "fundir ficción y realidad, historia y literatura" (312). Tacitus alters his ambitious history-writing project which so far had centred around Emperors, their families and other 'historical' characters, adding six books with the fictional Junius as a protagonist. Junius experiences and describes the decadent times in which he lives, travelling from Rome to Alexandria. The political situation is unstable: Domitian's cruel reign is at an end, and as he lies ill, different groups mobilise in order to seize power when the Emperor dies. Alexandria, moreover, has a number of prominent, competing ethnical groups and religions, most notably Jews and Egyptians. At the same time, sexual excess has become the norm among the wealthy Alexandria youth: orgies, perversions and aberrations are not uncommon. Immediately upon his arrival, Junius finds himself in demand with the women of Alexandria, and allows himself to be surprised and seduced by a young Egyptian woman who grabs him "por los genitales en mitad de la fiesta" (158). Just to what extent sexual morals are corrupted both in Alexandria and in the Roman capital is illustrated by the extravagant behaviour of Junius's friend Basilius Rufus, whose bestiality and perversion are shocking even to his own acquaintances.

Tacitus uses the fictional character of Junius as a way to make the reader familiar with the historical time he describes. He combines history with fiction, and a higher truth is the result. Luis Goytisolo, in another time and place, comes to the same conclusion. He discovers that by using autobiography to draw up a picture of certain historical circumstances, he may end up depicting collective experiences. What he describes is not merely his own childhood: it is the story of a family of an old, well-known Basque name that tries, and fails, to adapt to modern times. As Fernando Valls points out, this results in a departure from the individual and a shift to the collective:

> Empieza con la narración en primera persona de la infancia y adolescencia del protagonista (en este caso, narrador, protagonista y autor coinciden); el nacimiento de su vocación de escritor, en curiosa competencia con el descubrimiento de la sexualidad; el surgimiento de sus convicciones ideológicas, su antifranquismo; la visión y la crónica de su vida familiar, la relación con sus antepasados, con sus propios hermanos [...] y la merma del patrimonio familiar; para poco a poco ir abandonando lo personal y comenzar a incidir en lo público, en el trazado de unos anales de estos últimos decenios. (21)

Both Tacitus and Goytisolo have ended up finding the proper way of doing this. Tacitus has started writing historiographic fiction, a hybrid form which allows him to introduce the experience of the individual into the current of history; and Goytisolo has settled, first on the novel, "algo susceptible de transformar el mundo" (252), and now, on the interview: as he mentions to David, the novel is in crisis and he believes "en el porvenir de la entrevista como género literario", even if it is merely in the shape of an "entrevista a sí mismo" (330).

Yet the solutions that both narrator-protagonists have come up with also carry new problems with them. In spite of the fact that both Goytisolo and Tacitus have consciously decided to thematise the contrast between fiction and reality in their works and in spite of the fact that by doing this, they aim for a higher truth, their readers have instead always looked for the autobiographical in their works, treating these, rather, as individual accounts behind which the real authors are hidden. Narrator Luis Goytisolo complains: "Muchos son los críticos, sin embargo, que han creído detectar en mis obras elementos de carácter autobiográfico. [S]e equivocan al olvidar que, más de experiencias personales, se trata de experiencias colectivas" (259). Tacitus, in turn, suspects that he is banned from Rome because his protagonist, young Junius, ends up becoming Emperor – a fate holy books once predicted for Tacitus himself. Though Tacitus never wanted the reign of Rome, some enemies have interpreted Junius's fictional success as a sign of Tacitus's own ambitions:

> Lo irónico del caso es que un Blasio [...] adivinara la existencia de la conjura sin haber descubierto hilo alguno [...] por el significado que, con todo y ser un iletrado, desprendía de mis escritos. Es decir: por escribir la historia de un joven que había de terminar por convertirse en emperador, una biografía que Blasio juzgaba que tenía que ser entendida como autobiografía. (337)

The readers interpret the fictional worlds as autobiographies and do not pay attention to their fictional status.

Tacitus and Goytisolo are aware that they have become characters in their own fiction as a result of this reading. In the case of Luis Goytisolo, this status even surpasses his own texts: his brothers José and Juan have also written and spoken about their family, often embellishing stories or inventing them altogether, and narrator Luis Goytisolo tries to correct these falsities at length. Both Tacitus and Goytisolo find themselves involved in a struggle for autonomy within their texts: as they become characters, the borders between themselves and the characters they create become fuzzy. The final section of the novel reveals that Luis Goytisolo has really been a character in the novel all along, conceding an interview to a boy who believes he is his son. Tacitus wonders whether in future times, people will believe that it was Junius who wrote a work with Tacitus as the main character, instead of the other way round: "¿no convierte todo eso a su vez en Publio Cornelio Tácito en un personaje más de la obra? ¿No sería incluso lógico que en el futuro llegara a creerse que Junio Escipión había escrito una obra cuyo protagonista era Publio Cornelio Tácito?" (340). The independence of Tacitus's creation is most obvious when Junius starts manifesting himself as a narrator, albeit only in letters. And even Junius sets out to find his own voice: "La sensación que le poseía de haber encontrado su propia voz [...]. Ante todo, la convicción de haber estado tanteando una nueva forma de expresión, un tipo de creación literaria" (205). Literary characters become autonomous, then create their own style and their own fictional characters – and so on, *ad infinitum*.

The parallels between the Ancient-Rome-narrative and the modern Spanish one do not end with the shared occupation and concerns of Tacitus and Goytisolo or with the independence their creations gain at the cost of their authors. In both narratives, an important theme is sexuality – especially sexuality as an equivalent of writing. Junius's accounts of sexual abandonment among his peers and Goytisolo's frequent references to his love life go hand in hand with the literary preoccupations of all four narrators. In a telling fragment, Tacitus describes how Junius worries simultaneously about a writer's block caused by his extreme sexual activity, and about his fear of impotence later in life as a sort of punishment for his youthful excesses (129). Luis Goytisolo, on the other hand, explains how his sexual and his literary development went hand in hand, and how similar both impulses were to him (48). In either case, there is a connection between sexuality and literary creation, and impotence and writer's block.

The obvious parallel placement of contemporary Spain and Ancient Rome has had a marked effect on how scholars have looked at the novel. Many of them see the juxtaposition of both historical periods as a reason to read one as a commentary the other. For it could be argued that the decadence and chaos of the times of Junius (whose young age may well be the age Tacitus had at that time), followed by the stable period under Traianus of Tacitus's old age, is an allegory of recent Spanish history. Indeed, both Garrido and Weaver read the novel this way, but their interpretations vary. Garrido claims that there is an analogy between Franco and Domitian, and that the period of relative stability is analogous to Spain as a recent dictatorship (176). Weaver, on the other hand, sees the censorship that was typical of the francoist period in Spain mirrored in the imperial censorship of Tacitus's times (764), of which Tacitus himself becomes a victim under Traianus, forced to resign from his position as proconsul of Asia and to retire to his farm in Etruria. This would mean that the chaotic and bloody beginning of the Spanish dictatorship is equivalent to the equally bloody years of Domitian's reign, and that the later, more peaceful but still dictatorial decades are analogous to Traianus's more stable years as a *princeps*.

It is quite understandable that scholars such as Garrido and Weaver focus on the parallels between the two stories of *Estatua con palomas*. The similarities between the narrators and their literary struggles point towards such an interpretation, and so does the fact that the two periods appear to have a lot in common. In both cases, a period of crisis and decay asks for a new form of literature that can provide general knowledge of the world in its latest incarnation, and in both cases, the narrator-protagonists attempt to create such a new form of literature. Alicia Molero de la Iglesia mentions that *Estatua con palomas* (as well as other novels by Luis Goytisolo) investigates "la certeza de que el ser social sustituye un dios por otro igualmente tiránico, [...] la pérdida de los valores y la disolución de las costumbres" (372-373). But are these scholars right in looking, above all, for the parallels between the story set in Ancient Rome and the story set in dictatorial Spain?

The novel's ideological structure and its value hierarchy suggest the opposite. In *Estatua con palomas*, there are four main evaluators: Junius, Tacitus, Luis Goytisolo and his son David. As we have seen, Luis Goytisolo dominates the first one hundred or so 'autobiographical' pages of the novel, so that we read his judgment on a large number of subjects. Goytisolo talks about his youth under the francoist dictatorship, carefully describing his bourgeois family, their social surroundings and the norms and values of those times. He portrays with great detail the roles assigned to various family members: the bachelor uncles, the spinster aunts who were made godmothers of their nieces and nephews. He paints a lively picture of the holidays spent in the family's country home, and of the school years and friendships of himself and his brothers. He mentions an early development of "mis dotes de observación" (90): these allow him to see, also, the effects the Civil War had on his family. His mother's death in a bombing, which casts a "sombra de la muerte" (90) over the family, leaves him to be raised by a servant and by his grandmother, who suffers from Alzheimer's disease and harbours "una verdadera obsesión relacionada con el hambre pasado durante de la guerra civil, que la impulsaba a hacer acopio de toda clase de restos de comida" (84).

The narrator positions himself as an observer, a role that suits him particularly well when the novel progresses and the supra-personal gains importance. This shows, for example, in the objective tone he uses to analyse changes in Spanish society. According to him, the strict sexual morality of the first francoist decades was replaced in the 1960s by a period of "convulsiones" (283) and scandal, after which a normalisation of sexuality followed, giving way to a "consolidación del dinero como valor supremo" (284). Nevertheless, there are many places where the narrator is less objective and speaks on a more personal note. He describes his family as representatives of a certain class in a changing

160

world, but he also talks of his own coming-of-age, which is centred mainly around two important themes: that of sexuality and that of writing. It is in discussing these themes that the narrator pronounces the clearest judgments on the society he lived in – judgments that the reader would expect to find, rather, in the descriptions of his political activism. He admits:

> [L]a exaltación ideológica y las consecuentes actividades subversivas, anduvieron siempre relacionadas con la amistad. Y el tiempo de dedicación que me tomaban tenía más bien el carácter, en relación al resto de mis actividades, de tiempo muerto, una especie de contribución o tasa a la que moralmente me obligaban mis convicciones antifranquistas. A diferencia de lo que era patente en otros, mi toma de partido o, si se prefiere, mi compromiso político, no obedecía a ninguna clase de necesidad profunda [...]. (52)

The one place where Goytisolo really feels hindered by francoism is no doubt the domain of sexual morals. Goytisolo devotes numerous pages to his romantic conquests. His own sexual initiation is handily dealt with: "A mis diecisiete años, la iniciación sexual en un prostíbulo era la norma" (171). The girls, however, are expected to remain virgins until their wedding night – and it is there that young Luis experiences catholic francoist morals as oppressive. He describes, for example, his troubles with a girl named Lola whose constant escort of an aunt and a cousin "me hizo desistir de ir todo lo lejos que hubiera deseado" (164).

Interestingly, the other evaluators undermine this largely dominant discourse. There are numerous parallels between the four of them: they all write, and they all establish a connection between sexuality and writing, which share a dark undertone, an "oscuridad de sus orígenes" (257), as narrator Goytisolo puts it. But Junius, Tacitus and David express judgments on society's morals and, in particular, on sexual liberty, that differ greatly from those of Luis Goytisolo. Junius behaves as an onlooker who describes the decadence he sees all around him, yet he also participates in the orgies of his friends. Nevertheless, he writes to a certain Fulvia that he is naturally inclined to only have one lover at a time: "¿Seré yo, acaso, el único para quien, en el fondo, no existe más que una sola persona?" (170). In the places where he is a character and Tacitus's narration is focalised through him, Junius expresses wonder at the political unrest and the simultaneous sexual excess; this judgment is shared by Tacitus, who, also appearing briefly as a character in his own books, does not approve of the free sexual morals: "Costumbres en las que, al igual que en el afeminamiento cada día más frecuente entre los muchachos, Tácito distaba mucho de ver una manifestación de salud de la sociedad romana, un juicio en el que probablemente tenía razón" (185).

Junius and Tacitus as characters and narrators see the extreme lack of sexual morals as an unhealthy aberration. Roman society of Junius's youth is the opposite of post-war francoist Spain: it is decadent, excessive, and it lacks norms. These two narrators thus provide a different view on Goytisolo's love of women, which he brags about repeatedly. The third narrator, David, enhances this effect: he is the product of Luis Goytisolo's libido, not recognised by the writer and thus fatherless. Of course, David is to be seen as an invention of his father, the writer; sexuality and writing are comparable processes, and both the novel and the son are creations, children of the writer or father. But David is also an independent narrator who, in turn, can turn his father into a character. The Luis Goytisolo he calls up is not the flamboyant intellectual observer of the autobiographical part of *Estatua con palomas*. Instead, David sees a rather unsympathetic man who is quite aloof:

> La palabra apropiada era cortés, un hombre de una cortesía algo inquietante por lo que pudiera tener de compensatoria: la clase de cortesía que tiende a mantener distancias antes que a reducirlas. Fuera o no de su gusto, fuera o no del mío, esa era la impresión que ofrecía el novelista, no a través de las páginas de sus novelas, sino considerado en su propio ambiente [...]. (322-323)

The autobiographical narrator of the first pages is cast in another light altogether; and the parts of the novel set in Ancient Rome do not only break down the autobiographical pact, but they also offer a judgment different to that of the narrator.

But critics and scholars do not appear to mind much. It is remarkable how they follow the utterances of narrator Luis Goytisolo in their interpretations. By searching for parallels, they still try to read the contemporary Spanish part *through* the Roman story. Garrido, for example, points out that Tacitus mentions that he spent a short time in prison once, and reads this as a reference to a similar episode narrator Goytisolo talks of: "Experiencia que hay que relacionar con las cinco semanas de aislamiento que Luis Goytisolo pasó en el penal de Carabanchel" (175). Echevarría argues that "Lo que importa, con todo, es la afinidad de ese supuesto empeño [de Tácito] al del propio Luis Goytisolo" (88). Valls, as we have seen, calls Tacitus the "*alter ego* del autor" (121). In this novel, indeed, the value hierarchy is so structured that the apparent dominant, the value system of the autobiographical narrator, is counterbalanced by other, distinct ideologies. These, and especially that of narrator David, lessen the importance of Goytisolo's narration. Yet as we have seen, many of its readers see this differently and still consider his values and judgments as highest in the hierarchy.

It seems that in spite of the text's attempts at undermining the autobiographical narrator's claim to truth, at unbalancing it and showing that it was just as fictional as any other element of the novel, its readers and critics ultimately still favour the autobiographical narrator over the others. In the light of the shock effect that the interruption of autobiography causes here, it may safely be said that such a highly concordant reading is remarkable – as Weaver accurately asserts, "El engaño inicial de una imposición de lo autobiográfico, texto yuxtapuesto con otros [...] tiene el efecto de debilitar la fuerte presencia autorial inicial" (769). This text openly invites discordance, wanting to confront the reader with his or her expectations, exposing the fictionality of autobiography and complaining emphatically about the usual tendency of readers and critics to look for autobiographical pacts that are founded on equivocal assumptions. It seems that the surprising construction of the novel makes the reader *temporarily* aware of the fact that the autobiographical narrator has the same status as someone like Tacitus, that he is, in fact a fictional creation, but in the end, the reader is still drawn to this autobiographical narrator and subordinates the others to him.

Perhaps, the concordance that autobiography unwittingly imposes here is the result of the very fact that it is linked to the Spanish traumatic past. Put quite simply, scholars would like Goytisolo's narrator to be responsible, so that his non-fictional counterpart can also be said to fulfil his moral duty. They admire the complexity of the novel and the unreadability that is provided by the text, but ultimately, they would like to see it perform the very responsible task that it so openly rejects. Paradoxically, the force of autobiography's unmasked referentiality is so seductive that this aura attracts readers even if it is deconstructed within the very text. Here, then, autobiography works just as forcefully as in the novel of Marías, but the aura of authenticity ultimately leads to concordance and violent readings.

As a result, memory narratives become confused as well. The narrators, particularly Goytisolo and Tacitus, clearly steer away from an all too personal memory and want to sketch a society-wide decline. Both these narrators' explanations of their struggle in finding their own mode of writing, and the dramatic and shocking departure from a memory that is too personal, show how the aim must have been to overcome the personal and anecdotal, and to focus, rather, on society at large. This 'objective' view does not pay too much attention to personal sufferings, to crime, justice or punishment, but it wants to observe what once was. The novel, in other words, tries to portray pasts with distance and rationality, avoiding the unrepresentative and personal nature of autobiographical remembering, but also the focus on supposedly historical events and persons that turns history writing into something too abstract.

However, the possibility of reading the Roman past through the Spanish one has caused no few readers to see in one a critique of the other. This leads to a possible understanding of *Estatua con palomas* not as a work that wants to deal with the past 'from a distance', but as a novel which is, in fact, highly critical of the dictatorship. Unwittingly, it seems, the text has ended up becoming readable exactly as it claims it does not want to be read. It is seen as a complicatedly structured but ultimately autobiographical and personal comment on francoism, which, by comparison to an unstable era of Ancient Rome, is highlighted as a particularly unwholesome period. Luis Goytisolo and Tacitus, we find, were but too right in their fear of losing control of the text.

Javier Cercas, *Soldados de Salamina*

Soldados de Salamina by Javier Cercas (2001) is a novel that usually provokes the same question in its critics: why has it become so success-ful? What has caused its numerous reprints and translations? What made it a best-seller? In short: what makes this novel stand out? In their attempts to answer this question, critics and scholars alike tend to settle upon an aspect of the work that is the very reason why they themselves strongly criticise it. They seek the novel's success especially in the way it deals with its subject, the Spanish Civil War. Nora Catelli calls *Soldados de Salamina* "la primera novela histórica de la Guerra Civil": it uses the Civil War as if it were a "fichero que pone en marcha el mecanismo de la aventura". Catelli points out that this treatment of the War was a breaking point in contemporary Spanish fiction: "en 2001 toda narrativa de la guerra civil anterior a Javier Cercas pareció conver-tirse en pasado". Catelli even speaks of an "efecto Cercas", visible in novels by Manuel Rico and Juan Carlos Arce, which imitate his use of the Spanish Civil War as en exciting historical background.

Soldados de Salamina is thus the first novel to stop treating the traumatic past of the Civil War as a difficult theme, using historical data to construct a fictional, thrilling narrative. Many critics point out that this interplay of 'historical fact' and fiction in *Soldados de Salamina* determined its success. In *Soldados de Salamina*, the past is not a painful matter or trauma, on account of "la liquidación de la actualidad de la guerra civil y de sus consecuencias" (Catelli). The War simply makes for an exciting story that can be lifted above its context. Not for nothing does the book title refer to a wholly different war, the battle of Salamis between the Greeks and the Persians. In this war, "todas la guerras del mundo se rememoran simbólicamente" (Pozuelo Yvancos 278). Besides, the key scene of the novel itself, to which I will return shortly, has "una fuerza simbólica tremenda" (278).

This treatment of the Civil War as a background for a historical novel, which is considered highly innovative, has also been criticised severely. *Soldados de Salamina* has been called revisionist not only in

Spain, but also in Germany. It is accused of "acercarse a los verdugos de la historia sin descalificarlos" (Moreno), and of equalling the adventures of fascist ideologist Rafael Sánchez Mazas it narrates to the sufferings of the anonymous republican soldier who saves his life, which would be "una forma de convertir un indulto legítimo (el miliciano perdona la vida al jerarca falangista) en una amnistía mutua, casi deportiva" (Mainer 103). And finally, the plot of the novel has been deemed frivolous and exaggeratedly exalted, leaning on an archetypical hero and provided with a happy ending (103). *Soldados de Salamina* thus appears to be raising ethical questions. The work is felt to dwarf the importance of the particular historical circumstances it describes, and its hybrid form that openly fictionalises biographical and historical material is what makes it 'irresponsible'.

Soldados de Salamina is not only a controversial best-seller and a hybrid 'historical novel'. It is also a typical case of autoficción, where an autobiographical pact is called up, broken and, in that way, thematised. Although the protagonist has a lot in common with the author – his name, and the titles of the novels he has previously published –, the Cercas in the novel is different: he is divorced, childless, works as a journalist, and is of a different age than the author of the same name. The real Javier Cercas, by contrast, is a university lecturer and a family man (Pozuelo Yvancos 284). Remarkably, Pozuelo Yvancos is convinced that the autofictional nature of *Soldados de Salamina* has been "una razón de éxito", since it makes the story "muy actual, muy moderno" (281). Yet compared to the spectacular nature of the chosen historical material and the laborious process, described in the novel, of turning this material into fiction, the autobiographical material appears rather bleak by comparison. As we shall see, the suggestion that all this 'really happened' is provided extensively by countless references to historical data and historical characters, and by, for example, the inclusion of a photograph as 'evidence'. The autobiographical moments seem part of this enterprise, yet their role appears secondary. How, then, does autobiography function in this novel?

In Soldados de Salamina, a first-person narrator called Javier Cercas goes through a personal crisis: his wife has left him, his writing career has stranded before it even fully began, and his father has just died. By coincidence, this narrator-protagonist, a journalist, interviews writer Rafael Sánchez Ferlosio. Sánchez Ferlosio tells him the story of his father, Rafael Sánchez Mazas, "el primer fascista de España" (82), who was imprisoned by the republicans in the Catalan sanctuary-turned-prison of Santa Maria del Collell during the final days of the Civil War. He was to be executed by a firing squad along with other prisoners, but miraculously managed to escape. Upon fleeing the scene, he was overtaken by a republican soldier – but magnanimously, the soldier saved his life by telling the others that "¡Por aquí no hay nadie!" (20). After this incident, Sánchez Mazas managed to survive for days in the woods with the help of three local boys who had deserted from the republican army. Together, they waited for the nationalist troops to come.

Decades later, Cercas is asked to write a commemorative article about republican poet Antonio Machado's tragic death just over the French border in 1939. To enliven this well-known fact, he mirrors it with Sánchez Mazas's escape from death, which occurred more or less at the same time on the other side of the border. After the article has been published, Cercas receives a letter from somebody who claims to know more about the execution. Cercas concedes to a meeting, and from that point on, he starts investigating more and more seriously what exactly happened before, during, and after the execution. He speaks with the surviving two *amigos del bosque*, as Sánchez Mazas called the republican deserters; he discovers the diary Sánchez Mazas kept in those days; and gradually, he becomes obsessed with the story. After extensive research, he writes a detailed account of the whole event, based on facts and complemented with conjecture, in which the meeting of Sánchez Mazas and the merciful anonymous soldier who saved him occupies a central position.

Soldados de Salamina departs, as has become clear, from what may be called 'historical facts', as Cercas himself admitted ("Cercas se confiesa"). Rafael Sánchez Mazas actually existed, and he really did escape death at Collell. However, the story of his escape, and in particular, the part of the enemy who lets him live, is ripe for fiction. Indeed, in many places of the novel, the episode is described as "novelesco" (35, 198), and it is not surprising that many of the characters in *Soldados de Salamina* expect Cercas to turn it into a novel. Moreover, many elements of the episode as it is reconstructed in the second part of the novel are fictional. Though the narrator points out repeatedly that he has thoroughly investigated sources and compared versions of the same story, he is forced to admit that "lo que a continuación consigno no es lo que realmente sucedió, sino lo que parece verosímil que sucedió" (89). A delicate equilibrium of fact and fiction emerges that explains the generic title of 'relato real' Cercas gives to his retelling of the story.

Soldados de Salamina is a novel-in-the-making, as Pozuelo Yvancos calls it (284). In the work's first part, the narrator explains how he investigated the story of Sánchez Mazas, how he wrote and thus fictionalised it. The narrator presents himself as an unbiased and neutral journalist searching for truth. To underline this, he painstakingly documents where fabulation begins and fact ends. He repeatedly attempts to make his story credible by differentiating fact from fiction and pointing out how narration always replaces actual memory. As he first focuses on the story of Rafael Sánchez Mazas, which the man himself has recounted numerous times all through his life, journalist Cercas is aware of how it is repeated almost word for word: Sánchez Mazas ended up retelling "no [...] lo que recordaba que ocurrió, sino lo que recordaba haber contado otras veces" (43). He is very excited when he finds a film fragment of the writer telling the story just after it happened: "no pude evitar un estremecimiento indefinible, porque supe que estaba escuchando una de las primeras versiones" (42).

Having thus shown his ability to distinguish fiction from fact, the narrator attempts to make his story even more credible by documenting all kinds of minor details. For one, he faithfully renders the name of every single café he visits on his quest to solve the puzzle. He also includes proofs which may not be conclusive, but which strongly suggest that his own reconstruction of what happened has a factual basis: the pages of the diary Sánchez Mazas kept in the days he was hiding in the forest are reproduced photographically in *Soldados de Salamina* – as we have seen, an effective way of making the reader feel Barthes's *punctum*.

That the narrator-protagonist highly values evidential proof becomes clear on numerous occasions during his search. When he finds out that Pedro or Pere Figueras, one of the *amigos del bosque*, was imprisoned in Gerona, he visits the Historical Archive of the town and looks for Figueras's name on the list of prisoners. He is shattered when he does not find it, and considers giving up his quest: "pensé: 'Todo es mentira' [...] y ya me disponía a salir de la biblioteca, anulado por una sensación de vergüenza y estafa" (64-65). But when the librarian points out to him that Figueras's name figures on the list with a slightly different spelling, he moves from despair to cheerful optimism, happily concluding that "si la estancia de Pere Figueras en la cárcel no era una invención, tampoco lo era el resto de la historia" (66).

All the while, the narrator seems to avoid judging or evaluating the things he describes – consistent with his role of the independent and objective journalist. His only motivation appears to be curiosity and a lack of better things to do. He came across the story of Sánchez Mazas quite by accident, and follows up on it simply out of interest. There are places, nonetheless, where the journalistic investigation, realistic as it may appear, is not completely dry or objective. Some of the secondary characters Cercas encounters are portrayed as eccentric, due to their big appetite, for example. One of his informants "engullía grandes bocados de arroz empujados por vasos de tinto" (30), "examinando con avidez su enorme entrecot, con el cuchillo de carnicero y el tenedor en ristre, listo para atacarlo" (32), and after leaving his plate "tan limpio que relucía" (34), the young man takes his leave "con una mancha de chocolate" (37) in the corner of his mouth. Moreover, the segments in which the narrator describes his struggle to make his writing career take off and his budding relationship with tv astrologist Conchi provide the novel with the necessary comic relief. The overall theme appears to be a quest for truth, during which the narrator rather selflessly points out how much value he attaches to an unbiased approach of the painful past.

The result of the investigation described in the first part of the novel is a large essay on Sánchez Mazas's war experiences. This essay forms the second part of *Soldados de Salamina*. The narrator of this part is the same, Javier Cercas, the journalist – but here, the narrator leaves out all references to his own life, and concentrates on a precise reconstruction of what happened, hoping to accomplish an "interpretación del personaje [de Sánchez Mazas] y, por extensión de la naturaleza del falangismo o más exactamente, de los motivos que indujeron al puñado de hombres cultos y refinados que fundaron Falange a lanzar al país a una furiosa orgía de sangre" (143). This continuation of the objective, journalistic approach and the attempts of the narrator at supporting his story with facts or proofs all contribute to the effort of convincing any reader of the probability, if not factuality, of the story. Here, too, the cause pursued is that of impartiality and truth-finding.

As we have seen, the narrator admits that he cannot know everything that happened, and that he is often filling in gaps. However, even in these cases, he strongly argues that his version is at least acceptable. He refers to others: "como afirma Andrés Trapiello" (65). He presents alternative stories when they exist: "las versiones de lo que a continuación ocurre difieren" (94). He even comments on the reliability of Maria Ferré, a young girl who provided Sánchez Mazas with food and shelter, and of the two surviving '*amigos del bosque*'. One of them, Daniel Angelats, remembers waking up in the forest one night and hearing Rafael Sánchez Mazas telling the story of the soldier to Pere Figueras. Pere himself has died, and there is no one else to corroborate this scene. Nevertheless, the narrator deems it reliable, since "Angelats es un hombre sin imaginación; tampoco se me ocurre qué beneficio podría obtener él – un hombre cansado y enfermo, a quien no quedan muchos años de vida – al inventar una escena así" (119).

The narrator is obviously doing everything in his power to deliver a convincing reconstruction of what happened. But as his narration continues, it becomes more and more obviously fictional in nature. This does not only have to do with the lack of any concrete information, which forces the narrator at some points to use his imagination and fill in the blanks. Rather, the narration is embellished with passages such as this:

El autobús recorre en silencio Barcelona, convertida por el terror de la desbandada y el cielo invernizo en una desolación fantasmal de ventanas y balcones cerrados a cal y canto y de grandes avenidas cenicientas en las que reina un desorden campamental apenas cruzado por furtivos transeúntes que triscan como lobos por las aceras desventradas con caras de hambre y de preparar la fuga, protegiéndose contra la adversidad y contra el viento glacial con abrigos de miseria. (96)

The use of adjectives like 'fantasmal' and 'glacial', as well as the comparison of men to wolves, make the narration acquire a tone that is romantic or tragic rather than journalistic or matter-of-fact.

It becomes clear quite quickly that this change is caused by a focalisation shift. The story is narrated more and more 'through' Rafael Sánchez Mazas: we see what he sees, and how he sees it. The presence of Sánchez Mazas becomes increasingly explicit: "Sánchez Mazas siente que el corazón se le desboca [...]. Empieza a andar a la cabeza del grupo, desquiciado y temblón, incapaz de pensar con claridad, indagando absurdamente en la expresión neutra de los soldados armados que bordean la carretera una señal o una esperanza" (101). At this point, we are able to read Sánchez Mazas's thoughts: fiction definitely takes over. Whereas the reconstruction of Sánchez Mazas's feelings and thoughts is still rather predictable, the narrator later on allows the fugitive writer to become an independent fictional character – independent of actual facts, that is. When he can rest for the first time since his escape, his outdoor refuge appears paradisiacal to him and even reminds him of some poetry he once read: "le afloraron a los labios, como un brote incongruente de aquella imprevista plenitud, unos versos que ni siquiera recordaba haber leído: *Do not move / Let the wind speak / That is paradise*" (110). Perhaps, this focalisation of the narration through a falangist of high position has added to its scandal.

Yet, though the account of Sánchez Mazas's escape is thus fictionalised increasingly as the narration goes on, this second part of the novel keeps up a semblance of authenticity. Locations and time frames are scrupulously mentioned, and the choice of a protagonist who existed outside of fiction heightens the feeling that this is a very realistic reconstruction of what 'really happened'. The admission of the narrator that he had to use his imagination to fill in some gaps does not undermine, but rather enhance, this effect. The aura of authenticity is corroborated by the suggestion of an autobiographical pact that is not always maintained, but that is especially convincing exactly in the parts where the narrator-protagonist acts as a journalist-investigator – since we read the result of his investigations, we are easily brought under the impression that these investigations must really have taken place outside of the fictional world.

Clearly, the first two parts of *Soldados de Salamina* are dominated by the values of a narrator who, in spite of lapsing into downright invention, does what is in his power to give a truthful reconstruction of events. But all this changes in the third part, where Cercas embarks on a search for the republican soldier who saved Sánchez Mazas. This soldier gains importance due to an unlikely coincidence. During his search, Cercas has been informed that Sánchez Mazas recognised the heroic soldier and identified him as the prison guard who once, in a memorable scene, had started dancing in the rain and singing the melancholy pasodoble "Suspiros de España", to the entertainment of soldiers and captives alike. Cercas can hardly believe his luck when Roberto Bolaño, a befriended writer, tells him about a remarkable man he met while working, as a young man, at a camping site in Spain. This camping guest, Bolaño mentions, had fought in practically every war, was very probably in Collell at the time of the execution, and was known at the camping site for being a fervent dancer, especially fond of pasodobles. The description immediately brings to mind the unknown republican soldier, and Cercas decides to look for the camping guest. He finds him eventually in a residence in Dijon, and quickly discovers that he was not mistaken: though the old man, Antoni Miralles, will not admit to being the hero of Sánchez Mazas's story, he does concede he was one of the fascist's guards, and gives himself away precisely by admitting that the pasodoble Cercas's friend had seen him dance to was "Suspiros de España".

In this final part, the narrator lets go of his actively pursued role of a journalist who, as an outsider, tries to find out the truth. What has started as a journalist's curiosity ends up being a personal road to a sort of salvation. After completing his investigation and writing the *relato real* in the first two parts, the narrator feels something is lacking: "el libro no era malo, sino insuficiente, como un mecanismo completo pero incapaz de desempeñar la función para la que ha sido ideado porque le falta una pieza" (144). And he is not the only one. His girlfriend, Conchi, reads the manuscript and is not impressed. She blames the subject: "Ya te dije que no escribieras sobre un facha. Esa gente jode todo lo que toca" (144). As it turns out, she is right – the missing piece is in fact a republican.

All of the narrator's interest for objectivity has gone, by this stage. What started as the story of a fascist who survived his execution thanks to one of his executors now touches on something the narrator-protagonist deems essential:

> Pensaba en Miralles, al que pronto vería, y en Sánchez Mazas, al que no vería nunca; pensaba en su único encuentro conjetural, sesenta años atrás, a casi mil kilómetros de distancia, bajo la lluvia de una mañana violenta y boscosa; pensaba que pronto sabría si Miralles era el soldado de Líster que

salvó a Sánchez Mázas, y que sabría también qué pensó al mirarle a los ojos y por qué lo salvó, y que entonces tal vez comprendería un secreto esencial. (180)

Suddenly, the adventures of Sánchez Mazas and his *amigos del bosque* disappear to the background as the second character of the work's pivotal scene gains importance. There, the novel acquires, as Pozuelo Yvancos mentions, a generally ethical dimension:

> [La escena] no sería tan emocionante si fuese solamente literaria. En realidad si nos impresiona tanto es porque alcanzamos a ver en ella una dimensión ejemplar, profundamente ética: el subrayado que es imposible encontrar un heroísmo mayor en ese gesto que en todos los gestos de muerte. Miralles es un héroe anónimo y perdido y encarna y representa el sentido moral de muchos héroes de guerras perdidas. (278)

Antoni Miralles himself is the character who best expresses the ideology dominating the final part of *Soldados de Salamina*. The true hero of the novel realises quickly that he is to be converted into the hero of Cercas's book project, which annoys him greatly. He bursts out: "No hay héroes vivos, joven. Todos están muertos. Muertos, muertos, muertos" (199). Miralles makes it clear: the real heroes of wars are those young boys who lose their lives in battle, too young to have experienced the good things in life or to have become important enough to be remembered. Miralles, who has fought in very many wars after the Spanish Civil War ended and who, covered as he is in scars, represents the archetypal soldier, here phrases the inhumanity of war – *any* war – and the tragedy it brings to the lives of individuals.

Cercas's emotional involvement and his ethical turn are remarkable. Miralles becomes both a new father figure and an inspiration to this frustrated writer, as becomes clear from the downright cathartic final paragraphs of the novel. In these last lines, whose cathartic nature is mainly due not only to their rather emotional content, but also to the near absence of any full stops, combined with an abundance of commas and of the word "y", the narrator imagines how his life could be from now on: "y formaríamos una familia estrafalaria o imposible y entonces Miralles dejaría de ser definitivamente un huérfano (y quizá yo también) y Conchi sentiría una nostalgia terrible de un hijo (y quizá yo también)" (206). This value system resembles that of Javier Marías's *Tu rostro mañana* in that it incorporates the specific Spanish trauma into the traumas of other wars. What is different here, however, is that the Civil War does not actually haunt the narration. The one episode highlighted from the period instead stresses the nobility and courage of an individual, and thus conveys the rather optimistic message that even in the worst of circumstances, man can rise above himself and show pity. Every soldier in every war is a potential hero, as Miralles has pointed out. And, as the other protagonist of the pivotal execution scene shows, even the highest-ranked fascists were simple human beings, too.

The contrast between the narrator's value system here and in the first and second parts, where he is concerned with separating 'truth' from fabulation and refrains from evaluations or judgments, is great. At the beginning of the novel, the narrator values objectivity, truthfulness and historically correct representation – hard as this is to achieve – above anything. It is only in the last part of the novel that he realises that the *story*, its resolution, and thus, its *fictionality* is more important; and as he searches for his hero, he becomes concerned with an essence of general human knowledge. He does so reluctantly, and refuses, as Bolaño suggests, to invent a final scene with Miralles without having to go and search for him. He states that "mi libro no quería ser una novela, sino un relato real [...] inventarme la entrevista con Miralles equivalía a traicionar su naturaleza" (170). But, as Mario Vargas Llosa puts it: "lo literario termina prevaleciendo sobre lo histórico".

There are, thus, two opposing value systems at work here, and the last one ends up dominating the novel. The narrator changes his earlier ideas on how to write *Soldados de Salamina* and is immediately rewarded for this move with a happy ending. He is convinced, and tries to convince his reader by conveying his own emotions strongly at the end of the novel, that dry historical fact alone does not 'speak' to a reader; it needs to be fictionalised, provided with a hero, turned into a story. Then, a sort of mimetic representation of reality can be achieved, where an essential literary truth can touch and improve the lives of readers and narrator alike. The new perspective shows that *Soldados de Salamina* does not, or does no longer present us with a discourse of truth-finding. Rather, it seems to bank on an emotionality that surpasses the 'realistic'.

Along with this shift in values, the autobiographical pact is gradually abandoned. Though in some form, it is still maintained, the disappearance to the background of the semblance of authenticity in favour of the literariness of this story ends up undermining the pact strongly. No longer does the reader look upon the narrator simply as the investigator and writer of another person's story. His involvement, carefully introduced in the first part, is now complete, and the objective distance has been replaced by a more active role. The narrator-protagonist becomes more of a protagonist of his own story, which foregrounds the fact that he is a fictional construct not referentially linked to the author.

Interestingly, then, *Soldados de Salamina* shows the conviction that the authentic does *not* come with an aura which, on its own, provides for a truly fascinating narrative. It is the fictional that lifts a story above its realism, that is, so the narrator claims, capable of emotionally involving its readers. Cercas's novel ultimately rejects the authentic in favour of the fictional. Referentiality and (auto)biography do not have enough 'power' to the narrator. They are used, here, in a completely unsurprising way: they are not put into play to cause surprise or shock, but rather as a means of luring the reader into an autobiographical pact and thus into an acceptance of the story told without having to question the narrator's authority. While in the beginning, the role of the referential may well have been to evoke empathy, the narrator finally wants to rise above this 'weak' emotion and resorts to the fictional for reaching some sort of (to put it in Aristotelian terms) catharsis.

Ultimately, it may be exactly this choice of a narrative where the fictional ends up prevailing over the factual, that make some real readers protest. Of course, a large number are only too glad, probably, to find that their reading of *Soldados de Salamina* has turned out to be so satisfyingly cathartic, and this may be a further explanation for its becoming a best-seller. At the same time, though, the work's refusal to be satisfied with the actual truth, with historical facts, and its trading in of the investigation of a particularly Spanish trauma for a more comforting 'general' knowledge, must seem like unethical revisionism to other readers.

Soldados de Salamina is in fact a very dualistic book: it suggests two readings, consecutively. First, it stresses the importance of truth, and the need to find out how a historical reality was actually shaped. In this first reading, the choice of perspective is such that empathy is created both with the journalist-investigator, whose perspective is that of a non-participant, and, eventually, with the nationalist whose story he writes. Then, however, *Soldados de Salamina* takes a very moralistic turn, and it imposes a new reading that is supposedly better than the first one, because it is more gripping and touching – identification with the victim, and with the narrator, are strongly pursued here. This presence of two different ways of reading one and the same historical event makes the novel discordant and often contradictory. It is perhaps its own, openly stated choice for the second reading that makes this novel controversial.

Conclusion

At the beginning of this chapter, I suggested that autobiography might cause a *punctum*, a surprise, and that this surprise might surpass the Aristotelian rational emotion. In doing so, I – too quickly, perhaps – passed over a trait of autobiography that the analyses of two out of the three novels analysed here have brought to the foreground. Autobiography, it has become quite clear, does not only function discordantly in novels. Depending on the text and the way it puts autobiographical moments to use, it can also have a decidedly strong and influential concordant impact. The referentiality it endows the text with, and the credibility and authority it lends to the first-person narrator, both cooperate to suggest one reading only – and usually, this is the reading the narrator prescribes.

The analysis of *Soldados de Salamina* shows that a work of autofiction, which uses autobiography in a metafictional way, need not provide any *punctum* whatsoever. Though the novel consciously provides its readers with a feeling that what is described there 'really happened' (and autobiography is called upon to support such an impression), it goes on to conclude that the inclusion of such a truth claim in itself is not enough to make it a worthwile read. Any emotionality here is not provided by autobiographical or, for that matter, 'historical' moments. Emotion is not derived from *punctum*. Instead, real readerly involvement can only be reached, the novel concludes, by invention. Only in this way, a sort of 'meaning' may be derived from a work; and this meaning is valid for all human beings, rising above its local circumstances. Starting out as a novel that valued the search for truth and justice above all, the work replaces this democratic value system with an interest for the more generally human. In this way, it both suggests two different readings, thus showing its own discordant nature, and chooses the one that is (in the post-structuralist sense) the most violent and the least ethical one. This is a choice that has angered some of the readers of *Soldados de Salamina*, though others, of course, might well prefer the guilt-free and edifying reading experience the novel itself seems to advocate.

Estatua con palomas does use autobiography to surprise the reader. Goytisolo's novel does everything in its power to deconstruct autobiography and show its fictionality by brutally interrupting what began as an apparently conventional autobiography. Out of nowhere, the reality of the Roman Empire interrupts the descriptions of postwar Spain, and the novel turns into a confusing play where narrators, characters, and storylines show disturbing parallels. As it turns out, though, autobiography's seductive referentiality, its aura, manages to beguile the work's readers, even those trained as literary scholars. Though the autobiographical narrator's authority is undermined, inverted, and destabilised, they *still* fall into autobiography's trap, showing every inclination to follow the bruised and battered autobiographical narrator's instructions in their readings. What is worse, they actually read the narrations of the three other narrators *through* the autobiographical account, thus subordinating the former to the latter. The work, in the end, illustrates one of its central themes: the difficulties an author encounters in maintaining control over his text. Autobiography, here, is a force so strong that it seduces readers to perform a strangely concordant reading of a work that is asking for its very discordance to be recognised.

In Javier Marías's *Tu rostro mañana*, autobiography shows its discordant nature. Here, its aura allows a process of haunting to intrude on the work's structure. Of course, there are more auratic elements in *Tu rostro mañana*: estranging objects and uncanny occurrences that suggest the possibility of haunting. Yet the inclusion of photographs, particularly photographs of persons whose death is described in the accompanying text, creates the strongest and most direct possibility of *punctum*, and they provide the scenes they are connected to with the strongest autobiographical, referential semblance. Particularly the places that talk of the impact of the Spanish Civil War on Deza's family stand out, not in the least place because the earliest mention of this impact is accompanied by the first photograph, rendering the surprise effect strongest. But while the painful past is thus allowed to intrude on the novel and destabilise it through its felt absence, making the horror of that past *felt*, the very autobiographical and referential nature of these parts also allows a reading at odds with the novel's value system. While the novel thematises the fact that anybody can be a criminal as well as a victim, these parts allow the reader to identify with the victim, first and foremost. An empathic reading is made possible while it is discouraged at the same time.

That autobiography is a powerful force is thus beyond doubt. That the surprise it may cause when used in fictional settings may be connected to and perhaps enlarged by haunting, has also become clear. At the same time, though, it can be used as a concordant force, and in this case, the very attraction of referentiality that makes it so disturbing when used in a surprising way can now turn the autobiographical narrator into an authority figure whose narration can be followed unquestioningly. This authority can be so strong, in fact, that it can induce readers to perform violent, concordant readings even when the novel is openly discordant.

The authority of the autobiographical narrator-protagonist clearly makes his responsibility in dealing with a traumatic past all the more important. As we have seen, readers of Goytisolo *want* his novel to be more moralistic than it is – and Cercas's work is criticised for promoting a neutralising view of the past. Finally, *Tu rostro mañana*'s clever use of autobiography's aura of authenticity in the midst of fictional elements actually manages to call up the ghost of the traumatic past, so that the apparent neutralisation of that past is undone – but it also introduces a possibility of siding with the victims in a reading that does not match with the work's overall theme. It is clear that memory novels which play with autobiography and fiction will end up creating a contrast between the autobiographical and the fictional – and that certain parts of a novel, or certain narrators, may acquire more, or rather a different kind of, authority than others. Where fiction and referentiality struggle for dominance and recognition, a level of discordance and a rivalry of memory narratives become difficult to avoid.

CHAPTER 6

Fearsome Tropes and the Uncanny

Gothic, Uncanny and the Tropes of Fear

In fiction, the monstrous or the inhuman, which, Ricœur found, threaten concordance, can intrude in a text in a great number of ways, and processes of haunting are omnipresent in contemporary culture. But there exists a literary tradition that performs this intrusion in the most literal way imaginable – by allowing ghosts, the undead, and the haunted house a place in the narrative. This is certainly the case in the three novels this chapter investigates: a wide variety of terrifying tropes find their way into the works. So, in *Luna lunera* by Rosa Regàs, a villainous tyrant inhabits a spooky mansion, and in Carlos Ruiz Zafón's *La sombra del viento*, a deserted castle contains a crypt, a chapel with a Rasputin-like Jesus on a cross, a room where stains appear in the shape of faces, and a library where invisible hands move the books around. In *La casa del padre* by Justo Navarro, haunted houses once more abound, as well as truly monstrous, deformed characters. Are these motifs thus actually frightening, and do they really scare the reader? And if so, is this fear a reason for heightened discordance?

At first sight, it does not seem very likely that these tropes cause discordance, and the level of fear they produce seems rather limited. This is because all of these tropes belong to what Ruth Amossy describes as an autonomous field in contemporary culture, whose purpose it is to scare. According to her, fear has been industrialised and commercialised. The industrialisation of fear

> délimite un domaine culturel qui transcende les genres et les media. Elle s'accomode de l'image et du verbe, du film et du livre. Elle se nourrit d'œuvres tirées de catégories habituellement distinctes comme le conte fantastique, le roman d'horreur et la science-fiction. Elle récupère à son profit les textes du passé en s'incorporant le roman gothique de la fin du XVIIIe siècle, les contes de Edgar Allan Poe réédités dans des collections de poche, l'étrange fiction de Lovecraft utilisée comme trame de films nouveaux. Un brassage incessant s'y effectue à des fins commerciales avouées, une circulation perpétuelle où Dracula émerge indéfiniment de son cercueil, où toute horreur couronnée de succès se démultiplie automatiquement (*Halloween I*,

II et *III*) où le *remake* est de rigueur (*King Kong, La Mouche*, …). (Amossy, *Les idées reçues* 122)

Amossy sketches an extensive conglomerate of motifs in an ever-growing and commercially successful body of works. In this field, one trope is capable of calling up all other cultural products associated with fear. The domain of fear is not a static entity with a fixed place in history, but a body of all kinds of cultural expressions that imbue one another with new meanings, shaping and reshaping each other through mutual contamination. Genres and forms such as the science fiction novel, the vampire movie or the Gothic novel have been incorporated into this domain, loosening themselves from their origins. Since the domain is extensive as well as commercially viable, the tropes of ghost stories, horror movies, and science fiction have become overly familiar. They may appear predictable, banal, omnipresent, even boring – in short, they have become concordant elements in cultural narratives. In Amossy's words: the motif, or stereotype, of fear "contribue à delimiter un espace fictif hautement conventionnel où l'épouvante se donne comme jeu" (136). The reader recognises the narrative as one of fear and enters into a 'game of fear' by allowing him- or herself to get spooked.

The fear that scary narratives call up thus becomes linked to expectation, and it seems that for that reason, it is rather close to the Aristotelian tragic emotions of surprise, pity and fear. The reader empathises with the character, fears for him or her, and experiences shock and surprise when he or she is confronted with the monstrous or the inhuman. Indeed, this is a view on the fearful that was already expressed by Horace Walpole, author of *The Castle of Otranto* (1794). It is commonly agreed that the Gothic genre, "given principal expression through the novel, [with] a life span of approximately 56 years", was "given life in 1764 with the publication of Walpole's *The Castle of Otranto*", after which it gained enormous vitality and success until it "died allegedly somewhere around 1818 or 1820" (Wolfreys 8). Walpole, whose work thus stood at the basis of this highly successful genre, saw the fear his novel tried to inspire in its readers as a tragic Aristotelian emotion, as E.J. Clery notes (Walpole xx) in the first preface to *The Castle of Otranto*. According to Walpole, "Terror, the author's principal engine, prevents the story from ever languishing; and it is so often contrasted by pity, that the mind is kept up in a constant vicissitude of interesting passions" (Walpole 6).

In part, this interpretation of Aristotle may rest on an erroneous take on the tragic emotion of 'fear'. Walpole assumes that Aristotle's fear is the emotion his readers experience when, together with the protagonist, they are confronted with the supernatural and the inexplicable. Yet Aristotle speaks of "pity for the man suffering undeservedly, fear for the man like ourselves" (Aristotle, *Aristotle's Poetics* 57): the rational emotion of fear is provoked by empathy and concern for the protagonist, not by any supernatural event. James Hutton finds that "the two emotions [of fear and pity] form a pair [...] since they tend to be different reactions to the same kind of event" (95), and D.W. Lucas agrees: "Flesh may be made to creep by the portrayal of supernatural or infernal powers or by the suggestion of the uncanny [...]. But the majority of plays at all times make their impression by quite other means. A more universal effect of tragedy is, by revealing the precariousness of the human condition, to make men fear for themselves. This could be the point of the definition of fear [...] as being concerned with those like oneself" (Aristotle, *Poetics* 274). Yet even though Walpole's description of terror may not be in accordance with Aristotle's fear, it does seem to rely heavily on surprise – another one of the tragic emotions.

The question is, though, whether such mild surprise and empathic shock were the only experiences Walpole's readers went through upon their reading. Jacqueline Howard points out that this and other Gothic novels, most notably Ann Radcliffe's *The Mysteries of Udolpho*, effectuate "the recontextualization of superstitions, folklore, and a discourse of the sublime which operates as a more or less unproblematic extension of the 'real', and encourages belief in the uncanny" (6), and this was a real rupture in late-eighteenth century Europe. As a result, the novels of Radcliffe and Walpole might have frightened susceptible readers even when, at the end, the supposed supernatural often turned out to have a 'rational' explanation. The fearsome irrational was a new, surprising element, and as such, it might have caused what Amossy calls "La surprise qui annule l'esprit critique" (135). This type of surprise would certainly supersede the 'rational emotion'.

Be all that as it may: nowadays, the haunted castle, the tyrannical parent, the animated statue, the crypts and vaults, to name a few Gothic conventions (Howard 13), no longer belong to the Gothic novel only, and it seems that to use these stereotypes in a novel is not enough in itself to scare the reader. The genre has been integrated into the cultural domain of fear, as a part of its repertoire (Amossy 130). Julian Wolfreys argues that a broader view of the Gothic is now necessary: countering definitions of the Gothic in terms of 'genre', he reconceptualises it as a "gothic mode" (13) – the lower case is intentional – that exists independently of the genre, a mode being in Chris Baldick's definition "an unspecific critical term usually designating a broad but identifiable kind of literary method, mood, or manner that is not tied exclusively to a particular form or genre" (139-140). The advantage of perceiving of the gothic as a mode is "that the term *genre* [is] reserved for the study of individual works in their relationships to specific and historically identifiable traditions", Ulrich Wicks says. "Modal awareness allows us to see the *general* fictional makeup of the individual narrative work" (241). Like the ironic or comic modes, the gothic mode becomes something that can be 'called up' in any narrative. In due course, these motifs have lost their original meaning and no longer have the impact they could still impart in the original Gothic genre.

The gothic has thus lost its body, materiality, and attachment to a limited selection of literary works at the cost of its capacity to really disturb the reader or spectator. If we accept Wolfreys's definition, and talk of the "spectralization of the gothic" (7), we find that the gothic becomes "one proper name for a process of spectral transformation [...]. Cast out of its familiar places, the gothic is dematerialized into a somewhat unpredictable tropological play" (7). The domain of fear thus absorbs the Gothic genre and transforms it into a process of haunting. As such, it can leave its traces in any number of places: in the real world, and, for that matter, in a fictional world as well. Wolfreys reaffirms: "The gothic is thus one name for acts of spectral troping which we otherwise name the ghostly, the uncanny, the phantom" (14). Wolfreys sees the gothic mode as a particular form of haunting.

Whether this mode's spectral tropes actually scare a reader or viewer remains to be seen. The tropes within the cultural domain of fear have become familiar and predictable, and it seems that only those newly produced and suited to one's own era may rise above stereotypicality. Taking Edgar Allan Poe's "The Fall of the House of Usher" (1839) as an example, Amossy argues that fear does indeed have a historical dimension. In the days when Poe's story, in which a premature burial takes place, was published, the fear of being buried alive was "une obsession collective" (*Les idées reçues* 132): the difficulty of determining whether the deceased were actually dead, paired with the discovery of a number of cases where this problem had indeed led to live burials, inspired terrible fear in Poe's contemporaries. Amossy claims this story is not nearly as terrifying now that scientific and technological progress has greatly diminished the possibility of such mistakes. Even if the idea of a live burial may not appear particularly pleasant to us, this fear is nothing compared to the terror Poe's contemporaries experienced in knowing that this was a real risk threatening them. Amossy goes on to state:

> Chaque époque donne à ses obsessions des formes nouvelles. [...] Les objets d'épouvante ne se réduisent cependant pas aux seules formes qu'une époque donnée désigne explicitement à l'attention des contemporains. À côté des stéréotypes ancrés dans une réalité daté et qui expriment une obsession collective, on trouve des motifs anciens que l'actualité investit d'un sens nouveau. [...] En ce sens, les stéréotypes de la peur se rattacheraient à leur contexte socio-culturel propre alors même qu'ils semblent à première vue y échapper. (133)

The nature of fear, Amossy claims, depends on social and cultural circumstances. This goes not only for the choice of trope or stereotype as fearful, but also for the reappropriation of already existing tropes. The meaning invested in them differs according to the fears of each context. Amossy cites Stephen King to illustrate this premise: according to him, *The Exorcist* was a success because of its subtext of parents losing their children, a theme close to the hearts of the early 1970s American audience (133-134).

The historical dimension of fear places the fearsome tropes we find in contemporary Spanish novels into a new perspective. In themselves stereotypical, predictable, and not necessarily discordant in nature, their connection to a specific fear of Spanish society may make them scary nonetheless. On the one hand, of course, Spain's fears and preoccupations are those of the entire Western world. Whereas nowadays, the belief in irrational forces has greatly diminished compared to the heyday of the Gothic novel, the wars of the twentieth century and their aftermath have given us an entirely new frame of reference as to what we fear. It could be said that any connection to the mid-century 'trauma' of fascism might succeed in providing uncanny tropes with the necessary urgency. In the Spanish context, on the other hand, these fears know a very specific incarnation. In the case of contemporary Spanish novels, it is almost impossible *not* to think of the repressed past as a collective ghost, as my discussion of Isabel Cuñado and Jo Labanyi in chapter 2 illustrated. It seems possible that if a trope of the fearful manages to establish a connection with this past, or with another fear or preoccupation shared collectively by a contemporary audience, it may succeed in being frightening.

Even if this is the case, though, this in itself is not enough for such scary motifs to actually produce fear, as Freud's essay on "Das Unheimliche" illustrates. In this essay, Freud investigates the uncanny, a phenomenon he provisionally defines as "das Heimliche-Heimische [...] das eine Verdrängung erfahren hat und aus ihr wiedergekehrt ist" (75): the unfamiliar return of what was familiar once. He stresses that the experience of the uncanny is a decidedly human emotion, and claims that it is a consequence of a primitive, animistic phase we all go through early in life: "Es scheint [...], daß alles, was uns heute als 'unheimlich' erscheint, die Bedingung erfüllt, daß es an diese Reste animistischer Seelentätigkeit rührt und sie zu Äußerung anregt" (70). In the first place, the uncanny is thus an *emotion*, an unpleasant and creepy feeling of disturbance, uncertainty, and fear. Nevertheless, Freud's discussion of what we experience as uncanny takes as its main point of departure the uncanny *in literature*, and it centres around *motifs* that provoke this feeling. In an extensive analysis, he illustrates his concept of the uncanny by showing instances of it in a number of literary works – focusing above all on E.T.A. Hoffmann's 1816 short story, "Der Sandmann". Among the uncanny motifs he enumerates are *Doppelgänger* (Freud 63), severed body parts (73), and haunted houses (71); there is the "Motiv der belebt scheinenden Puppe" (61) and the damaged, hurt, or otherwise disturbed eye, since according to Freud, it is "eine schreckliche Kinderangst [...], die Augen zu beschädigen" (59).

As Freud himself admits, it is remarkable that a psychoanalyst like himself would turn to literature to describe such a generally human phenomenon. "Der Psychoanalytiker verspürt nur selten den Antrieb zu ästhetischen Untersuchungen", he notes. "Hier und da trifft es sich doch, daß er sich für ein bestimmtes Gebiet der Ästhetik interessieren muß, und dann ist dies gewöhnlich ein abseits liegendes [...]. Ein solches ist das 'Unheimliche'" (45). It seems that Freud feels that the experience of the uncanny is one that is best explained by looking at tropes and conventions, and these in turn are most easily found in literary works.

Of course, the uncanny's reliance on certain motifs brings to mind the gothic mode; its tropes, with their stress on the monstrous and the inhuman, could certainly be described as fearsome tropes. Indeed, they occasionally overlap: the haunted house, the *unheimlich Heim*, is a trope that we see both within the uncanny and within the gothic, and which is essential to the concept of haunting itself. After all, haunting is a disruptive element within a structure – and the mention of a structure (in the sense of a whole whose parts are related) indicates an importance of place within haunting. The haunted house is the most literal illustration of such a structure. We can thus see the uncanny as a mode that functions similarly to the gothic mode: its spectral troping can turn up in any contemporary text. Possibly, then, we might just speak of a 'mode of fear', a form of haunting that fills the text with the echo of all other texts belonging to the domain of fear. But this, then, would be a form of haunting that is only really disturbing if it touches upon a real fear within the reception context. Otherwise, the tropes of the uncanny, just as those of the gothic, might not lead to any fearful surprise at all.

However, unlike the gothic, the uncanny is not just defined by its motifs. It is, first and foremost, an experience: the experience of disturbance, or, as Freud himself calls it, the unfamiliar return of the repressed:

> So muß es unter den Fällen des ängstlichen eine Gruppe geben, in der sich zeigen läßt, daß dies ängstliche etwas wiederkehrendes Verdrängtes ist. Diese Art des ängstlichen wäre eben das Unheimliche [...] dies Unheimliche ist wirklich nichts Neues oder Fremdes, sondern etwas dem Seelenleben von alters her Vertrautes, das ihm nur durch den Prozeß der Verdrängung entfremdet worden ist. (70)

This, then, *is* an emotion of surprise that does away with the critical spirit – it is a feeling of terror that leaves the reader spooked. Such a feeling of disturbance and openness, if it is called up, is bound to make a novel seem indeterminate and discordant to a much higher degree than if it was merely the cultural domain of the fearful that would haunt through its motifs. Now, on the one hand, the tropes of the fearful are familiar, recognisable – but, on the other, they become estranged. As a mode, the uncanny is part of the domain of fear – particularly now that Freud's essay has become a 'classic' of the fearsome itself; as a feeling, however, it relies on the combination of and contrast between what is familiar to a reader and what is strange.

Unsurprisingly, Freud struggles with the connection of tropes and feeling. He has to admit that uncanny motifs in themselves do not always inspire the feeling of the uncanny in readers of literature. Freud refuses to conceive of *Hamlet*'s ghost as uncanny, for example: he reasons that in the realm of fiction a breach of real world conventions is to be expected, so that the appearance of a ghost is not really all that shocking. In a footnote of *Spectres de Marx*, Jacques Derrida finds this turn of thought remarkable – for it seems to imply that uncanny motifs cannot really disturb a work of fiction, precisely because it is fiction and allows for the supernatural within its boundaries. It seems rather odd, therefore, to go looking for it in the one place – literature – where it supposedly does not occur. And this while, Derrida exclaims, "tous les exemples de *Unheimlichkeit* sont dans cet essai empruntés à la littérature!" (275). But as John Fletcher remarks in his analysis of *Spectres de Marx*, Derrida is mistaken here: Freud does not suggest that *all* fiction prevents supernatural events from appearing uncanny. It really depends on the text's genre and its conventions (33): if the laws established *by* the text and *in* the text are 'realistic' enough to make a ghost strange to the novel's reality, then there is ample room for uncanny emotions to be evoked.

Derrida's mistake is understandable, however, for Freud's description of this mechanism leaves ample room for questions: he finds fairy tales so unrealistic that they exclude the uncanny, and states that only a work which presents us with common reality can produce the uncanny – not taking into account the fact that 'common reality' is a concept that moves in time, or that the primitive nature of a fairy tale may be so strange to us now that this very temporal distance operates as uncanny. It might be better to say, then, that the uncanny is called up in a text if its motifs create a certain ambiguity, if they are not unproblematic in the course of novelistic action. The uncanny is awakened precisely when it is *unclear* what the status of the fearful tropes is in the novel. What Freud's essay does show, however, is that the tropes of the uncanny (or rather, the tropes of the fearsome) do not *have to* disturb the text or narrative in which they appear. If the ghost, the haunted house or the vampire appear as perfectly natural, unambiguous elements of the fictional world, they inspire no fear inside or outside the work. Only if they break the work's internal rule or blur its boundaries, the *feeling* of the uncanny may be evoked. Here, we seem to have landed on a second quality of motifs of fear that heightens their chances to overcome their own stereotypicality and cause actual fear – besides, of course, the quality of their connecting to a collective fear or preoccupation in their reception context.

As a result, the motifs of the cultural domain of fear in contemporary Spanish novels may well be undisturbing parts of the fictional realm, not creating any particular discordance, fitting in with the general direction the works take and not disrupting the novels' realities. At the same time, though, the fear they inspire may rise above Aristotelian surprise or empathy with a literary character faced with something frightening. Then, as the reader's own fears are addressed, and feelings shared by a society called up, a novel's discordance may be enhanced greatly. This means that memory novels talking of the painful Spanish past, such as the three I investigate in this chapter, are quite likely to establish a link between the shared preoccupation with the past and the stereotypical motifs of the fearsome. Is this really the case? If it is, do the motifs actually create a sense of uncanniness and disturbance? And if they do not – do the novels really retain a semblance of concordance? The following chapter investigates what the consequences are of the tropes of fear in Spanish memory novels.

Justo Navarro, *La casa del padre*

Justo Navarro has called his 1994 novel *La casa del padre* a "novela gótica" (Echevarría 152); and indeed, it is remarkable how many fearsome tropes can be distinguished in the work. Most of all, though, the text is filled with the uncanny tropes Freud summed up – from *Doppelgänger* and haunted houses to war veterans missing body parts or characters who only have one eye or who wear the wrong glasses, so they "[entrecierran] siempre los ojos turbios" (Navarro 62). A boy suffering from frost bite appears "un ingenio mecánico" (66) who "crujía como un autómata" (65), bringing to mind the 'live doll' motif. It would seem that this work contains enough spooky elements to enable a very disturbing type of haunting. However, the novel can be said to contain a very clear hierarchy of value systems, so that it seems rather concordant at the same time. How, then, do these uncanny motifs function?

The story of *La casa del padre* revolves around an unnamed protagonist-narrator, who recollects an important episode of his youth: the six months he was supposed to have left of life on his return from hospital, decorated with a Second Class Iron Cross after fighting for the *División Azul*, the Spanish army division that helped Nazi-Germany on the Russian front. The protagonist's limited life expectations, due to machine gun pellets in his lungs, do not prevent his mother from sending him to his uncle in Granada to study law, because disease in their home town of Málaga is threatening to kill him even before the six months are over. On the drive to Granada, the protagonist makes some acquaintances: Portugal, a journalist, and an eccentric property hustler, the Duke of Elvira. Though the protagonist does not like Portugal in the least, he soon realises, once in Granada, that the reporter is his ticket to getting out of his uncle's big, dark house to spend many a happy afternoon with the Duke of Elvira and especially his wife Ángeles, with whom he has fallen in love instantly. Eventually, however, Elvira's vocation of blackmailing people into selling him real estate below market value results in his murder. Portugal also seems to disintegrate, and the only person who wins is the protagonist: he lives much longer than the allotted six months, finishes his studies, and marries Ángeles. At the end of his six months of life, moreover, he discovers that his uncle is actually his real father, which relieves him of having to remember a father who died ungraciously in a bar toilet.

In *La casa del padre*, the narrator's voice is the most important one, so that he is usually the evaluating instance. He looks back from modern, democratic times upon the first years of the francoist dictatorship, but he does so with surprisingly little critical distance. In spite of the fact that the narrator looks upon the past from a post-dictatorial perspective, he avoids passing judgment on the events and circumstances he talks of. Instead, the narration is consistently focalised through the narrator's younger self, and since this protagonist is firmly positioned as an outsider, a spectator, the picture he paints of the past is that which an observer would paint. This is not an entirely neutral observer, however: the young protagonist's view on life has been coloured by his war experiences. Since his return from Russia, the boy can only see the world around him conscious of the inevitable decay of all that is beautiful. Even when he gets to dance with an attractive young girl, he is suddenly overcome by an awareness of her fate: "Vi bailar a la hija del farmacéutico con muchos, y era emocionante: estaba predestinada, dentro de diez años habría envejecido, estaría fea, y luego se pondría más vieja y más fea, y luego se moriría" (58). The contrast between his tender age and lack of experience with women, and his already ample experience with putrefaction and death, becomes painfully clear. To make matters worse, he feels constantly stared at: "me miraban y querían descubrir en mí la marca de la muerte" (187).

The protagonist's decidedly nihilistic stance may serve as an explanation for his approach to the society he lives in. The period he describes is a moral vacuum, and this is something he seems to take as a natural state of things. Society as he describes it is a dog-eat-dog world. The protagonist himself is a coward who lives in constant apprehension of being harmed. Like most people, he avoids standing out and attracting attention for fear of what could be done to him: "Nadie se miraba dentro del tranvía [...]. Un hombre no desvió los ojos, y me imaginé que era uno de la policía secreta o un confidente" (153). He is afraid of being "interrogado sobre un asunto del que no sabía nada" (196). There are more cowards present on the pages of *La casa del padre*, towards whom focalisation shifts occasionally. There is, for example, Larraz, the director of the cinema in Málaga, who is terrified of being associated both with fascists with an all too cruel reputation, and with well-known *vencidos*, for fear of standing out: "porque no quería destacarse" (22).

There are those, however, who use the moral vacuum to their own good. Prime example is the Duke of Elvira, who cleverly enriches himself by making use of the situation of the immediate postwar. As a distinguished falangist who has met both Alfonso XIII, Franco and José Antonio Primo de Rivera, he is in the position of blackmailing the less fortunate with their pasts. All through the story, the protagonist professes great admiration for the Duke of Elvira, even though he realises all along that his behaviour is not, strictly speaking, very ethical. This sympathy for Elvira is understandable: amid a nation consisting mostly of cowards, Elvira is a flamboyant risk-taker who does not mind standing out. It is not surprising that the protagonist, a frightened, shy outsider, looks up to this worldly man. Journalist Portugal has also adapted to francoist society and writes propaganda for fascist newspapers, though before the war, the protagonist discovers, Portugal did not side with the nationalists. All in all, the world depicted is characterised by what Navarro himself calls "la atmósfera de grisura moral y mezquindad afectiva que impusieron los vencedores en los años cuarenta: un mundo de máscaras en estado de congelación" (Márquez). In such circumstances, one has to take advantage of others whenever one can, telling lies if necessary to save one's skin.

Towards the end of his six months of allotted time, the protagonist has learnt his lesson and develops from a scared liar into a happy opportunist. After Elvira has been murdered, it is the protagonist who ends up as the winner: he gains Elvira's wife and daughter, unscrupulously taking Elvira's place. What is more, upon Elvira's death, he comes into the possession of documents and photos painfully incriminating those whom Elvira tried to blackmail. No wonder, then, that he claims to have "muchos y excelentes amigos" (Navarro 294), including the King himself. He also suggests that he may have had something to do with the suicide of his childhood bully, the cousin of Elvira:

Sólo guardé por diversión algunos papeles del Duque de Elvira que recogían debilidades juveniles del ingeniero Espona-Castillo Creus, primo del Duque de Elvira y nuevo Duque de Elvira, mi antiguo condiscípulo en el colegio jesuita de Málaga. Espona-Castillo Creus [...] se pegó un tiro cuando se rumoreaba que dormía la siesta con un novillero [...]. Entonces destruí también los papeles que conservaba sobre Espona-Castillo Creus, porque hay que olvidar, la memoria feliz y limpia está hecha de olvidos. (295)

It is clear that the narrator-protagonist has managed to explain away any latter-day scruples or regrets by opting for the comfortable possibility of forgetting. He likes to state that "no tengo memoria", that "siempre he querido perder la memoria" (67) and that "sólo tengo memoria para lo bueno" (295).

But it is never possible to forget entirely, as the narrator's wish to tell us his life story makes plain. What also becomes obvious from his story, and particularly from the way he keeps stressing his own forgetfulness and happiness, is that he is aware that the discourse of amorality may not satisfy every interlocutor. Clearly, he knows that the value system he adapted to so well clashes with the value system of the society he lives in now, and that his past behaviour may seem right to *him*, but that it needs to be explained to a contemporary audience. Occasionally, therefore, he explains his choices in a way that sounds almost apologetic. He tells us how he used to lie constantly, mostly to please people – "sólo era para agradarle" (264), he remarks – and how he would invent stories to tell his uncle and make up tales about his life in Russia to impress Ángeles. Apparently feeling that this needs motivation, and that the narratee may judge this tendency to lie quite harshly, he clarifies why he felt the need to lie: "era agradable mentir: mentí por comodidad, por hablar lo menos posible. [...] Era insoportable decir la verdad: daba sueño" (232-233). The narrator here defends himself, stating that lying was the most comfortable option in those days. At the same time, he shows that the ironies of his paradoxical turns of fate – the coward becoming a war hero, the immoral opportunist a famous judge – are somehow uncomfortable to him, and that he prefers not to think through his past life all too much. "En cuanto uno se descuida", he says at the end of his narration, "recordar se convierte en aturdimiento, una invasión de voces dentro de la cabeza, voces que se rozan, se tocan, se empujan, se pisan, se atropellan, se aplastan entre sí, callan de pronto y te dejan vacío" (295). The latter-day narrator is not at ease where his memories are concerned.

It may be concluded, as a consequence, that there are two different normative discourses at work that determine the value hierarchy of this novel. First of all, there is the amoral discourse of the narrator. In his description of the early Spanish 1940s, the narrator makes it perfectly

187

clear that, in the absence of justice and morals, anything could get you killed, and that violence was frequent and random. The narrator does not openly attach any negative value to such amorality, by which he has been influenced to the point of incorporating it. In fact, on the final pages, he points out (in a tone that frequently sounds defensive) that his amoral value system has done him all the good in the world: he is influential, happy, and married to the woman of his dreams. Secondly, however, there is a normative discourse which is largely implicit: that of the narratee, that of the present. On the final page of the novel, the narratee is openly addressed by the narrator: "Mañana le seguiré contando" (295). Here, the real reader may feel spoken to, and in this way, the text indirectly incorporates his or her own normative discourse.

Unexpectedly, perhaps, the dominant discourse here is not that of the narrator. Though the text is apparently controlled by the narrator, and most of the characters adapt to this value system or behave according to it, this discourse can only be described *in relation to* what came before it or, in this case, after it: we can only speak of a moral vacuum when we define it through a discourse that is *not* a moral vacuum. One discourse thus implies the other. The narrator is an unreliable liar, whose admission of amorality reads, at times, defensive. The narrator knows that he is judged by his narratee; he explains his motivations, but realises where the narratee may disagree with him.

This hierarchy is, apparently, stable throughout the novel. Nevertheless, the novel contains gothic and uncanny elements that might perhaps lead to an actual feeling of uncanniness and rob the novel of its seeming concordance. Two of these motifs particularly leave a mark on *La casa del padre*: the Freudian *Doppelgänger*-motif and the typically gothic haunted house. The first is mostly remarkable because of its frequent occurrence in the text, and because of the ambiguity it creates. The second holds a central position in the narrative, as the title, which refers to it, shows. Interestingly, both motifs provide the text with 'phantom structures' – that of the house, and that of reproduction.

It seems almost everybody in *La casa del padre* has a double or pretends to pass as someone else. The young protagonist, though he is portrayed as an outsider, is no exception: he finds his double in the fellow soldier from Russia whose extremities are severely corroded by frost bite. The invalid does not know him, yet knows by which name to call him, the nickname all soldiers from their town had: "Málaga, ya has vuelto tú también" (Navarro 46). There is, it is suggested, no real difference between one and the other; they suffered similar fates and this makes them interchangeable. On a more uncanny level, there is Portugal's rumoured assumption of his brother's identity: "Muchos empezaron a decir que el Portugal que había muerto en un tejado de

Granada era el falangista y que el Portugal que vivía era el comunista que se había puesto las gafas de su hermano" (62). This suspicion is fed by Portugal's inexplicable behaviour: he brings a suitcase with him during the trip from Málaga to Granada which he got at an auction – the contents of which the protagonist recognises from an advertisement in the paper (104). Once in Granada, Portugal seems to be doing badly, appearing more and more dishevelled and drunk in his eternal summer suit. His troubled gaze through the spectacles that supposedly belonged to his brother makes him appear strangely distracted, always "mirándonos como si no nos viera" (76). However, it must be noted that the narrator is not to be trusted completely: his jealousy of Portugal's enviable rapport with women in general, not to mention Elvira's wife Ángeles, makes him an unreliable narrator. "Portugal hechizó desde la primera visita al Duque de Elvira y a la mujer del Duque de Elvira. [...] Y yo me moría de celos" (174-175), the narrator confesses. "[S]i no llevaba a Portugal, no me admitían en la casa del Duque de Elvira" (176). Whether Portugal really is masquerading as his brother, or whether the narrator merely suggests this out of jealousy, remains unclear for a long time. Even with the apparition of a photograph depicting the two brothers together, near the end of the novel, ambiguity remains.

The most uncanny doubles are the Bueso siblings, who inhabit the second floor of the building where the protagonist and his uncle live. They are a truly monstrous duo, abjectly impoverished and living amidst layer upon layer of filth. The *Doppelgänger*-motif is developed through chauffeur Don Julio's linking them to the Portugals, as well as to another pair of brothers, whose betrayal he relates. As the narrator recalls: "Don Julio sólo hablaba de parejas de hermanos, todos más o menos viles e infelices, dos hermanos, los Bueso" (108). The uncannily one-eyed Bueso sister is particularly hideous:

> Había vuelto a taparse el ojo derecho con una gasa, iba vestida con ropa de hombre [...] y las vendas y la carne de la mujer tenían el mismo color de la ropa [...]. La mujer tenía ceniza y telarañas en el pelo, y la gasa que le cubría el ojo derecho era como una telaraña tupida, y no se sabía si el olor agrio y corrompido de la casa impregnaba a la mujer [...] o si el olor [...] de la mujer impregnaba todas las cosas. (146)

All in all, the Buesos are hardly human. The only thing the reader discovers about them with certainty, through a comment of Don Julio, is that their father was executed (108). For the rest, these larger-than-life characters are a horrific presence in the narration; their roles in it are vague and disquieting.

Other pairs of siblings or friends who turn on each other cause similar ambiguity in *La casa del padre*. Most notably, the uncle of the protagonist turns out to be, and assumes the role of, his father (261).

Also, both Don Julio and the protagonist wear the uncle's old clothes, which creates a bizarre rivalry between them (135). The result of all this mirroring, reflection, and dis- or replacement, is that a sort of general ambiguity comes into being: no one is as he seems, and the reader is left in constant doubt about characters' identities, their lies, and their truths. The uncanny *Doppelgänger*-motif thus gives the novel a general feel of instability: the novelistic world is constantly unbalanced by the many masks its inhabitants seem to be wearing.

The haunted house-motif functions in a similar way. The narrator describes the house he and his mother inhabited in Málaga as asphyxiating: "[M]i madre [...] había empezado a transformarse: no podía respirar en aquella casa [...]. Fue pisar aquella casa y empezar el asma, el ahogo, el miedo a morir asfixiada" (82). What is more, "el piso que mi madre y mi padre compartían era el signo de la maldición" (83): it has come to represent the father's mistake of marrying a simple waitress and the shame of his being thrown out of the family house in Granada where the uncle still lives. The narrator thus explicitly attributes metaphoric meaning to the houses that appear in *La casa del padre*.

The actual 'haunted house', the house of the father or uncle, occupies a single floor in a large building. Initially, it does not come across as particularly scary, but it becomes a prison for the protagonist, where almost all doors are locked: "Todas las puertas tenían llave en aquella casa y todas las puertas estaban cerradas siempre" (144). To make things worse, his uncle obliges him to rest constantly, making him feel like "Houdini, un mago que se lanza al fondo del océano atado con cadenas [...] y ha de liberarse antes de que lo mate la asfixia" (144). Eventually, however, he manages to make copies of all the keys of the house, and one night, he starts investigating it. In the dark, the house reminds him of "la nieve, un laberinto sin muros en el que había estado encerrado una vez" (211) – a reference, as we shall see, to his experiences in Russia. Like a labyrinth, the house, massive and unknown in the darkness, turns out to have its own monster: the protagonist's demented grandmother, who is locked up and hidden in the middle. "Vi al monstruo, una vieja con la cabeza blanca, vestida de negro de pies a cabeza, deforme" (212). At night, the house is a "mundo de fantasmas" (215), yet it is no less strange in the daytime, with its eccentric, black-haired maid, Beatriz, whose face exhibits strange red spots: "las manchas rosa en la cara de Beatriz como mapas de Groenlandia y Gran Bretaña" (215), and its rather tyrannical owner: "todas las cosas estaban siempre como disponía mi tío" (135). Strangest of all, perhaps, is how the house is mirrored in that of the Bueso siblings on the second floor: "era una casa extraña porque era exactamente igual que la casa de mi tío, pero putrefacta [...]. En la pared [...] no había un cuadro como en la casa de mi tío, sino un gran rectángulo de un ocre más pálido que el ocre del resto de la pared"

(147). Here, the motif of doubling and that of the haunted house work together to create a strange sense of ambiguity.

The haunted house motif is further manifest in the description of the Duke of Elvira's apartment. This home clearly personifies Elvira's illusive splendour, hollowness and meaninglessness:

> Era como una película, como una casa que sólo es una fachada de telones pintados y bastidores de madera, en una habitación que quizá sólo tuviera las tres paredes que veías. Y quizá estuviera hueco el piano vertical con dos candelabros de plata y velas negras que no habían sido encendidas nunca. (154)

More than fictional settings, the houses reflect the characters and histories of their inhabitants. Accordingly, a house can feel like a prison, a labyrinth, or a symbol of shame.

A house can also be a tomb, a grave for the living dead. The Bueso siblings are said to have buried themselves alive in their own home: "se habían enterrado en vida" (108). The same goes for the grandmother, who hides as if buried in her own home. And the protagonist's limited life expectation makes him one of the living dead as well: "me quedaban seis meses de vida, […] era un fantasma, un muerto que salía de paso" (16). Believing he only has six months left to live, he feels he has no life to look forward to, and he discards his future, no longer making plans. Repeatedly, he mentions that people look at him to see "cómo operaba la muerte en mí" (187). Besides, he is paralysed by a fear of dying, which is all the more significant since his father died of fear: "se murió de miedo porque creía que llegaba la Marina nacional" (29). Aside from the haunted house-motif and the *Doppelgänger* with which the novel is filled, then, yet another convention of the gothic surfaces: that of the living dead.

The uncertainty that surrounds these fearsome tropes is actually increased because of their convergence with a personal trauma of the protagonist. This becomes clear when the narrator finally explains what happened in Russia, and why he won the Iron Cross. At a certain moment during his service in Russia, the protagonist, his sergeant and a wounded corporal got snowed in inside a shack in the town of Possad. In an attempt to get out of this desperate situation, the sergeant ordered the protagonist to try and repair the wire that provided radio contact with headquarters. But the protagonist, exhausted, confused and blinded by snow, did not follow orders but instead shot at one of the two hand grenades the sergeant had hanging around his neck, causing an explosion and the death of the two others. "Y entonces pensé: ¿si le disparo a una de las bombas, se estallará? Y apunté. Creo que disparé: me dormí, desaparecí. Y mucho después desperté en el Hospital de Riga con la Cruz de Hierro de Segunda Clase" (288), the narrator explains his action. It is clear from the text that the boy acted in a fit of insanity and that he had no murderous intentions, but the fact that his action was immediately rewarded with an Iron Cross is quite bizarre.

The traumatic episode in the Possad cabin is repressed, but haunts the protagonist all through the novel – and since this private trauma is connected to the Second World War and the francoist dictatorship, it is linked to a collective fear. We have already seen that the house of the father reminds the protagonist-narrator of that snowy 'labyrinth without walls'. He also mentions that his uncle smothers him: "Me cuidaba mi tío, me tenía entre algodones, y era muy cansada la vida cómoda y feliz" (143). Just as in the cabin, the protagonist feels muffled and mortally tired. As in Possad, he is waiting for death, and once again, he miraculously survives. The Possad episode, like any true trauma, is completely separated from the fictional world of Málaga and Granada where the protagonist now lives. It is distant both in space and time. Nevertheless, the Possad scene keeps intruding into the consciousness of the protagonist-narrator. All houses are potential graves, like the Possad cabin: a snow or cotton padding keeps out the outside world. It is clear that at least the protagonist of *La casa del padre* experiences the uncanny as his trauma causes disruption in the fictional world, making use of phantom structures like reproduction or a haunted house.

These uncanny houses and people are elements that disturb the fictional world and cause estrangement. Strictly speaking, it never becomes entirely clear whether these tropes of fear clash with the laws of the fictional world. They even appear quite integrated into the realm of the novel, where most of the characters, if they are not uncanny themselves, seem to take apparently supernatural and uncanny elements in their stride. The protagonist does not fail to remark, though, that the uncanny and gothic phenomena he encounters are strange, surprising and often downright scary – he is mortally afraid of the inhuman Bueso siblings. It remains ambiguous whether or not these appearances have a rational explanation, or whether they are portrayed as uncanny because we look through the eyes of an imaginative, unreliable, and traumatised narrator. It is a fact, however, that they disturb the fictional realm, investing it precisely with a haunting ambiguity.

The uncanny is called up and causes indeterminacy, not only where the status of the spectral tropes is concerned. In the ideological hierarchy of Navarro's text, the haunting uncanny works as an undermining force. We have previously established that in *La casa del padre*, two normative discourses are opposed: that of the narratee, with its democratic values, and that of the narrator-protagonist, which, in comparison, can be called amoral. The first normative discourse seems to be the hierarchical dominant, since the narrator defends his own normative system against it. Trauma, however, disturbs this hierarchy. The frightening presence of trauma actually justifies the narrator's holding on to the value system of a past era. In the Possad cabin, the protagonist felt trapped and excluded from the outside world, and he was driven to an act of insanity. Back in the world of the living, he receives a medal for his wartime performance. From this point on, behaving morally seems absurd to the narrator-protagonist, and his only development between the 1940s and the democratic present is from coward to opportunist. The continuous intrusion of the Possad episode in the narration makes this almost understandable: the feeling of being smothered and buried alive is constantly called up by spaces or situations that remind the protagonist of the cabin in the snow – labyrinth-like houses, or the bed that his uncle forces him to spend much time in. The haunting uncanny thus undermines the apparently concordant reading the work seems to invite. At first glance, the text appears to place the reader in a most comfortable position from which he may accuse the protagonist-narrator of hypocritically 'forgetting' about the unethical behaviour he displayed in francoist times. Thus, without taking into account the traumatic, uncanny undercurrent of the novel, Navarro's work allows for a very moralistic reading. Such concordance is aided by the pity called up by the poor, young and dying protagonist, and by the defensive tone of the narrator that suggests he somehow feels guilty or uncomfortable with his own story.

Yet the uncanny haunting of the trauma destabilises this reading and introduces discordance into the work, making it highly ambiguous. The amoral behaviour becomes much more understandable in the face of trauma, and ethical judgments are highly complicated. As Ignacio Echevarría remarks, *La casa del padre* "explora la sórdida atmósfera de la inmediata posguerra desde una perspectiva eminentemente amoral" (152). As a result, "se disipan los contornos morales de unos personajes desencajados, vistos como a través de una cornucopia en la que los objetos se exaltan y la realidad entera aparece desfigurada por una distorsión […] afín a la que tiene lugar en las novelas de terror" (153). In the novel, "indefinición moral" and "ausencia de culpa" reign (Márquez). In other words: the difference between right and wrong becomes fuzzy and problematic, the value hierarchy unstable.

La casa del padre shows that uncanny motifs can be activated by a connection to contemporary fears by introducing trauma, and particularly war trauma, into the novel. It also shows that as a consequence, it is perhaps still possible to read this work as condemning the immoral attitude and forgetfulness of the dictatorship's perpetrators. But this becomes only one (rather reductive) possibility among others. The protagonist's trauma is narrated in a way that appears to thematise the very fact that war situations do not allow heroic, 'correct' decisions, so that morality becomes a shady concept altogether.

Rosa Regàs, *Luna lunera*

In Rosa Regàs's *Luna lunera* (1999), such moral relativism is nowhere to be found. Right from the very beginning, the novel imposes a clear value system according to which the narration is to be judged. Already in the introduction, one version of the past is firmly instated at the cost of another. Things seem suspiciously peaceful at first, as an abbot at the death bed of one Pius Vidal Armengol ponders:

> [E]l anciano señor Vidal Armengol moría sin haber cometido un solo pecado mortal. Había sido un hombre generoso hasta extremos que bordeaban la santidad, había renunciado a su propia vida por los demás, era en verdad, tal como todo el mundo lo consideraba, un santo moderno, un santo de la vida cotidiana, de la responsabilidad y del bien hacer. (20)

This peace is disrupted in a violent manner when focalisation shifts to Anna, the granddaughter of the dying man, in a section separated from the rest of the chapter by a smaller font and asterisks that mark its contrast to what came before. Anna's thoughts betray a very different opinion of the saintly grandfather:

> Había llegado la hora tantas veces soñada y deseada, recreada y compartida día a día como un trasfondo al jolgorio o al silencio, a la fiesta y a las lágrimas, la hora de aquella liberación que habría sido para nosotros, sus nietos, la anhelada redención de tanto sufrimiento y de tanto desconcierto [...]. (24)

And when we turn the page and find that the rest of the novel is narrated by the very same granddaughter, it becomes plain that we must read the part about the 'saint of the everyday' with the necessary irony, and that we are entering into the story of a childhood ruined by a tyrant.

Luna lunera tells the story of the four grandchildren of Vidal Armengol, whose parents were *rojos* in the Civil War and fled with them into exile as the francoist troops reached Barcelona. When the Second World War breaks out and the children remain in France and the Netherlands, their grandfather pulls some strings and returns them to Barcelona. Narrator-protagonist Anna, her elder brother and sister, Elías and Pía, and her younger brother Alexis are quickly adopted by their grandfather. Their parents separate while they remain exiled in France, which makes it all the easier for the grandfather to gain custody over the children. As a good francoist and patriot he easily receives the *patria potestad*, and legally, the children are his now, while the absent parents cannot claim them anymore. Their grandfather then sends them to boarding schools, so that they only spend time at his residences in

Barcelona and on the coast during school holidays. Nevertheless, his presence has such an impact on their lives that even when he dies many years later, in 1965, they all make sure to be in his Barcelona home and share their relief over this event.

In interviews, Regàs has made clear that *Luna lunera* is a work of autobiographical fiction, and that it is based on what she describes as "una parte importante de mi propia y 'dickensiana' infancia" ("El juego de la memoria" 2). Narrator Anna says that she and her sister liked to impress their classmates at school by telling them about their experiences with their grandfather: the classmates found these stories "más deslumbrantes por más cercanos que los que encontrarían con el tiempo en los libros de Dickens, de Jack London y de Edgar Allan Poe que se alineaban en la biblioteca del colegio" (96). It is not surprising that both the author and the narrator should connect the difficult childhood of the four near-orphans to the works of Charles Dickens. The mention of Poe, however, gains special importance when one considers two gothic elements in *Luna lunera* that typically appear in many of his short stories: the haunted house, and the tyrannical parent.

Both elements are closely connected. There are actually two houses involved, the Barcelona home and the home in Tiana, a village outside Barcelona, which was built by the grandfather himself, and which represents his character and tastes. The description of this second house certainly calls up the image of a remote castle out of Gothic novels, which seems to rub off on the first one as well:

> La casa de un hombre es su Castillo, decía el abuelo a sus invitados, y la suya, de Tiana, un pueblo del Maresme, lo era más aún, un Castillo alto y separado de la calle y del pueblo como si estuviera rodeado de un foso. Estaba envuelta en un enmarañado y misterioso jardín elevado sobre las calles que la circundaban y al que se accedía por una verja de pesados barrotes de hierro y florituras en el cabezal que sostenían una orla con las iniciales de su nombre y apellidos [...]. Tanto la verja como el portalón permanecían siempre cerrados con llave [...]. (147)

The children are practically locked up in this 'castle': they have been appointed to the care of their grandfather and cannot leave until they reach adulthood. Sombre as the house is, though, it has a kitchen that is warm and homely, where the women of the household reign, the maids who cook, iron, clean, and, most importantly, gossip. Not surprisingly, the children prefer spending their time with them to staying with their grandfather: the women are part of a different reality which is more humble but less oppressive, and they form the only real relief from the dark atmosphere that governs the house. In a lecture, Rosa Regàs has stated that the kitchen maids are intended to function as a choir ("El juego de la memoria" 2), and indeed, they comment on what happens and provide background information to the children about their lives and those of other family members.

However, it is clear at all times that the kitchen is a temporary refuge only, and that the children cannot escape their grim surroundings. Their long periods at boarding schools always end in their having to return home, where they are once more delivered to the power of their grandfather. The house becomes their prison, from which the children dream to escape. Every day, they hear how a neighbour sings a song called 'Luna lunera'. Her sweet voice suggests the existence of an outside, and Elías even fantasises about marrying her, so she can sing for him every day. According to Regàs, "el significado de esta canción que oyen por las mañanas los días que están en casa de su abuelo, reside en su papel redentor dentro del ambiente opresivo en el que viven" ("El juego de la memoria" 2).

The children are forced to live in a gloomy castle of a house, and it is run by a tyrant. The extent of the grandfather's tyranny is clear from the novel's very first pages onwards, and it is further underlined by the exceedingly bitter tone narrator Anna uses whenever she talks of her grandfather. When Anna arrives to her grandfather's house in 1940, she is five or six years old, but her story is narrated from a present-day point of view, openly showing her current judgment of things she might not have completely grasped as a child. This combination of hindsight bias and the depiction of events through the eyes of a little child, results in a particularly harsh portrayal of the grandfather. The episode on the three wise men is a prime example of this. Whereas all Spanish children receive gifts on 6 January, the narrator states: "La primera noticia que tuvimos de la existencia de los Reyes Magos fue que para nosotros no habrían de venir" (Regàs 85). On the day itself, the grandfather gathers the entire household to witness the moment when the children discover there really are no presents for them. He then lectures them, saying:

> [L]os Reyes son los padres. Se detuvo, Bien, creo que no hace falta conti-
> nuar, en la situación en la que estáis no debéis ni podéis aspirar a lo que
> aspiran los demás porque no tenéis padres, es decir, rectificó, vuestros
> padres no están donde deberían estar. (93)

The scene is described mainly from a child's point of view, as the subject is one of the typical high points of a child's life. This choice of perspective highlights the cruelty that the grandfather displays. At the same time, the voice of little Anna is always mixed with the narrator's grown-up voice, which occasionally takes over:

> De hecho cuando ocurrió lo que ocurrió el día de Reyes no habríamos podi-
> do decir que no se nos había avisado, y tal vez por esto nuestra desilusión no
> fue tan desmesurada como creyeron que había sido las personas a las que
> más tarde contamos el suceso. (87)

In a very effective manner, the innocence of the children makes the grandfather's behaviour appear the more shocking, and the latter-day narrator's indignant commentaries reinforce this impression.

In spite of her young age, though, Anna already understands that her grandfather's behaviour is often hypocritical or contradictory, even when he does not think so himself. When the children discover him crying after he has beaten up their grandmother, she says: "No está arrepentido [...]. Lo que pasa es que se siente importante haciendo como que es un santo" (141). At this point, Anna's narration is interrupted by a prayer, printed in a smaller font, that seems to corroborate her supposition: it is the grandfather directing himself at God, admitting his weaknesses and recognising that God has sent him many tests on the path to sainthood (142). The grandfather clearly sees himself as a chosen one and identifies with Abraham – the biblical leader of the Jews, who, significantly, was asked to sacrifice his own son. Maid Francisca remembers that he "[h]abría querido morir como Abraham a quien estaba seguro de parecerse [...] por la elección de que ambos habían sido objeto por parte del Altísimo" (92). To the children, he rather resembles the God of the Old Testament. On the few occasions they break one of his rules, he always somehow manages to find out, causing the children to wonder about his omniscience and his divine status: "¡Cuantas veces, al comprobar esa infinita sabiduría del abuelo [...], nos preguntábamos si [...] él, igual que el terrible Dios justiciero en el que creía, no tendría también la facultad de verlo todo, oírlo todo [...]!" (280). Also, though they hope his old age may lead to his death soon, the fact that he never dies leads the children to conclude: "El abuelo era immortal" (296).

The cruelty and hypocrisy of the grandfather and his violent nature are thus constantly underlined. Narrator Anna connects the grandfather's behaviour and values to that of the Civil War's victors, particularly to the clergy, as she describes how her grandfather surrounds himself with prominent clergymen, and how he strives to give the impression that he is a devout catholic. In church, he is involved in a rivalry with another churchgoer as to who is the best catholic; usually, that week's winner is he who gets to communion first (135). The grandfather's pious behaviour and the size of his donations to catholic foundations contribute to his image as a 'saint of the everyday'. Nevertheless, his behaviour within the walls of his house contrasts with this image: he regularly loses his temper completely, which results in outbursts of violence. One day, he works himself up into a rage after his wife has bought sweets for lunch:

El abuelo seguía mirando a la abuela mientras se le iba poniendo la cara más roja, los ojos más vidriosos, las mandíbulas más contraídas. [...] Luego lentamente, con los ojos fijos en la abuela aunque sin verla, se desabrochó el cinturón [...] y sin darse el menor descanso azotó una vez y otra y otra la espalda de la abuela [...]. (138-139)

Outbursts like this occur quite often, but this time, it is suggested the grandfather even has an orgasm while punishing his wife; at least, such is Elías's conviction (135). When the grandmother later commits suicide, the grandfather considers it a shame upon his family and uses all of his power to hush up the scandal.

Typically, the grandfather changes his political opinions as the times change. After a few years, in 1946, he starts becoming less openly francoist, and more pro-Catalan. He even removes the picture of his son Miguel, who died in battle on the nationalist side, and which was until then displayed with the utmost care, stating: "El hijo Miguel murió por Cataluña" (268). Along with him, the church changes: priest and eternal house guest Hilario Mariné quickly changes his name to the Catalan Ilari Mariner. Narrator Anna calls these political opportunists "una clase social que comenzaba a olvidar, a ocultar o a tergiversar su pasado" (267).

It is the social class of the grandfather, the clergymen and other victors of the war which is criticised most vehemently in *Luna lunera*. Its members are all portrayed as villains, each in their own way. Hilario Mariné, for one, is a sexual deviant who violates Elías, Pía, their uncle Santiago, and finally Anna herself. When she confides this to her school priest, he accuses her of seducing and tempting Mariné. We are thus dealing with a novel where the narrator imposes a clear value system through numerous evaluations, and where the morally inferior grandfather and his hypocritical behaviour come to stand for the abusive behaviour of all those in power.

At the same time, though, strange elements are present in the novel that are reminiscent of the gothic. The work contains more fearsome tropes than just the haunted castle and the tyrannical grandfather, be it that these are metaphorical to a degree: a number of characters are portrayed as rather ghostly creatures, and their ontological status is surrounded by just a hint of ambiguity. They are the members of the generation between that of the grandfather and that of his grandchildren. The one son who has lived up to his grandfather's expectations, Miguel, died in combat, but his photograph is on the wall and he is the hero of the household. Manuel, the first-born and father of Anna and her siblings, got involved in republican politics and had to flee the country when the national troops entered. Juan and José, two other sons, also chose the republican side: José was imprisoned, disowned by his father, and executed; Juan survived the war, but his father rejected him too. He is forced to hide in his apartment during the daytime, getting up at night only. Santiago, the youngest, returned from the war traumatised and psychologically damaged. Santiago is the only son who has not been forbidden entrance to the house. The memory of the deceased sons is repressed or manipulated, and the living ones are, each in their own ways, living dead.

The parents of Anna are also ghostlike creatures, though they are both still alive and the children's father even returns from France to live with them for a year and a half, until he is thrown out for maintaining relations with a 'bad woman'. He is depicted as an admirable but unhappy man who has lost everything, even his children. The narrator regularly praises him, stating, for example, that he was "la única persona que nosotros conocíamos que en aquel tiempo parecía tener las ideas claras, las mismas ideas de siempre por lo menos" (167). He even inspires Anna to rebel against the grown-ups: when she has to sing a patriotic song at school, she is too frightened to stop singing, but she does fall down, pretending to faint (172). Nevertheless, the father of the children is not capable of preventing their grandfather from harming them. Essentially, he is a defeated man, waiting for better times which never arrive: after Franco's death, he experiences profound disillusion with the new democracy and "se dejó morir" (256).

The children's lovely mother, whom they hardly ever see and never get to speak to in private, is the one who seems to resist authorities and the grandfather most, but in doing so, she puts her children at risk. She tries to get custody of them, but always loses the legal battles. Therefore, she urges the children to meet her in secret. They escape to meet her twice, and their grandfather always finds out. The first time, only Elías is sent to a juvenile prison. The second time, they are all sent there. The younger children stay only for three months, but Elías is sent to Madrid and has to serve longer. His prison years practically ruin his life and distance him from the other three. Even so, the mother is portrayed as an angel. Before her return, the children do not remember her – but when they see her again, they are not disillusioned or disappointed. The angelic image they have constructed of their mother is actually reinforced. On reappearing in their lives, she wears a hat with fine gauze, which the children think must be made of "la materia de las alas de los ángeles" (77). The mother's angelic figure serves as a contrast to the perverted mind of the grandfather. In fact, the thought of that beautiful and stubborn woman, who dares to resist him, drives the grandfather to extremes of anger. Narrator Anna speaks of a secret passion, an obsession, which causes him to reach "esos extremos de violencia" (190).

All in all, *Luna lunera* is a novel that imposes a value system which strongly condemns the dictatorship. It exposes those who adapt to changing circumstances by silencing what came before. In the narrator's angry and accusatory style, the disillusionment with the forgetfulness of democracy is visible: she openly rejects the narrative of forgetting she detects in society, and instead, forcefully confronts her readers with the past's most brutal sides. In this light, it is surprising that the narration includes fearsome tropes and grotesque images which appear to undermine such a direct and confronting view of the past, favouring invention over apparent referentiality. For in many ways, the characters of this novel are strange, unrealistic and uncanny, even if it is to a lesser degree than the tropes of fear in *La casa del padre*. The grandfather is a stereotypical tyrant, the mother an angel, the living sons seem to be in an undead state – the quiet, broken-spirited father; traumatised Santiago, who is in love with a statue of the Virgin Mary; and Juan, living in silence and darkness, away from the world. If we add to this the isolation of the haunted house, they could, indeed, easily be part of a Dickensian novel or a story by Poe.

Judging by the author's own commentary, she purposefully constructed this uncanny atmosphere, and she is aware of its connections to gothic novels and other works that are part of the contemporary 'industry of fear'. It is imaginable that these elements are to have the same impact on the real reader as they did once on narrator Anna's classmates, and that they are to dazzle and shock him or her. Apparently, though, Anna introduces them with a mind to reinforce her own, dominant normative discourse. The gothic elements serve to justify the narrator's anger at the tendency of forgetting that she claims came with democracy, which brings her to a vehement narration of how her young life was ruined. Clearly, she suggests that the *naming* of the painful past is preferable to the comfortable option of forgetting. This preference for a normative discourse, and, accordingly, for a memory narrative, is corroborated rather than undermined by the spectral tropes she introduces. The spectral, here, must make the reader feel sympathy for Anna and her siblings.

But it could be said that the tropes in *Luna lunera* actually open up the novel to discordance. The ambiguity they call up leads to an experience of the uncanny: the tyrant in himself is still a human being, and his ghostly children are not actual ghosts, but their characters maintain a sort of stereotypicality that removes them from a clear 'humanity' like that of Anna, her sister and brothers. The unclear borders between what is real and what is not, enhanced by the child's perspective, create a strangeness that allows multiple readings at the same time. As a result, whereas the ideological dominant suggests that silencing must be replaced by talking, the presence of gothic tropes does the opposite: they do not define or describe anything, but rather, they allow a different reading based on otherness and uncertainty. The terror of the little girl who cannot yet grasp with full rationality what surrounds her is combined with the inexplicable and the strange, so that childhood fears are called up. As a result, the castle, the omnipotent grandfather who sees and hears all, the silent suffering of the ghostly adults and the occasional fairylike relief brought by the angelic mother – they all seem like the stuff of childish bad dreams.

In this sense, *Luna lunera* shows how the inclusion of spectral tropes and their ambiguity may interfere with a plot's concordance. It seems that the spectral motifs were introduced to produce sympathetic fear in the real readers, allowing them to empathise with little Anna while arriving at one, concordant, reading that condemns the grandfather in particular and francoist society in general. However, the tropes actually give rise to multiple readings which undermine the value hierarchy. As the grown-up characters are enlarged to truly uncanny dimensions, this move accidentally disturbs the moralistic tone entirely.

So, whereas this novel wants to be read concordantly because it deals with a matter as important and conflictive as the negative forces of the dictatorship, it simultaneously allows a reading that strays from this 'message' and thus undermines the value system of the work. It is possible to read the ghostly elements as unreal or to see them as realistic, and this duality causes an uncanny feeling and makes for discordance on the plot level. The anger *Luna lunera* seems to want to stir up in the reader, the indignation we are supposed to share with the narrator – these are lessened by the option of reading the novel as a frightening ghost world, as a child's nightmare.

Carlos Ruiz Zafón, *La sombra del viento*

When Daniel Sempere is ten years old, his father, a bookshop owner, takes him to a place called the Cemetery of Forgotten Books. It is a sort of borgesian labyrinth library, where, as a *rite de passage*, young Daniel gets to choose and keep one of the forgotten books. The work he takes home turns out to be called *La sombra del viento*, and was written by a certain Julián Carax. Daniel embarks on a quest to find out more about the mysterious circumstances that surround the author and his works. Carax's novels are very rare, since a mysterious stranger has been buying up and destroying them all. Little is known of their author: only that he was born in Barcelona in 1900, moved to Paris later and worked as a bar pianist. Rumour had it that in 1936, he disappeared on the eve of his wedding to a wealthy elderly lady after a duel on Père Lachaise cemetery. Apparently, he died, though it is unclear whether this happened in Paris or in Barcelona, where he was supposed to have returned just at the outbreak of the Spanish Civil War.

Carlos Ruiz Zafón's *La sombra del viento* (2001) thus recounts two stories. The first is that of young Daniel, who, on trying to find out what exactly happened to Carax, encounters a number of people who either help him or work against him, and who, in the process, grows up and experiences his first loves. The second is that of Julián Carax, which Daniel unravels bit by bit. The novel can consequently be read as a truth-finding quest which echoes memory narratives of openness and justice. Daniel finds out about Julián's tragic love for Penélope, daughter of his benefactor Ricardo Aldaya, who sent him into French exile, and her into an early grave; about his enemy, Fumero, a former classmate turned police inspector under Franco; about the story behind the burning of all Carax's books and his return to Barcelona. Daniel's quest is set between 1945 and 1955, and it is told in retrospect, from the year 1966, by the narrator, Daniel Sempere. It contains an exciting intrigue full of mysteries that get solved; it also contains lots of comical characters and plenty of funny scenes. And, as mentioned, it encompasses the coming-of-age of young Daniel. All the ingredients are there to turn *La sombra del viento* into the best-seller it was to become. Then, there are other, mysterious elements to the novel which perhaps add to the tension of the quest; and many of these, it turns out, may be considered uncanny and gothic motifs. As Stephen King puts it: "If you thought the true gothic novel died with the 19th century, [*La sombra del viento*] will change your mind".

Right at the beginning of the novel, the scene is set: "caminábamos por las calles de una Barcelona atrapada bajo cielos de ceniza y un sol de vapor" (Ruiz Zafón 7). Postwar Barcelona is "una ciudad de tinieblas" (37). Against this sinister backdrop, a mysterious figure walks around at night: "Aquel personaje no tenía nariz, ni labios, ni párpados. Su rostro era apenas una máscara de piel negra y cicatrizada, devorada por el fuego" (69). From the start, he reminds Daniel of a character from Carax's novel:

> El extraño permanecía allí, con la mano derecha enfundada en el bolsillo de una chaqueta negra, para luego alejarse, cojeando. En la escena que yo acababa de presenciar, aquel extraño hubiera podido ser cualquier trasnochador, una figura sin rostro ni identidad. En la novela de Carax, aquel extraño era el diablo. (48)

Frighteningly enough, this leather-faced figure tries to pry the novel of Carax from Daniel; also, he calls himself Laín Coubert, the very name of the devil in Carax's book.

When later on, it becomes clear that Laín is really Julián Carax, that his face got burnt because he set on fire a warehouse with his own books in it, and that he really is not all that scary, the indeterminacy surrounding this figure is not lifted completely. Though Carax has turned out to be alive and well, he lives by night, and hides from the world. And at the end of *La sombra del viento*, he mysteriously disappears, so that his ontological status remains vague. Equally disturbing is the strange connection there seems to exist between Julián Carax and young Daniel. Daniel strongly identifies with the frustrated writer, especially when his own love story with a girl named Bea threatens to take the same turn for the worse as that of Julián and Penélope. He is usually very pleased when somebody points out that he physically resembles Carax: "Se parece usted un poco a Julián" (196). Carax turns out to feel the same way about him: he claims that "ese muchacho me recuerda a mí mismo" (526) and even sees him as the son he never knew, "una nueva página en blanco para volver a empezar aquella historia que no podía inventar, pero que podía recordar" (527). More mysteriously, even, little Daniel has always longed to have an expensive fountain pen on display in a shop window of his neighbourhood; eventually, his father gives it to him. It turns out to have belonged, once, to Carax.

The strange connection between Carax and Daniel, their strong resemblance, and their temporarily overlapping fates are not explained, and evoke Freud's *Doppelgänger*-motif. And there are more aspects of *La sombra del viento* that may be called strange. There are, for instance, not one, but two haunted houses. One of them is the family house of the Aldayas. It is called "El ángel de bruma", and it is cursed. Seven months after its construction, its owner, a rich and eccentric businessman, was found poisoned along with his wife by their Cuban maid, who was rumoured to know witchcraft; the maid had subsequently committed suicide by cutting open her veins, smearing her blood all over the walls of the house. When the Aldayas move in, they find that the house is, indeed, haunted:

> Los recientes inquilinos se quejaban de ruidos y golpes en las paredes por la noche, súbitos olores a putrefacción y corrientes de aire helado que parecían vagar por la casa como centinelas errantes. El caserón era un compendio de misterios. Tenía un doble sótano, con una suerte de cripta por estrenar en el nivel inferior y una capilla en el superior dominada por un gran Cristo en una cruz policromada al que los criados encontraban un inquietante parecido con Rasputín, personaje muy popular en la época. Los libros de la biblioteca aparecían constantemente reordenados, o vueltos del revés. Había una habitación en el tercer piso, un dormitorio que no se usaba debido a inexplicables manchas de humedad que brotaban de las paredes y parecían formar rostros borrosos, donde las flores frescas se marchitaban en apenas minutos y siempre se escuchaban moscas revolotear, aunque era imposible verlas. (284)

Later, when Daniel discovers the empty Aldaya home and uses it for secret rendezvous with his girlfriend Bea, he does not realise that the house is haunted by new as well as old ghosts. Julián Carax lives there, hiding from the world, and in the previously unused crypt stand the coffins of Penélope Aldaya and her stillborn son.

A second haunted house in *La sombra del viento* is the asylum of Santa Lucía, where Penélope's old nurse Jacinta is locked up. Daniel visits her there to find out more about what happened to Julián and Penélope. This asylum is a castle that has been put to various uses: it has been a prison, a sanatorium, and a *Tenebrarium*, a collection of rarities and deformities. As Daniel enters into the asylum, he notes: "Un portón de madera podrida nos condujo al interior de un patio custodiado por lámparas de gas que salpicaban gárgolas y ángeles cuyas facciones se deshacían en la piedra envejecida. [...] Se escuchaban lamentos y se adivinaban siluetas entre la rejilla de los cortinajes" (298-299). Dark, smelly and full of poor, abandoned old people, the castle conserves a dantesque feel: "La penumbra velaba lo que a primera vista me pareció una colección de figuras de cera, sentadas o abandonadas en los rincones, con ojos muertos y vidriosos que brillaban como monedas de latón a la lumbre de las velas" (299). Its inhabitants no longer belong to the world of the living, and they can only await their deaths in the most depressing of circumstances.

Apart from these two haunted houses and the doubling of Daniel and Julián Carax, *La sombra del viento* contains another trope of fear: a villain called Francisco Javier Fumero. This Fumero displays suspicious behaviour from an early age: "*Caza gatos y palomas y los martiriza durante horas con su cuchillo*" (255). His evil nature, rooted in but not entirely explained by his unhappy childhood, first surfaces when he tries to kill Julián, the secret lover of his adored Penélope – but also one of his few friends. After the Civil War, Fumero becomes a feared inspector of police, who is known for his cruelty. Daniel's friend, the tramp Fermín who comes to work in his father's bookshop, has been tortured by him:

> Fumero y un tipo que sólo hablaba alemán me colgaron boca abajo por los pies. [...] A un signo de Fumero, el alemán me inyectó no sé qué en el muslo y esperó unos minutos. Luego, mientras Fumero fumaba y me observaba sonriente, empezó a asarme concienzudamente. Usted ha visto las marcas. (383-384)

Fumero's evilness is obviously innate. The narrator makes it very clear that he is a morally inferior being, belonging to one side, then the other, during the war, working as a spy – and, to make matters worse, cooperating with the Nazis, whose experience in torturing he gladly makes use of. Fumero has no conscience: rather than as a human being, he is portrayed as a spider that patiently catches all his enemies in his web. Already in their school years, Julián's best friend Miquel warns him that "Ese muchacho [...] tiene alma de araña" (257). Fumero "sentía veneración por [...] los insectos en general" (462), and physically reminds Daniel of a spider (544). Fumero is driven by hate: "La gente como

Fumero nunca deja de odiar" (513). No wonder, then, that he has always remained resentful towards Carax and still wants to find him, interfering frequently with Daniel's search.

All these fearful tropes are embedded in what may be called a firm hierarchy of values. This may seem surprising if the novel's complex build-up is taken into account. Of course, narrator Daniel does much of the evaluating, but there is also another, intradiegetic narrator, and focalisation frequently shifts. Moreover, the actions and comments of a host of minor characters also lead to multiple evaluations. Such a large number of evaluators suggests a variety of normative stances, but *La sombra del viento*'s value hierarchy is homogeneous and simple. Nuria Monfort, the novel's second, intradiegetic narrator, is the Cemetery keeper's daughter and assistant to Carax's Spanish publisher. She dies relatively early on in the novel, but she leaves Daniel a manuscript in which she relates her story, her romance with a bitter Julián in Paris, and her marriage out of pity to Julián's friend Miquel. The manuscript is reproduced entirely: a narration within the narration. Nuria focuses more on the developments around Carax than on the other characters and events. Nevertheless, it is clear whose side she is on. After the war, she struggles to make ends meet and experiences the postwar period as a bleak and depressing time:

> 1945, un año de cenizas. Sólo habían pasado seis años desde el fin de la guerra y aunque sus cicatrices se sentían a cada paso, casi nadie hablaba de ella abiertamente. [...] Eran años de escasez y miseria, extrañamente bendecidos por esa paz que inspiran los mudos y los tullidos, a medio camino entre la lástima y el repelús. (515)

Also, she openly speaks her mind about her eventual murderer, Fumero, who she thinks is only capable of hate. Nuria's testimony is that of the defeated, and therefore, it lacks the humoristic touch of Daniel's narrative; her values, however, are the same as those of Daniel.

Daniel, the older narrator, occasionally evaluates the circumstances under which he grew up. Such is the case, for example, when he mentions that the Spain of his childhood was "un mundo de quietud, miseria y rencores velados" (45). His opinions become much clearer, however, in his descriptions of the behaviour and nature of other characters. Fermín is the sympathetic friend who helps Daniel; his having been tortured by Fumero already casts a bad light upon the dictatorship that allows for such practices. Then, there is the arrest and torture of the neighbourhood's friendly, homosexual, watchmaker. Of course, it is often made clear that many francoists, like the happy Falangist barman who treats Daniel and Fermín to a cigar on the occasion of the birth of his first son, are only people; that, in Nuria's words, "quienes [...] hacían [la guerra] también habían sido niños" (512). But the circumstances which allow an unscrupulous man like Fumero to work with Nazis and to torture and murder at will, are considered morally despicable – though never too explicitly described.

Both in Daniel's and in Nuria's narration, focalisation shifts from the narrator to one of the characters in the story. These parts of the novel are printed in italics and easy to distinguish. Since the narrator remains the same, the consequences for the normative system are limited, however. When Nuria's manuscript adopts the viewpoint of Jorge Aldaya, it starts with the following line: *"Diez años después de desembarcar en Buenos Aires, Jorge Aldaya, o el despojo humano en el que se había convertido, regresó a Barcelona"* (460). It is Nuria's judgment we read in the term "despojo humano", not that of Jorge Aldaya. Similarly, the opinions and evaluations of narrator Daniel are clearly felt in the places where the narration is focalised through the eyes of others. In Daniel's narrative, these places are usually stylised versions of what he is told during his investigation of the tragic life of Julián Carax. Some characters tell their own story, like nanny Jacinta; some, like the concierge of Julián's father's house, tell that of others. The italicised parts of *La sombra del viento* might cause the impression, precisely because they are italicised and seem to represent a new voice and outlook, that their perspective is limited to the focaliser. But the narrator inserts plenty of comments through which he explains and evaluates their actions and thoughts: *"Antoni Fortuny había visto a su propio padre golpear a su madre infinidad de veces e hizo lo que entendía procedente"* (153).

In spite of the multiple narrators, focalisers and characters, the novel's ideology is thus surprisingly straightforward. The narrators' evaluations are very similar, and they are reflected in the actions of all characters as well as in the sections of the novel with a different focaliser. Clearly, the dictatorship is condemned, as it allows cruelty, torture and a general atmosphere of misery and greyness. The older Daniel points out that in 1966, the year from which he writes, "me parece que la luz se atreve cada vez más, que vuelve a Barcelona" (573). Daniel, Nuria and all those who help them are on the 'good' side; Fumero is the bad guy. Yet, there are the uncanny and gothic elements, and these might overthrow the seemingly concordant structure and make way for one that is obviously discordant. Actually, it appears that this is bound to happen, judging by the presence, within one and the same narrative, of gothic and uncanny tropes and a shared, painful past.

But the gothic and uncanny do not actually *disrupt* the fictional world. Though Daniel and the other characters do find the uncanny elements they encounter in their world rather frightening, at no point do they show any disbelief in their possibility. When Daniel enters into the gloomy, slightly anachronistic castle of the Aldayas or is led into the monstrous old people's home, he accepts them unquestioningly, just as he did the notion of the book library and the idea that it contained one work that was destined to be picked by him. The novel's realm clearly and unambiguously allows this sort of element. For that reason, if we follow Freud, these uncanny conventions are not actually uncanny.

This does not mean, however, that these in themselves perhaps stereotypical elements aid in the construction of a concordant plot. They actually construct a reading that is simultaneously at odds with other elements of the novel and in accordance with them – most notably, in relation to the comical elements that abound in the work. Many characters of low birth and humorous description populate the pages of *La sombra del viento*, and their obvious fictionality lays bare the fictional nature of the text as a whole – including that of the fearsome tropes. Prime example of these characters is Daniel's roguish friend and helper, the eccentric Fermín Romero de Torres, the tramp turned book detective with the heart of gold, who knows his way around the obscurest layers of society, and who is remarkable through his strange use of language and his colourful behaviour. Then, *La sombra del viento* is full of taxi drivers, bartenders, concierges and other locals. Their direct speech is transcribed as it sounds: "Siento comunicarsus, en nombre de la diresión, que no queda ni veta de jamong. Pueo ofresele butifarra negra, blanca, mixta, arbóndiga o chitorra" (212). This type of characters, the focus on their oddities and the faithful rendering of their speech often provide *La sombra del viento* with a strong contrast to the dark and uncanny mood of the gothic stereotypes – while at the same time heightening the degree of unrealism that determines this novel. While they thus stress the fictionality they have in common with the uncanny tropes, the characters' airiness at the same time contrasts with the dark atmosphere these call up.

It may be concluded, as a consequence, that gothic and uncanny tropes contribute to the discordance of *La sombra del viento*, in the sense that they allow the work to be read in various ways. They *both* support the value system of the work, judging francoist times and portraying them as dark and gloomy, *and* they suggest another reading through their fantastic nature, which focuses much more on fictional elements than on historical realities. They both contrast with the comical and share its unrealism, and as a result, the dictatorship turns out to be of atmospheric rather than historical importance – while at the same time, of course, a reading of *La sombra del viento* as critical of the past is still allowed.

The focus on atmosphere is perhaps what has caused many readers to protest against this work's portrayal of the Spanish past. The work loses itself as it were in the creation of a certain atmosphere, and the attention for depictions of the actual, historical reality is quite small. Richmond Ellis, for one, finds that in *La sombra del viento*, "The past remembered, though concurrent with the Spanish Civil War and its aftermath, is depoliticized" (839), and complains that especially "Fumero [...] is emblematic of how the Ruiz Zafón text depoliticizes history, transmuting the violence of the war into a personal vendetta rooted in psychological trauma" (846). Others, however, do not mind the way the novel invites its reader to enjoy the work as fiction while simultaneously letting him or her read it as a critique of the dictatorial past. This, at least, is what may be deduced from Richard Elder's review of *La sombra del viento*'s English translation in the *New York Times*:

> Throughout, in fact, the residue of the past's fraternal horror is the grave thematic substratum beneath capers and mystifications. [...] We are taken on a wild ride – *for* a ride, we may occasionally feel – that executes its hairpin bends with breathtaking lurches. But there is more to say. Return a moment to the civil war. Ostensibly an undertheme to the pyrotechnics, in fact it is *the* theme – an enduring darkness that the pyrotechnics serve to light up.

So, it turns out that even in this work, where the uncanny is no more than a tropological play, its tropes contribute to discordance and multiple readings. While the novel's reliance on the pleasantly creepy gloom of the gothic comes to stand *in the place* of the actual horrors of the reality described, it still maintains a moralistic stance that is condemning enough of the past to still allow a more comfortable reading of this novel as 'responsible'. It may even be argued, as Elder's comment shows, that this work plays down and trivialises the past, but that its very processes of trivialisation make the past return as a ghostly undercurrent. Besides as a story of personal vendetta, then, *La sombra del viento* can be read as a responsible work that takes on collective trauma.

Conclusion

As we have seen, gothic and uncanny tropes can have a considerable effect in a novel. Particularly when they themselves have an ambiguous status in the text that leads to an uncanny feel, while giving way to a haunting process that is connected to the shared, traumatised past, the spectral tropes acquire a highly disturbing dimension. Such is the case in Justo Navarro's *La casa del padre*. In spite of its normative stance, where the unreliable narrator's value system is implicitly criticised by and subordinated to a moralistic viewpoint, the intrusion of trauma through gothic and uncanny motifs disturbs this possibility of a concordant reading. As the Possad episode is revealed, it becomes clear that the experience of trauma allows other approaches to the past than that of the narratee who judges the narrator. Such a judgment becomes difficult in the context of the Possad episode, a trauma that stops the reader from being able to identify with the narrator-protagonist, and it becomes the more difficult in the light of the bizarre outcome of the incident, which turns the crazed murderer into a war hero.

The novel manages to drive home this point particularly well by casting the protagonist's day-to-day reality in the light of his earlier traumatic experience, making use of disturbingly uncanny motifs in the process. In this way, the reader is confronted with the sensation of being stuck in a muffled, snowlike world long before the accident in Russia is related, and haunted by a host of characters who all seem to be hiding something, often endowed with decidedly uncanny traits. Houses mirror one another and monstrous creatures inhabit them. This work, then, can thus also be read as a plea for the narrator-protagonist's choice of values, which becomes understandable in the light of his trauma, or as a statement against morals in general, undermining either value system through uncanny haunting.

In *Luna lunera* by Rosa Regàs, gothic and uncanny motifs create an uncanny feeling, precisely because they can be explained rationally as well as interpreted as strange. This hesitation between readings, between the realism of the work and the possible lack of realism introduced by the gothic and uncanny elements, creates discordance. Judging by statements made in interviews by author Rosa Regàs, and most of all by the vehemence with which her narrator Anna comments on her childhood memories and criticises the grandfather who ruined her youth, such ambiguity may not be intended by *Luna lunera*, a novel which relies on a loudly proclaimed value system.

In this novel, it is immediately clear who the villain is, and with which innocent little children the reader is to side and empathise. The work criticises francoist society, particularly those in power, as it goes along, sparing neither church nor Law. The presence of gothic and uncanny motifs is perhaps surprising, in this sense. While they obviously aid the novel in constructing a truly horrific, 'dickensian' childhood, they also interrupt harsh reality and in this way lessen the force of the narrator's indignant and thoroughly bitter eloquence. *Luna lunera*'s value system and the concordant reading it enables are undermined, it turns out, by the presence of gothic motifs. Ambiguity and uncertainty enter into the novel, and in the process, the harsh historical reality comes to appear distorted. It is no longer a reality, but a terrifying ghostly realm that stands in strong contrast to the unpleasant, but at any rate normally-sized world outside of the grandfather's castle.

Clearly, the gothic and the uncanny make for a high degree of discordance when they evoke an uncannily indeterminate feeling. In *La sombra del viento* by Carlos Ruiz Zafón, the spectral tropes do not have such an uncanny effect, because the fictional realm allows for them to seem normal. That does not mean, however, that this novel is concordant in any way. In fact, even without evoking the uncanny, the stereotypical tropes undermine concordance: they acquire an atmospheric importance that permits a complicated double reading. The pleasantly scary atmosphere both supports the narrative dominant that judges the past *and* makes that past appear interesting and exciting at the same time.

While it can thus be said that tropes of fear, such as the gothic and uncanny tropes, do not always allow the uncanny to be evoked by a novel, and while they frequently remain an unproblematic aspect of the novel's plot, a work containing such motifs certainly does not gain concordance: many readings are possible. What is more, in the case of these memory novels, the lack of realism and the 'scary' feel the tropes give a novel can go against a work's intention to 'deal with' the past. The memory of the francoist past may even be neutralised and mitigated by these tropes, as many conclude in the case of *La sombra del viento*; the motifs may undermine a value system as firm as that of *Luna lunera*; and they may unfold the complicated ethical questions raised by a novel such as *La casa del padre*.

PART III

CONCLUSION

CHAPTER 7

Conclusion

In the contemporary memory paradigm, against the background of the international memory boom, the role of literature as a memory medium has become one of the focal points. Under the effect of the paradigm's post-Holocaust legacy, though, scholars of collective memory often show a tendency to describe this role in psychoanalytic terms, and this tendency makes fiction appear as a medicine against 'forgetting' and a therapy for 'working through' a 'traumatic' past. As a consequence, scholars of memory in literature often side with the victims of the processes they describe, so that they become participants in the debates who copy some of their normative discourses rather than consider the place of their objects of study in relation to these debates. Instead of discussing the role of literature in the memory culture and as a memory medium, they run the risk of stating what the role of a work of fiction *should* be.

In itself, of course, this is a pertinent question. Literary works that touch on memory debates, particularly where these concern painful and neutralised aspects of one's own past, can be said to have some sort of ethical obligation. Their relation to historical events is by necessity not one of playfulness or carelessness – a view which is, unlike what some memory scholars appear to assume, shared by memory scholars and post-structuralists alike. Moreover, many are convinced that literature's particular nature, its fundamental potential to let Otherness remain Other, its portrayal of many different norms, values and narratives that are a part of a discourse it shares with the outside world, and its overall complexity and unreadability, make it more suitable than other forms of writing for addressing difficult pasts. But the question of ethics should not lead to any prescriptions, to claims that a memory novel 'should deal with the past' and 'not silence it'. Such prescriptions, indeed, can be considered unethical themselves: they suggest that works of fiction can somehow control and neutralise the past, and that they generate a healing process. These types of assumptions do no justice to the experiences of the actual victims of the past, and indeed exclude their voices as literature speaks for them.

I have tried, in the above, to avoid a similar approach to the contemporary Spanish memory novels I have discussed here. This does not

213

mean, of course, that I have been objective where others were subjective, exchanging the dependent participant-position for a neutral place above the discourse on memory, from where I could study the complex network of memory debates and those who are involved in them. Rather, I have tried, from a position inescapably *inside* the discursive formation, to look upon the novels as utterances in a field of rules and norms, as unique statements dependent on, but also possibly imposing and exhibiting the limits of, these norms as to what may and can be said about the past, by whom, and in what way. In doing so, my aim has been to avoid adopting the dominant narrative of healing and working-through that can especially be found in many scholarly studies about memory and the Spanish past, a narrative which would reduce the novels to simple utterances which, in a chain of cause and effect, either contributed or failed to contribute to the memory boom at the end of that chain. Instead, I have approached these works as specific memory media that appeared at specific moments, and investigated both the normative system ranking their memory narratives and the places where they escaped or inverted that very hierarchy.

As a consequence, I have distanced myself from a perception of ethics which I have called Aristotelian here, and which can be felt in many of the statements and assumptions of those memory scholars stuck in the dominant narrative of health and healing. Aristotelian ethics induces scholars to read novels as *concordant* entities, which, by using empathy and mild surprise, lead the reader to a clear and simple meaning and interpretation. Instead, I have looked upon these literary works as complex and fundamentally *discordant* works, whose possible readings lay bare conflictive memory narratives and value systems. This much more post-structuralist approach assumes that every text, and certainly every literary text, is discordant – that it does not just obey rules and makes clear normative suggestions, but that it contains multiple problematic, even conflictive meanings and readings and is uncontrollable both to the reader and to the author. It is the works' Otherness I want to expose, so that their complexity and inconsistency as memory media comes to the foreground, rather than the measure in which they obey or fail to obey later readers' expectations.

I have started out by demonstrating the fallacy of the Aristotelian model of literature, which assumes that a narrative can be kept concordant (and that this is a good thing) by means of the use of tragic emotions. First, I have tried to show that even elements which make a narrative predictable, and which provide its readers with comfortable reading tools, do not always aid a work of fiction in maintaining at least an appearance of simplicity and straightforwardness. One such stereotype, that of the *Bildungsroman* (a genre frequently called up in the context of memory novels), proves that its use in a narrative in combination with its disruption can easily lead to a degree of discordance. Critique, irony or parody expose the stereotype: it is ridiculed and its workings are laid bare. Nonetheless, it still remains present in the text itself and is not entirely dismissed. Then again, the very stereotypical nature of the genre form and its dependence on tropes allow it to be called up in a novel, even if the novel itself clearly deviates from the standard generic work – we may now perhaps reintroduce the concept of mode to describe this process. In such a case, a simple reading is by no means the only option: readerly expectations are called up, then broken, and the coherent reading remains present even where another one is finally pursued. It seems, then, that only the works that do not stray from the prototypical plot of the *Bildungsroman* (in either of its five Bakhtinian guises) can appear openly concordant; but since the prototypical plot is a matter that is under debate, who knows how concordant they can ever really get?

Then, I turned my attention to the so-called rational emotions of fear, pity, and surprise by looking at nostalgia and autobiography. A frequent phenomenon in memory novels, nostalgia is often a very effective way of making a reader feel empathy for a character, and the autobiographical moment as it is often used in memory fiction is highly suitable for building a surprise effect into a plot. As it turns out, these emotions also prove unreliable when called up in a novel. As a rule, their force exceeds the merely rational, so that their workings in a narrative turn out to provoke discordance. Though it could be said that nostalgia causes compassion and empathy, it has become clear that its 'ethical' use in the Aristotelian sense does not entirely neutralise its force. Whether it is accompanied by critique or evoked with irony, the feeling of nostalgia is not lessened as a consequence, and it constitutes a seductive double meaning within the novels, suggesting a pleasantly melancholy and enjoyable reading of the past at odds with the more critical versions of memory advocated.

The emotion of surprise does not guarantee concordance either, as the case of autobiography shows. Autobiography calls up a certain form of authority – the reader is induced to believe the autobiographical narrator, and his narration is provided with an aura of authenticity. The autobiographical pact is not maintained in autobiographical fiction, though, and the alternation of 'truth' and fiction turns out to be a struggle that increases discordance. Autobiography's authority can get undermined by the claim of fiction to a fictional kind of 'truth' that might seem more 'honest' than the aura of authenticity that surrounds autobiography. Particularly when the surprise of the interruption or intrusion of autobiography gives way to a process of haunting, fictionality may come to compete with the claim to 'realism' of autobiography. The narrative can thus come to contain a struggle for ultimate authority, and in the process, a double reading.

Finally, tropes of the fearsome, such as the gothic and uncanny, can introduce uncertainty and complexity into a narrative, a feeling of the uncanny. The work can arouse a terror that supersedes the 'rational', tragic emotions of either fear or surprise. It can do so by surrounding the status of the tropes with ambiguity – and by connecting them to a real fear or preoccupation (which is not hard to find in the context of the difficult past that the Spanish memory novels talk of). The tropes then become indeterminate and strange, and this strangeness extends to the memory narratives and the value hierarchy that ranks them. But even if these tropes just remain tropes of the fearsome, their fictional and familiar nature can already cause a high degree of discordance in novels in which painful historical realities are remembered. After all, they call up a reality that is attractive because of its dark atmosphere, and this attraction contrasts with critical approaches to that same past.

It has thus become abundantly clear that none of these novels have only one, simple reading. Instead, they all contain forces that contradict each other, undermining the apparent ideology of the work or inviting an opposite perspective to an advocated memory narrative. The importance of reading these novels like this, as contradictory and discordant, becomes clear if we compare this reading to other readings these works have received, particularly from the moment the memory boom took off and the question of ethics gained importance. Remarkably, Spanish novels often seem to obey the complex normative systems in which they came to exist to quite an extent, sticking to and holding up a largely implicit set of rules as to how the past might be addressed. Very frequently, however, scholars insist on reading works as critical comments on the past, even if such a reading is refused openly by the work itself.

Such is the case with Luis Goytisolo's 1992 novel *Estatua con palomas*. It carefully describes the narrator-protagonist's youth under the francoist dictatorship, as one would expect of a work written in times when careful neutralisation was still the norm. It seems to want to provide us with a 'collective', that is to say depersonalised and neutralised view of the dictatorial past, for while such an approach naturally avoids a narrative that is too topical or small-scale, it also suggests a wish for distance and objectivity that reduces the dictatorship to just another historical period. Later on, scholars like Garrido (1995) or Molero de la Iglesia (2000) have wanted to credit the author with an even more responsible attitude. Even though they are aware of the work's complexity, they perform a reductive reading upon the novel, relying on the autobiographical narrator by comparing and equating a period of political instability in Ancient Rome to francoist Spain. The novel itself, though, undermines narrator Goytisolo quite enough to make the work seem more discordant and less responsible than it is made out to be.

Of course, there is something to be said for this view on things, because memory novels often *do* play a role in advancing real world collective memory processes. Considering its context, Goytisolo's novel can be called progressive for its treatment of the past alone. Yet it seems that this and other memory novels of the early 1990s choose to deal with the past not solely out of a concern with transitional 'forgetting', but because the authors' lives, their youths, and their development into writers took place under the dictatorship. A great number of these novels describe, following the *Bildungsroman*-format, the coming-of-age under francoism of a young man who in some ways resembles the author. The texts become invested with a fundamental difficulty: the confrontation of nostalgic, happy, 'autobiographical' memories and the knowledge acquired later that these memories were shaped against the backdrop of a cruel and unjust regime. Even though ethics thus becomes a theme or preoccupation in these works, they still tend to allow for a rosy, nostalgic view of the past. This is not so much the case in Goytisolo's novel, which attempts to avoid a too personal view of the dictatorship and to knock its autobiographical narrator off his pedestal. But the narrator in Julio Llamazares's *Escenas de cine mudo* (1994) shows a deep feeling of guilt as he recognises that his rational, adult view of the past does not change the way nostalgia still seduces him. Manuel Vicent's *Tranvía a la Malvarrosa* (1994) suggests that his later insights into the nature of the dictatorship do make the narrator feel guilty, but the way the work combines nostalgia, eroticism, sensorial pleasure and a hint of decadence, clearly invites the real readers to let go of their scruples and indulge in this past.

Other novels are more obviously critical in nature and bank less on the individualist, autobiographical and nostalgic tone. Antonio Muñoz Molina's *El dueño del secreto* (1994) resembles the nostalgic novels in many ways: it is also a semi-autobiographical *Bildungsroman*, and shows a tendency toward melancholy and occasional nostalgia. It contains a particularly forceful autobiographical moment when the narrator learns about fear, 'real' fear, as he faces the francoist police. At the same time, the novel is also critical of the way francoism ended and of the silence of the *Transición*, and many readers have seen it as a work that combines nostalgia with a strong social and political critique. Such readers tend to overlook the fact that the narrator's authority is dubious, and that the *Bildungsroman* stereotype is parodied – so that a downright moralistic reading is rendered more complicated. Álvaro Pombo's *Aparición del eterno femenino* (1993), also a *Bildungsroman* with autobiographical traits, comments on the past, parodying the behaviour

217

of the nationalist and pro-francoist adult characters and allowing the young protagonist's happy world to be haunted by history. In Justo Navarro's 1994 novel *La casa del padre*, the unreliable narrator's discourse of forgetting obviously serves as a handy excuse for him to cover up his own crimes. At the same time, though, uncanny and gothic elements create disturbing ambiguity, and it becomes clear that while Navarro's work denounces the silence of the *Transición*, it does not replace this with a memory narrative that would approach the later, democratic one.

In general, then, many of these novels of the early 1990s deal with the difficulty of remembering a personal past, while acknowledging the fact that the society which forms a background to that past was not exactly perfect. They also criticise the process of *desmemorización* of the transition to democracy, with its tendency to portray itself as a glorious step into a revolutionary future, and of the dictatorship itself. The novels thus seem to fulfil their roles as forerunners in broaching new subjects and transgressing norms, but they do so in the most careful way possible. The works incorporate and comment on various memory discourses, often in a critical way, but their nostalgic tendencies, their use of parody or their undermining of the narrator's authority may soften such criticism. They do not offer a loud counternarrative or search for justice and compensation. In this sense, all of these novels seem typical products of their time, where the one, transitional memory narrative seemed to have lost much of its vigour, but still was not confronted directly with that other, the democratic one.

The three novels from the second half of the 1990s suggest hat this new memory narrative gained importance, though. They each express a clear will to be critical and to challenge fiercely the transitional tendency to hush up the painful past. Much more than the earlier novels, these could be called, if not responsible, then *aware* of a responsibility. Both Andrés Trapiello's *El buque fantasma* (1998) and Rosa Regàs's *Luna lunera* (1999) are highly polemical novels that try to assert certain shared conceptions of the past. Neither text is actually successful when it comes to constructing a concordant reading to this purpose: Regàs's novel is disturbed by the uncanny, and Trapiello's sinks back into nostalgic reminiscing when it claims to combat revisionism. *El buque fantasma* even caused readers to protest massively, to such an extent that the author deemed an added, defensive epilogue necessary. However, the responsible tone and moral outrage of these two works' narrators contrasts with the earlier novels' melancholy stance. Félix de Azúa's *Momentos decisivos* (2000) also resorts to a strongly critical tone, and abandons the *Bildungsroman*-form in order to do so.

This line of criticism was first continued as the memory boom unfolded. Rafael Chirbes's *Los viejos amigos* (2003) is similar to the works of Regàs, Trapiello and, particularly, Azúa, as it polemically challenges the narrative of forgetting and tries to undo the myth of the revolution. *Tu rostro mañana* by Javier Marías (2002-2007) seems to balance a neutralising, transitional narrative with a more democratic one, in favour of justice, but it also confronts the reader directly with the past through its haunting autobiographical moments, where the cruelty of the Civil War transpires. However, another direction emerged as a part of the memory boom, which seems like a return to a neutralisation of the past in spite of its now being a central theme instead of a taboo. A number of novels appeared which treated the painful past as something to be dealt with, but also, as past in general. This tendency of using Spain's difficult history as a neutral background, a reservoir of stories of heroism and anguish, is visible in Carlos Ruiz Zafón's 2001 *La sombra del viento*. It is also the turn that is taken by Javier Cercas's influential *Soldados de Salamina* of the same year, even if this novel responds to and incorporates a discourse of finding justice and truth.

Notably, each of these two novels can be said to contain a critical memory discourse that responsibly put francoism in its place. Nevertheless, their obvious pleasure in the fictionalising of history, in the appropriation of it to the education or enjoyment of the reader, stands at quite a distance from the more serious, even bitter shades of Regàs's or Azúa's texts. For this reason, and perhaps also because of their enormous commercial success, they have raised ethical questions, causing discussion inside and outside Spain. Enrique Vila-Matas's *París no se acaba nunca* (2003) does not show such a perceived disconcern for the weight of the painful past. His novel refers to it, but otherwise actually manages to ignore it almost entirely. It could be said that this lack of treatment of the past is necessary, for without this weight, the novel can be 'allowed' its postmodern playfulness.

All in all, it seems that with Vila-Matas as a notable exception, we might carefully conclude that Spanish authors show the same wish of dealing with the past that Spanish society as a whole seems to have shown. As they look for ways to thematise it, they incorporate some of the main contextual memory narratives into their works, to challenge, expose or defend these. And as the memory boom brought with it the commercial interest of the past as a literary theme, the novels did not lag behind but profited by it, too. Spanish literature has thus not played the very progressive, taboo-breaking part Bernecker, Winter and others expect of literature in general. Instead, it has followed more or less the increasing call for a renewed dealing with the past that marked Spanish society at large. As society started to commemorate, so did literature; as society developed a new memory discourse to counter an old one, so did literature; and as society started developing what some call a veritable memory market, literature reaped its benefits.

The view that thus emerges of contemporary Spanish memory literature may, perhaps, anger some of its scholars. Literary texts cannot escape the memory narratives present in their society. Instead, they struggle with these, allowing one to dominate the other accidentally, abandoning them both, or letting them all be present at the same time. To read them in an ethical way, that is, to allow them their fundamental discordance and to look for contradictory and competing possibilities of reading, is to exhibit the difficulties, the norms and the values that compete with each other in contemporary Spanish memory discourses. These fictional worlds show the complexity of the difficult past and the contradictions, rules, and problems that any memory of such a past is faced with. This, of course, is the ethical potential of literature: it does not simplify the Civil War and francoism, arguing for one particular version of 'truth', but by incorporating rivalling narratives and showing their flaws, it illustrates how complex and unknowably Other that past is even to those who lived it.

But the Spanish case also shows that while works of fiction latch on to social processes in an utterly indirect and complicated way, they *do* take memory narratives and newly organise them. This organisation may be discordant, conflictive and often contradictory – but perhaps, this is precisely what the function of literature as a memory medium is all about. Fiction demonstrates how complicated such narratives, such value systems are, and it shows how their combination and confrontation leads to a lack of clarity and a lot of confusion. It places them in surroundings other than the 'real world' and stresses their fictionality. Rather than picking elements from their context and thus presenting a reduced, simplified, concordant plot, so that they can advocate one value system, one view on memory against all others, these Spanish memory novels present us with a mapping of the inner complexities of narrated memory as a whole.

Thus, a work of fiction can play its very own role in society. It can be read in reductive ways, it can be criticised for certain impressions it makes on certain readers, and it can be appropriated by different groups, or collectives, of readers, as each puts it to use in its own memory context. Altogether, though, fiction shows not only its own inherent discordance, but also the inner discordance of memory narratives themselves. It is not surprising, then, that authors of Spanish memory novels often fail to produce a straightforwardly concordant reading of the past, and *that* responsibility must not be asked of them.

Works Cited

Adorno, Theodor W., "Kulturkritik und Gesellschaft", in *Prismen. Kulturkritik und Gesellschaft*, Frankfurt am Main, Suhrkamp, 1969 [1955], pp. 7-31.

Adriaensen, Brigitte, *La poética de la ironía en la obra tardía de Juan Goytisolo* (1993-2000): *Arabescos para entendidos*, Madrid, Verbum, 2007.

Aguilar Fernández, Paloma, *Memoria y olvido de la guerra civil española*, Madrid, Alianza, 1996.

Alberca, Manuel, "Las vueltas autobiográficas de Javier Marías", in Irene Andres-Suárez and Ana Casas (eds.), *Javier Marías*, Madrid, Arco; Neuchâtel, Universidad de Neuchâtel, 2005, pp. 49-72.

Alcalde, Soledad, "Fomento retira de madrugada la estatua ecuestre de Franco de Nuevos Ministerios", in *El País*, 17 March 2005.

Alphen, Ernst van, *Caught by History: Holocaust Effects in Contemporary Art, Literature, and Theory*, Stanford, Stanford University Press, 1997.

Amossy, Ruth, *Les idées reçues: sémiologie du stéréotype*, Paris, Nathan, 1991.

——, "Introduction to the Study of Doxa", in *Poetics Today* 23.3, 2002, pp. 369-394.

Anderson, Linda, *Autobiography*, London/New York, Routledge, 2001.

Aristotle, *Aristotle's Poetics*, James Hutton (trans.), New York, W.W. Norton, 1982.

——, *Poetics*, D.W. Lucas (ed.), Oxford, Clarendon, 1968.

Assmann, Aleida, "Four Formats of Memory: From Individual to Collective Forms of Constructing the Past", in Christian Emden and David Midgley (eds.), *Cultural Memory and Historical Consciousness in the German-Speaking World Since 1500*, Bern, Peter Lang, 2004, pp. 19-38.

——. "Gedächtnis als Leitbegriff der Kulturwissenschaften", in Lutz Musner and Gotthart Wunberg (eds.), *Kulturwissenschaften: Forschung – Praxis – Positionen*, Wien, WUV, 2002, pp. 27-45.

Assmann, Jan, *Das kulturelle Gedächtnis: Schrift, Erinnerung und politische Identität in frühen Hochkulturen*, München, Beck, 1992.

Ayala-Dip, J. Ernesto, "Amor, decoro y confianza", in *El País*, 21 June 2003, Babelia.

Azúa, Félix de, *Momentos Decisivos*, Barcelona, Anagrama, 2000.

Baker, Peter, *Deconstruction and the Ethical Turn*, Gainesville [etc.], University Press of Florida, 1995.

Bakhtin, M. M., "The *Bildungsroman* and Its Significance in the History of Realism (Toward a Historical Typology of the Novel)", in *Speech Genres and Other Late Essays*, Vern W. McGee (trans.), Caryl Emerson and Michael Holquist (eds.), Austin, University of Texas Press, 1986.

——, "Forms of Time and the Chronotope in the Novel", in *The Dialogic Imagination*, Caryl Emerson and Michael Holquist (trans,), Michael Holquist (ed.), Austin, University of Texas Press, 2004 [1981], pp. 84-258.

——, *Problems of Dostoevsky's Poetics*, R.W. Rotsel (trans.), Ann Arbor, Michigan, Ardis, 1973.

Baldick, Chris, *The Concise Oxford Dictionary of Literary Terms*, Oxford, Oxford University Press, 1996 [1990].

Ballesteros, Isolina, *Escritura femenina y discurso autobiográfico en la nueva novela española*, New York, Peter Lang, 1994.

Bannasch, Bettina and Holm Christiane (eds.), *Erinnern und Erzählen: Der spanische Bürgerkrieg in der deutschen und spanischen Erzählliteratur und in den Bildmedien*, Tübingen, Gunter Narr, 2005.

Barthes, Roland, *La chambre claire: note sur la photographie*, Paris, Gallimard Seuil, 1980.

Baudrillard, Jean, *Simulacres et simulation*, Paris, Galilée, 1981.

Benjamin, Walter, "The Work of Art in the Age of Mechanical Reproduction", in Meenakshi Gigi Durham and Douglas MacKay Kellner (eds.), *Media and Cultural Studies: Keyworks*, Malden, Massachusetts, Blackwell, 2001, pp. 48-70.

Bernecker, Walther L., "Demokratisierung und Vergangenheitsaufarbeitung in Spanien", in Bettina Bannasch and Christiane Holm (eds.), *Erinnern und Erzählen: Der spanische Bürgerkrieg in der deutschen und spanischen Literatur und in den Bildmedien*, Tübingen, Gunter Narr, 2005, pp. 9-23.

Blakeley, Georgina, "Digging up Spain's Past: Consequences of Truth and Reconciliation", in *Democratization* 12.1, 2005, pp. 44-59.

Booth, Wayne, *The Rhetoric of Fiction*, Chicago, University of Chicago Press, 1967 [1961].

Boym, Svetlana, *The Future of Nostalgia*, New York, Basic Books, 2001.

Bradu, Fabienne, "*El dueño del secreto* de Antonio Muñoz Molina", in *Vuelta* 221, 1995, pp. 46-47.

Braese, Stephan and Holger Gehle, "Literaturwissenschaft und Literaturgeschichte nach dem Holocaust", in *Text + Kritik* 144, 1999, pp. 79-95.

Brockmeier, Jens, "Remembering and Forgetting: Narrative as Cultural Memory", in *Culture and Psychology* 8, 2002, pp. 15-43.

Buckley, Jerome Hamilton, *Seasons of Youth: The Bildungsroman from Dickens to Golding*, Cambridge, Massachusetts, Harvard University Press, 1974.

Burke, Séan, *The Death and Return of the Author: Criticism and Subjectivity in Barthes, Foucault and Derrida*, 2nd ed., Edinburgh, Edinburgh University Press, 1998.

Caballé, Anna, "La escritura autobiográfica: seguir los hilos", in *Quimera* 240, 2004, pp. 10-13.

Cardús i Ros, Salvador, "Politics and the Invention of Memory. For a Sociology of the Transition to Democracy in Spain", in Joan Ramon Resina (ed.), *Dis-*

remembering the Dictatorship: The Politics of Memory in the Spanish Transition to Democracy, Amsterdam, Rodopi, 2000, pp. 17-28.

Catelli, Nora, "El nuevo efecto Cercas", in *El País*, 9 November 2002.

Cercas, Javier, *Soldados de Salamina*, Barcelona, Tusquets, 2001.

"Cercas se confiesa ante los alumnos", in *El País*, 12 May 2006.

Chirbes, Rafael, *Los viejos amigos*, Barcelona, Anagrama, 2003.

"Chirbes alerta en 'Los viejos amigos' de que no se puede aparcar la vida", in *El País*, 16 October 2003, Valencia ed.

Cifre Wibrow, Patricia, "Literatura, memoria y olvido. La narrativa española y austríaca de los ochenta", in *Anthropos* 196, 2002, pp. 174-194.

Cook, Pam, *Screening the Past: Memory and Nostalgia in Cinema*, London, Routledge, 2005.

Critchley, Simon, "On Derrida's *Specters of Marx*", in *Philosophy & Social Criticism* 21.3, 1995, pp. 1-30.

Cuñado, Isabel, *El espectro de la herencia: la narrativa de Javier Marías*, Amsterdam, Rodopi, 2004.

DeKoven Ezrahi, Sidra, *By Words Alone: The Holocaust in Literature*, Chicago and London, University of Chicago Press, 1980.

——, "Representing Auschwitz", in *History and Memory* 7.2, 1996, pp. 121-154.

Derrida, Jacques, *De la grammatologie*, Paris, Minuit, 1967.

——, "Marx, c'est quelqu'un", in Marc Guillaume, Jacques Derrida, and Jean-Pierre Vincent (eds.), *Marx en jeu*, Paris, Descartes & Cie, 1997, pp. 9-28.

——, *Spectres de Marx: l'état de la dette, le travail du deuil et la nouvelle Internationale*, Paris, Galilée, 1993.

——, "Violence et métaphysique: Essai sur la pensée de E. Levinas (première partie)", in *Revue de métaphysique et de morale* 69.3, 1964, pp. 322-354.

——, "Violence et métaphysique: Essai sur la pensée de E. Levinas (deuxième partie)", in *Revue de métaphysique et de morale* 69.4, 1964, pp. 425-473.

Doubrovsky, Serge, "Autobiographie/vérité/psychanalyse", in *Autobiographiques: de Corneille à Sartre*, Paris, PUF, 1988.

Dufays, Jean-Louis, *Stéréotype et lecture*, Liège, Mardaga, 1994.

——, "Stéréotypes, lecture littéraire et postmodernisme", in Christian Plantin (ed.), *Lieux communs, topoi, stéréotypes, clichés*, Paris, Kimé, 1993, pp. 80-91.

Eaglestone, Robert, *The Holocaust and the Postmodern*, Oxford, Oxford University Press, 2004.

Eakin, Paul John, *Touching the World: Reference in Autobiography*, Princeton, Princeton University Press, 1992.

Echevarría, Ignacio, *Trayecto: un recorrido crítico por la reciente narrativa española*, Barcelona, Debate, 2005.

Eder, Richard, "In the Cemetery of Forgotten Books", in *New York Times Book Review*, 25 April 2004.

Ellis, Robert Richmond, "Reading the Spanish Past: Library Fantasies in Carlos Ruiz Zafón's *La sombra del viento*", in *Bulletin of Spanish Studies* 83.6, 2006, pp. 839-854.

Erll, Astrid, *Kollektives Gedächtnis und Erinnerungskulturen*, Stuttgart, J.B. Metzler, 2005.

Evans, Mary, *Missing Persons: The Impossibility of Auto/Biography*, London/ New York, Routledge, 1999.

Faber, Sebastiaan, "The Price of Peace: Historical Memory in Post-Franco Spain", in *Revista hispánica moderna* 58.1-2, 2005, 205-220.

Felman, Shoshana and Laub, Dori, *Testimony: Crises of Witnessing in Literature, Psychoanalysis, and History*, New York/London, Routledge, 1992.

Ferns, Chris, *Narrating Utopia: Ideology, Gender, Form in Utopian Literature*, Liverpool, Liverpool University Press, 1999.

Ferrán, Ofelia, "Memory and Forgetting, Resistance and Noise in the Spanish Transition: Semprún and Vázquez Montalbán", in Joan Ramon Resina (ed.), *Disremembering the Dictatorship: The Politics of Memory in the Spanish Transition to Democracy*, Amsterdam, Rodopi, 2000, pp. 191-222.

Fletcher, John, "Marx the Uncanny? Ghosts and Their Relation to the Mode of Production", in *Radical Philosophy* 75, 1996, pp. 31-37.

Foucault, Michel, *L'archéologie du savoir*, Paris, Gallimard, 1969.

——, *L'ordre du discours*, Paris, Gallimard, 1971.

Freud, Sigmund, "Das Unheimliche", *Das Unheimliche: Aufsätze zur Literatur*, Frankfurt am Main, Fischer, 1963 [1919], pp. 45-84.

Friedlander, Saul, *Memory, History, and the Extermination of the Jews of Europe*, Bloomington and Indianapolis, Indiana University Press, 1993.

García-Abadillo, Casimiro, "11-M: sin rastro de la marca Al Qaeda", in *El Mundo*, 25 June 2007.

Garrido, Rosa María, "Una lectura posmodernista de *Estatua con palomas* de Luis Goytisolo", in Miguel Ángel Vázquez Medel (ed.), *Luis Goytisolo: el espacio de la creación*, Barcelona, Lumen, 1995, pp. 168-182.

"El Gobierno confirma la 'reconversión' del Valle de los Caídos, pero reconoce que aún no hay propuesta formal", in *ABC*, 29 March 2005.

"El Gobierno convertirá el Valle de los Caídos en un 'centro de interpretación' del franquismo, según ICV", in *ABC*, 28 March 2005.

Gómez López-Quiñones, Antonio, *La guerra persistente: memoria, violencia y utopía: representaciones contemporáneas de la Guerra Civil española*, Frankfurt am Main, Vervuert, 2006.

Goytisolo, Luis, *Estatua con palomas*, Barcelona, Destino, 1992.

Green, Peter, "Doom, Gloom, and Suspense", *Los Angeles Times Book Review*, 3 May 2004, p. R6.

Graef, Ortwin de, "Onbeslecht geweten: literatuur, sympathetiek en hermeneutisch geweld", in Bart Philipsen, Ria van den Brandt and Elianne Mulder (eds.), *Verbeeldingen van de Ander: over literatuur, filosofie en religie*, Budel, Damon, 2002, pp. 21-46.

Grohmann, Alexis, *Coming into One's Own: The Novelistic Development of Javier Marías*, Amsterdam/New York, Rodopi, 2002.

Halbwachs, Maurice, *Les cadres sociaux de la mémoire*, Paris, Albin Michel, 1994 [1925].

Hamon, Philippe, *Texte et idéologie*, Paris, Presses Universitaires de France, 1984.

Hirsch, Marianne, *Family Frames: Photography, Narrative, and Postmemory*, Cambridge, Massachusetts, Harvard University Press, 1997.

Howard, Jacqueline, *Reading Gothic Fiction: A Bakhtinian Approach*, Oxford, Clarendon, 1994.

Hutcheon, Linda, "Irony, Nostalgia and the Postmodern", in Raymond Vervliet and Annemarie Estor (eds.), *Methods for the Study of Literature as Cultural Memory*, Amsterdam, Rodopi, 1997, pp. 189-207.

——, *A Theory of Parody: The Teachings of Twentieth-Century Art Forms*, New York, Methuen, 1985.

Huyssen, Andreas, *Twilight Memories: Marking Time in a Culture of Amnesia*, New York/London, Routledge, 1995.

Ibáñez Ehrlich, María-Teresa, "Memoria y revolución: el desengaño de una quimera", in María-Teresa Ibáñez Ehrlich (ed.), *Ensayos sobre Rafael Chirbes*, Madrid, Iberoamericana; Frankfurt am Main, Vervuert, 2006, pp. 59-79.

Intxausti, A., "Rafael Chirbes describe el desencanto de una generación en 'Los viejos amigos'", in *El País*, 5 June 2003.

Iser, Wolfgang, *Das Fiktive und das Imaginäre*, Frankfurt am Main, Suhrkamp, 1993.

——, *Der implizite Leser: Kommunikationsformen des Romans von Bunyan bis Beckett*, München, Wilhelm Fink, 1972.

Izquierdo, José María, "Memoria y literatura en la narrativa española contemporánea. Unos ejemplos", in *Historia y memoria*, spec. issue of *Anales nueva época* 3-4, 2001, pp. 101-128.

Jameson, Fredric, "Marx' Purloined Letter", in Michael Sprinker (ed.), *Ghostly Demarcations: A Symposium on Jacques Derrida's Specters of Marx*, London, Verso, 1999, pp. 26-67.

Jauß, Hans Robert, "Literaturgeschichte als Provokation der Literaturwissenschaft", in *Literaturgeschichte als Provokation*, Frankfurt am Main, Suhrkamp, 1970, pp. 144-207.

Jeffers, Thomas L., *Apprenticeships: The Bildungsroman from Goethe to Santayana*, New York, Palgrave MacMillan, 2005.

Jouve, Vincent, *Poétique des valeurs*, Paris, Presses Universitaires de France, 2001.

"El juego de la memoria: Luna lunera", in *El Correo Digital*, 2 December 1999 [El Correo Digital, 18 January 2008, http://servicios.elcorreodigital.com/ \\auladecultura/regas1.html].

Kammen, Michael, Rev. of *Frames of Remembrance. The Dynamics of Collective Memory* by Iwona Irwin-Zarecka, in *History and Theory* 34.3, 1995, pp. 245-261.

Kansteiner, Wulf, "Finding Meaning in Memory: A Methodological Critique of Collective Memory Studies", in *History and Theory* 41, 2002, 179-197.

Keunen, Bart, "Bakhtin, Genre Formation, and the Cognitive Turn: Chronotopes as Memory Schemata", in *Comparative Literature and Culture* 2.2, 2000, 15 pp. [27 May 2008 http://docs.lib.purdue.edu/clcweb/vol2/\\ iss2/2/].

King, Stephen, "It's Alive! Alive!", in *Entertainment Weekly* 766, 21 May 2004.

Labanyi, Jo, "El cine como lugar de la memoria en películas, novelas y autobiografías de los años setenta hasta el presente", in Joan Ramon Resina and Ulrich Winter (eds.), *Casa encantada. Lugares de memoria en la España constitucional (1978-2004)*, Frankfurt am Main, Vervuert, 2005, pp. 157-171.

——, "History and Hauntology; or, What Does One Do with the Ghosts of the Past? Reflections on Spanish Film and Fiction of the Post-Franco Period", in Joan Ramon Resina (ed.) *Disremembering the Dictatorship: The Politics of Memory in the Spanish Transition to Democracy*, Amsterdam: Rodopi, 2000, pp. 65-82.

LaCapra, Dominick, *History and Memory after Auschwitz*, Ithaca/London, Cornell University Press, 1998.

——, *Representing the Holocaust: History, Theory, Trauma*, Ithaca/London, Cornell University Press, 1994.

Lang, Berel, *Holocaust Representation: Art within the Limits of History and Ethics*, Baltimore/London, Johns Hopkins University Press, 2000.

Langa Pizarro, M. Mar, *Del franquismo a la posmodernidad: la novela española (1975-1999): análisis y diccionario de autores*, Alicante, Universidad de Alicante, 2002.

Langer, Lawrence L., *Holocaust Testimonies: The Ruins of Memory*, New Haven, Yale University Press, 1991.

Lejeune, Philippe, *Le pacte autobiographique*, Paris, Éditions du Seuil, 1975.

Lipovetsky, Gilles, "Time against Time: Or the Hypermodern Society", trans. Andrew Brown, in Gilles Lipovetsky, Sébastien Charles and Andrew Brown (eds.), *Hypermodern Times*, Cambridge, Polity, 2005, pp. 29-71.

Llamazares, Julio, *Escenas de cine mudo*, Barcelona, Seix Barral, 2000 [1994].

López Bernasocchi, Augusta, and José Manuel López de Abadía, "'Lo que va de ayer a hoy'. Hacia una caracterización de los personajes principales de *Los viejos amigos*, de Rafael Chirbes", in María-Teresa Ibáñez Ehrlich (ed.),

Ensayos sobre Rafael Chirbes. Madrid, Iberoamericana; Frankfurt am Main, Vervuert, 2006, pp. 105-133.

Lowenthal, David, "Nostalgia Tells It Like It Wasn't", in Cristopher Shaw and Malcolm Chase (eds.), *The Imagined Past: History and Nostalgia*, Manchester, Manchester University Press, 1989, pp. 18-32.

Luengo, Ana, *La encrucijada de la memoria: la memoria colectiva de la Guerra Civil Española en la novela contemporánea*. Berlin, Walter Frey, 2004.

Lyons, John D., "The Ancients' Ironic Nostalgia", in *Paragraph* 26.1, 2006, pp. 94-107.

Lyotard, Jean-François, *Le différend*, Paris, Minuit, 1983.

Maier, Charles S., "A Surfeit of Memory? Reflections on History, Melancholy, and Denial", in *History and Memory* 5.2, 1993, pp. 136-152.

Mainer, José Carlos, "Antonio Muñoz Molina ou la prise de possession de la mémoire", in *Études*, February, 1994, pp. 235-246.

——, *Tramas, libros, nombres: para entender la literatura española, 1944-2000*, Barcelona, Anagrama, 2005.

Man, Paul de, "Autobiography as De-Facement", in *The Rhetoric of Romanticism*, New York, Columbia University Press, 1984, pp. 67-81.

Marías, Javier, "La huella del animal", in *Vuelta* 220, 1995, pp. 43-45.

——, *Mañana en la batalla piensa en mí*, Barcelona, Anagrama, 1994.

——, *Tu rostro mañana: I Fiebre y lanza*, Madrid, Alfaguara, 2002.

——, *Tu rostro mañana: II Baile y sueño*, Madrid, Alfaguara, 2004.

——, *Tu rostro mañana: III Veneno y sombra y adiós*, Madrid, Alfaguara, 2007.

Márquez, Héctor, "El mundo está lleno de canallas felices", in *El País*, 29 May 1994.

Masoliver Ródenas, Juan Antonio, *Voces contemporáneas*, Barcelona, Acantilado, 2004.

Mitscherlich, Alexander and Mitscherlich, Margarethe, *Die Unfähigkeit zu trauern: Grundlagen kollektiven Verhaltens*, München, Piper, 1970 [1967].

Moa, Pío, *Franco: un balance histórico*, Barcelona, Planeta, 2005.

——, *Los mitos de la Guerra Civil*, Madrid, Esfera, 2003.

Molero de la Iglesia, Alicia, *La autoficción en España: Jorge Semprún, Carlos Barral, Luis Goytisolo, Enriqueta Antolín y Antonio Muñoz Molina*, Bern, Peter Lang, 2000.

Mora, Rosa, "Andrés Trapiello gana el Plaza y Janés con un libro sobre la Transición", in *El País*, 26 March 1992.

Moreno, Javier, "Javier Cercas provoca un duro debate en Alemania sobre la recreación de la historia", in *El País*, 19 November 2002.

Moretti, Franco, *The Way of the World: The* Bildungsroman *in European Culture*, London, Verso, 1987.

Muñoz Molina, Antonio, *El dueño del secreto*, Madrid, Castalia, 1997.

Navarro, Justo, *La casa del padre*, Barcelona, Anagrama, 1994.

Nora, Pierre, *Les lieux de mémoire (1984-1992)*, rev. ed., Paris, Gallimard, 1997.

Nussbaum, Martha C., *Poetic Justice: The Literary Imagination and Public Life*, Boston, Beacon, 1995.

Olick, Jeffrey K., and Robbins, Joyce, "Social Memory Studies: From 'Collective Memory' to the Historical Sociology of Mnemonic Practices", in *Annual Review of Sociology* 24, 1996, pp. 105-141.

Oropesa, Salvador A., *La novelística de Antonio Muñoz Molina: sociedad civil y literatura lúdica*, Jaén, Universidad de Jaén, 1999.

Ors, Ines d', "Escenas de cine mudo: Un álbum de fotos sin rostro", in *Cuadernos de narrativa* 3, 1998, pp. 135-149.

Pageaux, Daniel-Henry, *La littérature générale et comparée*, Paris, Colin, 1994.

Pérez, Martha, "El acontecimiento autobiográfico", in Juan Orbe (ed.), *Autobiografía y escritura*, Buenos Aires, Corregidor, 1994, pp. 89-94.

Pérez Miguel, Leandro, "Vila-Matas no se acaba nunca", *El Mundo*, 10 November 2003.

Perry, Jos, *Wij herdenken, dus wij bestaan: over jubilea, monumenten en de collectieve herinnering*, Nijmegen, SUN, 1999.

Pickering, Michael, and Keightley, Emily, "The Modalities of Nostalgia", in *Current Sociology* 54.6, 2006, pp. 919-941.

Pittarello, Elide, "Haciendo tiempo con las cosas", in Irene Andres-Suárez and Ana Casas (eds.), *Javier Marías*, Madrid, Arco; Neuchâtel, Universidad de Neuchâtel, 2005, pp. 17-48.

Pombo, Álvaro, *Aparición del eterno femenino contada por S.M. el Rey*, 2nd ed., Barcelona, Anagrama, 1993.

Pozuelo Yvancos, José María, *Ventanas de la ficción: narrativa hispánica, siglos XX y XXI*, Barcelona, Península, 2004.

Prado Biezma, Javier del, Castillo, Juan Bravo, and Picazo, María Dolores, *Autobiografía y modernidad literaria*, Cuenca, Servicio de Publicaciones de la Universidad de Castilla-La Mancha, 1994.

Ravenet Kenna, Caridad, "Con la cámara en la novela, o el enfoque de Julio Llamazares", in *Revista hispánica moderna* 50.1, 1997, pp. 190-204.

Regàs, Rosa, *Luna lunera*, Barcelona, Plaza y Janés, 1999.

Resina, Joan Ramon, Introduction, in Joan Ramon Resina (ed.), *Disremembering the Dictatorship: The Politics of Memory in the Spanish Transition to Democracy*, Amsterdam, Rodopi, 2000, pp. 1-15.

——, "Short of Memory: The Reclamation of the Past since the Spanish Transition to Democracy", in Joan Ramon Resina (ed.), *Disremembering the Dictatorship: The Politics of Memory in the Spanish Transition to Democracy*, Amsterdam, Rodopi, 2000, pp. 83-125.

Ricœur, Paul, *Temps et récit*, Vol. 1, Paris, Seuil, 1983.

Rigney, Ann, "Portable Monuments: Literature, Cultural Memory and the Case of Jeanie Deans", in *Poetics Today* 25.2, 2004, pp. 361-396.

Rodríguez Marcos, Javier, "Las novelas se escriben contra la literatura", in *El País*, 21 June 2003, Babelia.

Rosa, Isaac, "Empacho de memoria", in *El País*, 6 July 2006.

——, *La malamemoria*, Badajoz, Del Oeste, 1999.

——, *¡Otra maldita novela sobre la Guerra Civil!: lectura crítica de La malamemoria*, Barcelona, Seix Barral, 2007.

Ruiz Zafón, Carlos, *La sombra del viento*, Barcelona, Planeta, 2004 [2001].

Sagarra, Joan de, "Enrique sonríe", in *El País*, 19 October 2003.

Saussure, Ferdinand de, *Cours de linguistique générale*, Charles Bally and Albert Sechehaye (eds.), Paris, Payot, 1949 [1919].

Schoentjes, Pierre, *Poétique de l'ironie*, Paris, Éditions du Seuil, 2001.

Schlant, Ernestine, *The Language of Silence: West German Literature and the Holocaust*, New York/London, Routledge, 1999.

Sedgwick, Eve Kosofsky, *The Coherence of Gothic Conventions*, New York, Arno, 1980.

Shaffner, Randolph P., *The Apprenticeship Novel: A Study of the Bildungsroman as a Regulative Type in Western Literature with a Focus on Three Classic Representatives by Goethe, Maugham, and Mann*, New York, Peter Lang, 1984.

Steenmeijer, Maarten, "El tabú del franquismo vivido en la narrativa de Mendoza, Marías y Muñoz Molina", in Joan Ramon Resina (ed.), *Disremembering the Dictatorship: The Politics of Memory in the Spanish Transition to Democracy*, Amsterdam, Rodopi, 2000, pp. 139-155.

Stewart, Susan, *On Longing: Narratives of the Miniature, the Gigantic, the Souvenir, the Collection*, Baltimore, Johns Hopkins University Press, 1984.

Strümpel, Jan, "Im Sog der Erinnerungskultur. Holocaust und Literatur – 'Normalität' und ihre Grenzen", in *Text + Kritik* 144, 1999, pp. 9-17.

Su, John J., *Ethics and Nostalgia in the Contemporary Novel*, Cambridge, Cambridge University Press, 2005.

Toonder, Jeanette den, *'Qui est je?': étude sur l'écriture autobiographique des nouveaux romanciers*, n.p., n.p., 1998.

Trapiello, Andrés, *El buque fantasma*, Barcelona, Destino, 2003 [1992].

Tyras, Georges, "'El dueño del secreto': la dualidad como secreto", in *Ética y estética de Antonio Muñoz Molina*, Neuchâtel, Université de Neuchâtel, 1997, pp. 139-159.

Valls, Fernando, *La realidad inventada: análisis crítico de la novela española actual*, Barcelona, Crítica, 2003.

Vargas Llosa, Mario, "El sueño de los héroes", in *El País*, 3 September 2001.

Vicent, Manuel, *Tranvía a la Malvarrosa*, Barcelona, Suma de Letras, 2000 [1994].

Vila-Matas, Enrique, *París no se acaba nunca*, Barcelona, Anagrama, 2003.

Voloshin, Beverly R., "The Ethical Turn in French Postmodern Philosophy", in *Pacific Coast Philology* 33.1, 1998, pp. 69-86.

Weaver, Wesley J., III., "Usos y abusos de la autobiografía en *Estatua con palomas* de Luis Goytisolo", in *Hispania* 78.4, 1995, pp. 762-772.

White, Hayden, *The Content of the Form: Narrative Discourse and Historical Representation*, Baltimore/London, Johns Hopkins University Press, 1987.

Wicks, Ulrich, "The Nature of Picaresque Narrative: A Modal Approach", in *Publications of the Modern Language Association of America* 59.2, 1974, pp. 240-249.

Wimsatt, W.K., and M.C. Beardsley, "The Intentional Fallacy", in *The Sewanee Review*, 1946, p. 468.

Winter, Jay, and Emmanuel Sivan, *War and Remembrance in the Twentieth Century*, Cambridge, Cambridge University Press, 1999.

Winter, Ulrich, "'Localizar a los muertos' y 'reconocer al Otro': 'lugares de memoria(s)' en la cultura española contemporánea", in Joan Ramon Resina and Ulrich Winter (eds.), *Casa encantada. Lugares de memoria en la España constitucional (1978-2004)*. Frankfurt am Main, Vervuert, 2005, pp. 17-39.

Wolfreys, Julian, *Victorian Hauntings: Spectrality, Gothic, the Uncanny and Literature*, Basingstoke/New York, Palgrave, 2002.

Yoldi, José and Rodríguez, Jorge A., "Las acusaciones de la conspiración sostienen que ETA o una trama policial están detrás del 11-M", in *El País*, 5 June 2007.

Young, James E., *Writing and Rewriting the Holocaust: Narrative and the Consequences of Interpretation*, Bloomington/Indianapolis, Indiana University Press, 1988.

Peter Lang – The website

Discover the general website of the Peter Lang publishing group:

www.peterlang.com